Soul Signs
from the Other Side

Rita,
Thanks for much
for helping my kids out.
Much appreciated
♡ God Ahead

ISBN: 9781937721640
Library of Congress NO. 2018964840

Published by Jetty House
An imprint of
Peter E. Randall Publisher
Portsmouth, New Hampshire 03801
www.perpublisher.com

Book Design; Tim Holtz

Soul Signs
from the Other Side

A Spiritual Memoir
and Love Story

By Gail Durant

Jetty House
Portsmouth, NH
2019

I dedicate this book to my late husband, Robert Maurice Durant, Jr. (MOOSE!.)

Thank you for taking the chance on me and for loving me the way you did.

This book may never had happened if we didn't cross each other's path.

Please stop telling me to find a boyfriend when you visit me in my dreams, because there will never be another love quite like ours! Until we meet in Heaven, I will always love you.

Love,
Wifey.

Contents

Introduction

My name is Gail Durant (my maiden name was Adams.) I was brought up in the Elmwood Gardens Projects with twelve other siblings, including my sister, Brenda Lee, who died in infancy. We lived with my mother, Doris, who everyone knew as Coffee. We went to Blessed Sacrament Church on Sundays and catechism on Monday nights. I hated catechism and wondered how it would ever benefit me.

I went as far as tenth grade in high school, so my writing may not be perfect. I quit school at sixteen after entering tenth grade for a third time, so at least I made it past freshman year! I hated school and played hooky for seven weeks before getting caught.

At that time in my life, I didn't have a care in the world. I was just being a teenager and doing what I wanted to do. I hung out with my friends. I babysat for many moms in the projects to buy myself new clothes. With so many children in my family, we didn't have fancy wardrobes.

Dad left my mother when I was seven or eight years old, leaving us to depend on the welfare system. That was a good thing for us, since it meant we always had a full belly. Mom made sure of it. She was a great cook and fed many. I take after her in that way.

Eventually, Mom met a man named Ray who took her and my family under his wing, into his home, and out of the projects. That was a highlight for all who were still living at home, but not for me. I asked my social worker if I could stay behind, and over time I lived with two different families, as I didn't want to leave the friendships I had made.

I first stayed with a Spanish woman named Osbie and her children. I learned to sew, make cakes, and cook. She also taught me how to play a mean tambourine. When Osbie moved, I went to another home with a couple named Fred and Anna and their children. There I learned how to play the horses and gamble and decorate a home. Both Osbie and Anna loved the color red, and I think my love for the color red comes from them. I did a lot of babysitting for Anna, but I didn't want to be a built in babysitter, so I moved back home for a short time.

I got my first job working for the City of Manchester, N.H. Most families with low income could have their children work for the City, and kids could start working at the age of fifteen. The program was called Model Cities, and it was a summer job only. We painted fences and mailboxes and put bark mulch down where it was needed. It was the first time I had interacted with other people and learned a strong work ethic. The job lasted through the summertime, but I would soon be sixteen and needed to get a job—a real job, full-time. I knew I wasn't going back to school. I could quit at that age.

I started working at J. F. McElwain shoe shops. I was there for eight and a half years and loved it. I was a box toe gal and an insert counter in men's shoes. I had freedom there. They had a bowling team and a softball team, both of which I joined and began to overcome my shyness. I started making friendships that would last a lifetime.

When the shoe shops phased out, I immediately went where others without a high school education had gone before me. I worked four and a half years at E & R Laundry. It was hard work, but it paid the bills in the small apartment I had rented. I loved my co-workers and remain friends with some still to this day.

One day, a new friend named Helen came into my life who would alter my life. I met her at the roller-skating rink through another friend. Helen told me about a company that would pay me double what I was earning, and she brought me an application form to fill out. Six months later, I got a call saying that they had a job for me.

I was scared to leave all my friends behind, but I believe that God sometimes shows you the way, and you have to seize opportunities that come your way. This new job at GTE Sylvania (later called Osram Sylvania) began my journey for the next twenty-six years.

That was a testing ground for me, working on the finishing line with moving conveyor belts and hot glass. Boy, was I afraid of fire! I almost walked out after three weeks because I never thought I would get the hang of it. After a year and a half in the finishing department, I was bumped to a mount line and became a welder. That experience changed me as a person. I didn't understand it then, but I do today. Out of thirty people, I was chosen to train each of the new operators coming in to work on the third shift they had recently added. I was scared as heck and marched into the office upset.

"Why me?" So many out there, "Why me?"

I didn't like their answer because I really didn't want to do it.

"Gail," I was told by my boss Jane, "your work is perfection, and you work well with others."

This was a decision made by many in staff. I had no choice. Little did I know that teaching others would turn out to be what I love doing most. This was a turning point in my life, but at the time I had no clue. I always thought I would be a teacher, but I thought that it would be in a school, not in manufacturing. I realized that if I taught others all the tricks I had learned and made their job easier, then it would also make my job easier.

To me, working for GTE Sylvania was not a job. I loved going to work. I taught songs to the newcomers as I taught them welding. We sang loud like a drill sergeant with his men. How many times did we get caught dancing to a tune out on the floor? How many higher-ups would laugh as I imitated a munchkin from the *Wizard of Oz*? They would just turn around shaking their heads: Gail will be Gail.

Out of everyone that I had trained, only one didn't make the cut for the job. It was a decision I had to make, to let her go. It was hard for me to tell the boss she wouldn't make it. Still, that was pretty good odds for a growing company. I was confident and good at what I did.

When GTE was sold, and we became Osram Sylvania, the pace became faster and more demanding. It didn't matter to me. I always did my best wherever I went. I gave it my all. I demanded respect and fought when it wasn't received. I was a little person with a BIG mouth. I found that I couldn't be shy anymore and stood up for my rights with some unruly bosses. I didn't care if I would lose my job. I demanded the same respect they expected of me.

I could read between the lines. I knew ten years earlier that the place had shown signs of closing. I felt it and told myself to prepare. I started saving more money and investing because I knew what lay ahead.

I've had these feelings for most my life and I've learned to trust in them. This was gnawing at me, so I knew it was real. When I would pass the word around, I was called a Negative Nellie. It was then that I realized that all I could do was inform a few friends and do my best to save. Every raise was put in my 401K account. I allowed myself just $2.50 a week in spending money. I used that to make a 50-cent phone call to my husband, Bob every weeknight from a payphone at work to let him know how much I loved him, and to ask how his day was.

Every night like clockwork I called to say I loved him. I would even sing him that song, "I Just Called to Say I Love You" and he would chuckle and tell me not to give up my night job. Even when he wasn't home I sang to him that song in the recorded message. I brought my own meals to save money. In my last year, I worked so much overtime, I surprised my husband. He knew I hated overtime. He hated it too.

"I don't see you anymore" he would say.

One day I asked him, "What would you say if I leave work and we move to the lake house?"

He told me that he wanted me to be happy and to do whatever I wanted, and he would support me. He said that he knew I hadn't been happy for a while and that he was on board with any decision I would make. It was settled, I would retire. I saved up plenty of money for my next move. It was coming soon.

The tension at work was getting thick, and I knew it was time for me to go. The pull was strong to leave, and then it happened. I received a sign in a book a neighbor had given me for a yard sale. I flipped it open to read a page. It said, "It's not work if you love your job. If you're not happy with your job, leave it." I was happy when I first started working at Sylvania, and I would reminisce about how much I had loved going to work, but that was not the case anymore. I got my sign. The time was now.

I made a few calls and went to the front office the next day. I told them, "I want to retire, and I want no one to know except for my boss."

I wanted my retirement date to be on my mother's birthday, December 2. With all of my paid days and holidays still left, it meant that I had just five more working days before I could leave. I was told that I wouldn't receive my first check for three months and that most people normally just continued working for those three months. I just smiled. December 2 it is. I am leaving.

I got home that night and knew it was the best decision I had ever made. My husband was sleeping, and he had no idea yet what I had done. I would tell him in the morning. But first I wanted to write up a good-bye letter for all of my Sylvania family. I was scared but ready for a new chapter in my life, a new journey in a new home that my husband and I had built together, with the help of many others.

We were moving to a log cabin on Emerald Lake. We had purchased the land many years earlier; after looking at so many places for over a year, this place had called out to me. This would be our retirement home. Bob agreed, and we purchased it right away.

Now God was showing me the way. On that last day of work, I got home and poured myself a glass of wine. Thank you, Sylvania, for giving me some of the best years of my life. I hit the send button to deliver my retirement letter and prayed that the remaining days would have hope for all still left there. I wanted nothing but the best for my Sylvania family. I believe it was four years later that the plant closed. I couldn't worry about them anymore. On December 2, 2010, I retired. I started packing the next day.

In April of 2011 we moved to our log cabin in Hillsborough, New Hampshire, a new beginning and a journey of retirement for me. My husband Bob was too young to retire. Or so I thought.

Here is OUR love story illustrated with all the signs visual and spiritual, that I received from my husband Bob and a few other loved ones that have moved on to heaven. I can only share what I feel and interpret for myself. I can also share with you what friends and family have shared with me. I am hoping that with visual signs and pictures I can show you how to recognize when a sign hits you. I am hoping that after you read this book, you will be able to understand and receive signs for yourselves or to at least see them as such. I hope that the teacher in me can show you how to finally see for yourself that there is life on the other side.

I can truly say, without a doubt, that Mother Mary has accompanied me at least four times in my dreams. I finally realized that she would appear when I was heading to the other side because of my sleep apnea and breathing issues. She always flew with me and brought me to safety. I would only know that she came in a time of need, just like in the song, "Let It Be." When "Mother Mary comes to me," she comforts me.

Since having surgery to open my airway, I have not seen her again, though her message to me then was loud and clear. She told me she is disguised as a nun on this earth and that she goes by the name of Mary. She just watches. She told me that children (orphans in orphanages) needed me. She told me that my husband would go before me. She needed my full concentration.

I was flying with her and told her she had to slow down as I couldn't breathe, and so she did. I was in awe of the beauty that I saw. I wished I could take pictures in my dream, but my memory holds onto this beautiful vision. I knew I was seeing MY heaven. I saw balconies on both sides with people dancing and laughing, and there was music. We flew over calm water. I saw flowers over the window ledges, and the sun was shining. I saw my relatives who had passed before me, and friends, all waving and smiling at me. I saw my mother wave at me. She was so happy. I remember asking where Uncle Bobby was, and they replied that he was coming soon. (He had died six months earlier.) There must be some kind of test to go through before you get to your heaven!

Mother Mary was not dressed as a nun on this day. She was in her white gown, and it was flowing in the air as we flew. You could feel the air hit our face and feel her presence of love. I wasn't afraid of flying with her, though I hate flying. After all, she was Mother Mary, why should I be scared?

The beauty and the colors were brilliant in heaven. It was like a saturation of vibrancy that one has never seen before. I could feel the tears running down my cheeks as I waved to all the ones who had passed before me, and I woke up sobbing uncontrollably. I was crying out loud and turned to make sure Bob was okay. I had woken him up, and he was wondering what was wrong. I could barely speak. I told that I was having a hard time breathing and I had gone to Heaven.

I saw my Heaven with everything I love on Earth. I saw the sun, the flowers, and the calm waters; there was music and those that had passed before me. People were happy.

Bob just hugged me because he had never seen me sobbing like this. He always listened when I spoke of the other side. He used to tell me, "When you talk out loud to the universe, someone listens to you."

I loved that my babe believed in me and understood what I said. He had felt it numerous times, and the belief that there is a heaven was a comfort to him,. We all need to believe, and this was no different.

Today I look back and I thank my mother for those catechism classes. That is what held me together in a most difficult time in my life:

The HOPE, that I would have a miracle

The FAITH that there is a heaven

The LOVE, which I still feel to this day from those who have gone before me

The SIGNS, I hope all of you will understand after reading this book, to help and give you comfort about those that have gone before you.

The NEED, as in "We all have the Need to Believe"!!!!!

The GOAL is that the profits from this book will be given away to help children in need, just as Mother Mary showed me in my dreams.

CHAPTER 1

In the Beginning

MOST TIMES, I THINK BACK TO THIS MOMENT;

"Everything will be alright. Everything will be okay" Bob said, as he patted my hand through the bars of the hospital bed that was in our living room. I always sat by his side and slipped my hands through the bars and held his hand tightly. I couldn't look at him as I didn't want him to see the tears running down my face. He must have known his days were limited and his end was coming soon.

"You have to go on alone, Gail. You will be okay. Everything will be okay."

Oh, how I couldn't look at him. I was thinking how I would miss his smile and his infectious laugh, our Sunday nights in the hot tub, his gentle kiss, his hand always patting my butt, calling me his "sexy babe," his jokes, his naked dancing jig just coming out of the shower, the way he said "I love you" so many times a day, his Santa Claus cheeks, his warm touch and his soft hands (for a man, they were so soft), his holding me tight, and the smell of his cologne. We never went anywhere without holding hands. He gazed into my eyes, staring at me with those beautiful baby blues. So much was going through my mind that day. I turned and blew him a kiss, and he blew one back as he always did.

"I am going to miss you so much," I said. It didn't matter how many tears were running down my cheeks. "I love you so much. Make sure you send me signs because you know I will receive them." He shook his head yes as his tears started falling. "Can you promise me one more thing?" I asked. "Can you make sure you are the first to come and get me when it's my time to meet you in heaven?"

Again, he shook his head and said, "Yes, you can count on it!"

I had one more question. "How am I to know it's you? What sign will you send me?"

He thought about this for a minute and said he would send me bad smelly farts.

"Really" I said, "You're gonna give me bad smelly farts?"

"Yep," he said, with the biggest shitty grin ever!

"Okay smelly farts it is!"

We didn't talk much more that afternoon. We sat holding hands watching *Who Wants to Be a Millionaire?* It was quiet. Nothing more needed to be said. We just had to keep remembering, "Everything will be okay!"

Four months after Bob had passed, I had to go to the hospital for tests. I had time to kill and went into the gift shop where I saw a sign that read: "If you're waiting for a sign, THIS IS IT!"

I had to get it, it made me chuckle. I asked the clerk to hold it for me while I continued to shop.

But something more meaningful was about to hit me square in the face.

"How could I have missed this?" I was thinking to myself as a second sign came into view. Written on it were the words of comfort Bob had spoken to me on that day four months ago, "Everything will be okay."

Photo by Gail Durant

I cried seeing that silly sign. The owner came over and asked if I was okay. Oh, my goodness, I laughed. She's asking me if I am OKAY!

"I have to have that sign," I tell her.

"It's the last one," she said, getting it down for me. Bob was surely with me this day. I just knew it.

Let's start from the beginning . . .

CHAPTER 2

Meeting Bob

THERE HE WAS, STANDING IN THE DOORWAY of the breakfast restaurant, waiting to be seated with his buddies. My friends and I were already settled, and I happened to look up just as he walked in. He had a terrific smile, and he was so cute. Our eyes connected, and I yelled to him, "You're cute, come sit with us!"

I couldn't believe I just blurted that out! Having a few drinks earlier had made me daring and not so shy.

A few acquaintances and I were having breakfast after dancing the night away at the Jameson's Club in Manchester, New Hampshire. It was our favorite hangout for listening to good music and meeting new friends. The club was just a few blocks from my home, which was convenient, because I didn't drive. I could walk home at night on Wilson Street to get to my house on Silver Street without worrying about being attacked by anyone. It was a pretty good neighborhood, and we all knew one another.

This good-looking man took me up on my offer and came to sit with us. He said his name was Bob. We all introduced ourselves and talked non-stop during breakfast. His friends were having fun from the other table, drunk and yelling stuff at him. I think they were jealous that he was the chosen one and not them. He was getting all our attention.

Soon it was time to go. He seemed interested in my red-headed friend, and they exchanged phone numbers. It didn't bother me because I had just met him. Good for my friend! He was a doll and was very nice to talk with.

For the next year and a half, I kept running into Bob at many different dance halls. He would always make sure to come by and say;

"Hello Gail."

I couldn't believe he remembered my name.

In town, out of town—it didn't matter, we always ran into each other. One night, when I was on a date, Bob stopped by my table just to say hi. That got my attention. I said, "Oh my God, he's so cute!" as Bob was walking away.

I guess my date noticed because he never called me back for a second one. Though I continued to run into Bob at dance clubs all around Manchester, he never once asked me to dance, even when I was just sitting with my friends.

Fast forward a year and a half; I was at the Music Hall in Concord, New Hampshire, with my girlfriends, ready to dance the night away. This was our newest hangout. It was set-up in a huge barn. I got to know the owner, and he would let me shake my tambourine to any song that I liked because he knew I would get the crowd going.

I'd get up on stage and grab the mike to get the party started, yelling, "Let's go, get out of your seats, let's dance!"

People would roar as I shook my tambourine. I wasn't shy—not after a few drinks anyways! I loved being up on stage, shaking my booty and bells! I had great confidence being up there. It was easy for me to get people out of their seats and on to the dance floor.

I always set up at least three tables for my group of friends wherever we went, and that night was no different. We were in the back, near the second bar, enjoying the night.

Later that evening, I saw Bob walking down our way with his buddies, looking for a place to sit. He saw me but didn't come over right away, and I wondered why.

I danced with anyone who asked me. I could see Bob watching me just as I was watching him. Our eyes connected once again. He finally came over when I sat down, and he said, "Gail! Your name is Gail. I wasn't coming over until I remembered your name, and after a few beers it came to me!"

I laughed and said, "If you're in a dancing mood come and ask me."

Before long he did ask. We never separated again that night. It was as if no one else were there. One song would lead to another, and in between we sat together at my table, his friends forgotten.

Soon the DJ called me up on stage, and Bob got a taste of how I could get the crowd going. I think that may have surprised him.

He was dancing to a fast song with my sister, but his eyes were on me! This scene reminded me of something from my past, something that had happened with my first love, on the night we first met. It felt like *déjà vu*, but this time was different. Bob didn't walk out. Let me explain.

Twelve years earlier I had broken off an engagement to a man who I loved deeply. We had met in that same way, when I was twenty-one years old, at The Venice Room in Manchester, New Hampshire. We had been dancing together for most of the night when I was called up on stage to join the band and shake my Ludwig tambourine. I was wearing hot pants. I had long hair and a sexy body to boot. While I was up there livening up the crowd, I watched him walk out, and stupidly, I chased him.

I quickly fell deeply in love with this man. After about a year together, he was jailed for a petty robbery involving food. I stayed by his side, but something seemed to change in him during the time he was incarcerated. He turned out to be verbally and physically abusive when he got out.

I was afraid of him now and only stayed in fear for my life. He would put guns to my head, knives to my throat, and suffocate me with a pillow if I dared to rebel against him. I would wake from passing out finding him apologetic. He always told me that it would never happen again, but it always did. I was scared.

I never told my friends or family any of this because he threatened to hurt them if I did. I took his abuse for a long time, but I finally found a way out, and he was the one to hand it to me.

The last straw was learning that he was cheating on me with a woman whom I had considered a good friend, and that she was carrying his baby. I knew I had to end it after I asked myself one question, "Did I want to live this way for the rest of my life?"

I knew in my heart that I had had enough, and I demanded that he move out—after all it was my apartment! Soon his rifle was at my head, one last shot at controlling me, but I couldn't live like this any longer. This time I took control and grabbed the gun. I wanted to make sure that his threat was carried out, so I put the barrel under my chin. I told him that I would pull the trigger, because I didn't care anymore if I lived. It must have scared him because he pulled it away immediately.

At last, I had found a way of letting him go. I thought I would feel relieved that it was finally over, but instead I went into a deep state of depression for the next year and a half. I had never felt so bad in my entire life. He was my first love. I didn't know how it had gotten so out of control or why I never saw it coming.

I had never understood the real meaning of the word *depression*, but it hit me hard when I realized that it was over between us! My problem was that I kept going back to our first year together and how happy we were then. I kept playing our favorite songs and re-reading his love letters. What I should have been thinking about was the abuse of the last two and a half years.

It was so hard for me to let him go while still loving him, but I hated the way I was being treated and thought that someday he might kill me. If this was love, I wanted nothing more to do with it!

After I threw him out, he began stalking me, threatening to bomb the apartment building where I lived. He would show up at my work-place and called me constantly until I had to change my phone number. He almost ran me over once, but my sister Diana pulled me out of the way as he sped past.

I prayed to God that he would find a new love and leave me alone. My prayers would soon be answered, and this nightmare would be over.

Today this man who had walked out on me when I danced on stage sits in a jail cell, and I don't want to give him any more notoriety. I learned the difference between love and control and how much better love truly is. I learned a valuable lesson from him, and I will never regret our relationship because of that. He made me the strong woman I am today. Because of him, I learned what kind of man I didn't want in my life.

I wrote to him in jail once, just to forgive him and then I moved on. He kept writing to me, a lot of crap about love, but I knew deep down in my heart that it was not real and that I could finally let him go.

I didn't receive any signs while I was with this man. My thoughts were just to stay alive and breathe easy again! It was one of the hardest and toughest times I've ever gone through in my life, but I did come out of it stronger. I could finally stand on my own two feet, all by myself. I didn't need or depend on him anymore.

I was afraid of losing my apartment without another paycheck, so I took a part-time job at Summit Packaging at the airport. I worked five hours every night while putting in a full shift at the laundry during the day. I did this to pay the rent and feel comfortable enough to relax.

I knew that if I had my sister move in with me, I wouldn't be tempted to take him back ever again! My kid sister, Ann Marie, lived with me for the next six years, and things were finally starting to fall into place.

I didn't have any love interests for the next twelve years after breaking it off with my first love. I did have a few sexual encounters here and there, very few and far between, but I wanted no love connection. Sometimes I went two years without anyone in my life because the wall I had built was very high. I didn't want to get hurt ever again. I didn't want to ever love again either.

But Bob watched me on the stage as I play to the crowd, with a smile on his face. He didn't walk out.

I was afraid of *déjà vu*, but I had to give him a chance. He made my heart flutter for the first time in twelve years. I was really scared of history repeating itself. I didn't know much about him, but I felt a connection, and part of me wanted to take a chance and get to know him better.

We danced the last song, a waltz, and he kissed me for the first time. I kept thinking what a great looker and kisser Bob was, just like my first love. I was afraid that he was going to shatter my wall. I had to be strong because I hadn't had any sexual activity for quite some time and knew that I would be vulnerable. I decided that we were going to get to know each other first.

I let him drive me home. When he dropped me off, I asked if he wanted to come up for coffee or tea, but not me so Bob understood that sex was not in the plans that night. He did come up, and we ended up talking all night long about anything and everything. I finally got to ask him, "Whatever happened to my red-headed friend that you exchanged numbers with at the breakfast restaurant?" I was kind of curious because I hadn't run into her again.

He told me that he never called her. Lucky me!

He wouldn't be a man if I said he didn't try to put his hands on me that first night, but sex wasn't part of my plan then, nor for quite some time to come. I wanted him to know me first. I was at a point in my life where there would be no more one-night stands. If he didn't call me back after that night, I couldn't be hurt because I hadn't given into temptation.

That was the beginning of our falling in love. Bob told me that himself. He said, "If I had gotten you that first night, I wouldn't have come back!"

He told me that he got to know me better because of our long talks about things that were going on in our lives. Those discussions and his patience were what made me fall in love with him. He did a lot of listening.

He told me he was worried that he had lost his touch because he never had to wait that long for any woman that he wanted sexually! It made him fall in love with me. He also told me it helped that I had a cute apartment that was clean and presentable, because no one he dated had kept a clean house.

Bob was a laid-back kind of guy and a businessman when I first met him. I was a hard worker and outgoing, but rather shy with men. We complemented one another perfectly. He made it easy for me to come out of my shell. At first we saw each other only on weekends, but soon we were missing each other so much that he started coming by in the middle of the week.

It was very obvious that we were becoming an item. We didn't have to say it. It was almost like we could read each other's mind.

Because I had been in an abusive relationship twelve years ago, I had built my wall pretty high. This beautiful man had broken the barrier and stolen my heart. I had to give into what I was feeling because I knew that I loved him. We never spoke that word *love*, but we both felt it!

I loved the way he held my hand when we were walking. He listened with his heart. Neither of us had ever married, so that was a great start!

I was happy that he showed patience with me. One afternoon, it was time for me to show how much I loved him. I took his hand and led him to my bedroom. We called that day "Afternoon Delight!" It was magical to be in love again and not be afraid to let it show just how much!

Soon we began saying "I love you" to each other many times a day and always before we went to sleep at night, whenever he would stay over.

"Bob," I would ask him, "do you remember the date we had our first dance and kiss, and became an item?"

He would tell me that it was on January 12, because I wouldn't let him forget. I gave him a greeting card on the 12th of every month for a full year to remind him of our love. Soon it would be just a yearly card on that day in January, and we would always celebrate that special day by going out to dinner and having a few drinks.

A little over a year and a half into our relationship, Bob took some time off to be with me on my July vacation from Sylvania.

He said, "Come with me, I want to show you something."

He took me to look at some homes that were for sale. He never said why, just asked me if I liked them or not.

I said, "It doesn't matter if I like them or not. If you're buying, you should be the one liking them, not me!"

Still he said nothing and kept hounding me for my input.

"Pretend it's going to be your home," he said.

So stupid me, I do just that, not realizing then that he was trying to make it *our* home.

During that vacation, we bought a little cape on a busy street. It was close to work for me to walk, because I didn't drive. It had a small, fenced-in backyard for a dog, a garden, and room for a pool. It had the largest bathroom I had ever seen and a huge Jacuzzi.

Some would say that we bought the house just for the Jacuzzi. How wrong they were. I would have gone anywhere just to be with Bob. In the end, the price was right. I remember going back to work after vacation was over and joking with my co-workers, telling them that we had just bought a Jacuzzi. They said, "What on earth would you buy that for?"

I said, "It came with the house!"

They congratulated me and were very surprised because I had never said a word about buying a house when we left for vacation.

I said, "You're in shock? I had no idea!"

That's how Bob liked to do things. He never told me that we were going house hunting for ourselves, but I knew after a while what he was up too!

I did make a deal with him though. We would each put in an equal share for the down payment, right down to the penny. He agreed. I made more than he did at the time, and I was going to help with the cost, no matter what!

We became first-time home buyers on September 30, 1992, and moved in right away!

It was probably then that I learned I was a cougar. I had just assumed that Bob was my age because of his salt-and-pepper hair. At the signing, I found out that he was eight and a half years younger than I was! Had I known this when we first met, I probably wouldn't have dated him at all. Too late now, I loved this man with all my heart, and we had just bought a Jacuzzi together! No turning back now!

It was time now to make memories, living together in sin. We made a lot of them in our small cape, memories, not sin! The best was Sunday night Jacuzzi night. All our friends and families knew not to bother us after 8 p.m.

A little candlelight, music, champagne, and Avon® bubbles became our Sunday night ritual in the Jacuzzi. It was *our* time alone, to relax and talk about our week since we worked different shifts. We hardly ever saw one another, so we used this time to make up for that. It was quality time and of course, love-making time. That tub was huge. Maybe our friends were right—we bought the house just for the tub!

We were becoming one as a family. He had one son and another boy that he thought of as a son. I loved that. I was also close to a young girl who I thought of as a daughter. We also had many nieces and nephews between both families and spent a lot of time with all of them. Wow, this man loves children as much as I do, I thought. This is awesome!

Two years after we bought the house, Bob took me on a vacation to North Conway, New Hampshire. We both loved going up north. We found a place to eat and dance the night away and fell in love with the area. No matter where we travelled, we always got a hotel with a hot tub, and this trip wasn't any different! That was a given!

This night changed my life forever. Spirit didn't even give it away!

We were at Barnaby's Steak House, and in the middle of dinner, Bob said;

"Give me your hand."

He started fumbling with something, trying to get it out of his pants pocket. It finally hit me, and I blurted out, "Are you going to ask me to marry you?"

He said; "Gail, please, let me do my job!"

He opened a tiny black box and pulled out a heart shaped ring. He asked me to marry him, right there at the dinner table!

"You've got to marry me before you're forty years old, or I will throw you out of the house!" he said, laughing.

"You can't throw me out of my own house, and of course I will marry you!" I told him.

I was tearing up as I told him, "Yes."

I stood up to give him a kiss from across the table, and some folks who had overheard the proposal started clapping for us. The wait-staff came over to congratulate us, and I asked one of them if they could take a picture of us with my camera on our special night.

That was a night that I will never forget!

After dinner, we went across the hall to listen to some country music. I wasn't big on country music then, but it was something to dance too. When Bob got up to go to the restroom, I stared at my ring again. I couldn't believe that this was happening to me! I was thirty-nine years old and had finally found someone to return the love that I had to offer. I was in awe and very happy because I hadn't seen this coming. It truly was a great surprise for me, and I thanked Spirit for not letting the cat out of the bag!

It wasn't long before we went back to North Conway, bringing the staff of Barnaby's Steak House the photo of us getting engaged. They remembered and told us that they would hang the picture of that special night on their wall. We loved that place, and now it was a must to stop there every time we went to North Conway!

Photo by Anonymous

A year later, on May 27, 1995, Bob and I were married at The Yard Restaurant, in the gazebo outside. We invited 185 family members and friends to our celebration. Our wedding party was huge and included family from each side, including two flower girls and two ring bearers. In all, the total was eighteen counting Bob and me.

I couldn't believe that I was getting married and had found someone who was willing to give me a chance to love them.

I never felt that I was beautiful, but on this day, I could feel the love so much that I felt like the most beautiful bride ever on the planet. My Bob was so handsome and the way he looked at me with his baby-blue eyes pierced my heart.

I asked him not to shave his beard till after the wedding because he had such a baby face. I wanted him to look more my age, at least for the wedding photos. He had no problem pleasing me, and you could tell that we were happy and in love on our wedding day. It shows in our pictures!

Photo by Helen Hiltz

Bob dedicated a country song to me called "Forever and Ever, Amen," and the song I dedicated to him was called, "Power of Love," which I sang and recorded for the wedding. The tape was playing as I walked down the aisle. I worked hard on that number as I am *not* a singer. I played it for Bob before we got married, and he said he was quite impressed. I think he was just being the nice guy that he always was! Our taste in music was so different then, but it wouldn't be long before I would be loving country music too.

We had already been living together but now it would be as husband and wife. It felt so weird to use the word *husband* for the first time ever in my life. Good things come to those who wait!

It had been one hell of a ride; from the control of an abusive man to being with the most generous and kindest man on earth. Now I knew what real love was all about. Bob told me that we both got lucky.

I always thanked Bob for giving me a chance to show my heart. I had so much to give and he saw that. Oh, how this man loved me. He showed it in the way he held my hand, the way he kissed me, the way he always aimed to please me, always playfully patting my butt and never being afraid to say "I love you" at any given moment. He was always trying to make me happy, and I did the same for him, so we were a match made in Heaven!

"Did I tell you today that I love you?" he would say.

I would say "Yes, many times," and he would say it again.

The day after our wedding, we left for our honeymoon to Las Vegas for a week, and it was then that Spirit would visit me in a good way—a very good way!

CHAPTER 3

Las Vegas Honeymoon

THE MORNING AFTER OUR WEDDING, we packed our suitcases and headed off to the Manchester Airport. Takeoff would be in the early afternoon.

My foster mom, Osbie, had taken me under her wing when my family moved out of the projects so many years ago, and I wanted Bob to meet this family that I had lived with for over a year! This would be my fourth time visiting them in Las Vegas, and I couldn't wait to see what new hotels and skyscrapers had gone up since the last time I had been there.

Bob was game for anything as long as he stayed cool. Mom picked us up at the airport and brought us to our hotel. We were staying in the honeymoon suite off the strip at the Rio Grande. We planned to take cabs to the strip to see shows and the neon lights. We had booked a hotel off the main drag hoping it would be a little quieter, and it was.

We asked Mom to plan a barbeque for the weekend so that the whole family could meet Bob. We handed her $200 and told her to keep $100 for herself and to use the rest for food for the barbeque, Bob's beer, and my red wine.

They used my foster sister Brenda's place, because she had a pool. The family did an outstanding job preparing the food. They really made Bob feel welcome. He fit right in. The temperature gauge that day read 120 degrees, so Bob and I mostly stayed in the pool just to try and keep cool.

We got to meet all the friends that Mom always talked about on the phone. How nice that they wanted to meet Bob and me. We had a good time and made plans for the rest of the week. Mom would be our tour guide and take us wherever we wanted to go.

The next day she took us to a ghost-town attraction that had go-carts and jail cells, where you could take pictures behind the bars but not much else. It was so hot there and felt deserted because the heat kept people away.

Mom also took us to Laughlin, Nevada, on the Colorado River. It was a beautiful, miniature Las Vegas, and quite a sight to see! Some of the hotels boasted $14 rooms! The place we entered had a huge water fountain at the front entrance. It was spectacular! At the back end was a beach on the river, and you could take water taxis to and from any hotel. Bob and I had never seen anything like it in our lives, and we were in awe of all its beauty.

We enjoyed a meal in Laughlin and spent an entire afternoon just watching all of the activity on the river. I think that was the first time I ever heard of a thong bathing suit, and there were plenty of bathing beauties for Bob to see.

Soon we would be heading back to our hotel so that we could book some trips on our own without having to bother family, most of whom had to work during the week. We also booked night shows so that we could include Mom. She would pick us up, and we'd then be a threesome together, the Three Musketeers. Bob and Osbie hit it off right away, and you could tell that she loved him as much as I did! We would never let her take any money out of her pocketbook, it was the least we could do to show our appreciation. She was kind enough to spend time with us and show us the ropes, which also meant filling up the car with gas. She wasn't spending any money on our watch!

Osbie took me under her wing as a teenager, and I could see her doing the same with Bob. Osbie is a kind woman, and I was happy that Bob didn't mind spending our honeymoon with people that I loved. He was so easy like that. What a great week it was, despite the heat!

Back at the Rio, Bob was looking at brochures and asked me if I wanted to try out some tours.

"What do you have in mind?" I asked.

"Babe, they got this river rafting tour that will take you to the Hoover Dam wall. It's about four hours long, and they will serve sandwiches and drinks. Would you want to do this tomorrow?" Bob asked.

I was game. Bob made the call, and we were booked. We got picked up at the front entrance of the hotel as part of the package. It was an awesome day, except that it was very hot sitting on the black rafts with the sun directly shining on us the whole time. It was impressive being right in front of this massive wall. The guide told us that if the damn broke, we would need to hold our breath for a long time because we could end up in Mexico before we came up for air. He was pretty funny, but I could tell Bob hated being in the heat. This was not his thing, and he let me know, "Gail, when we get back, I want to get into the air conditioning and stay there all afternoon until the sun goes down. I want to have a cold drink, smoke my cigars and just relax. Maybe we can hit up a casino and just chill."

When he called me by my first name I knew that he wasn't too pleased with this heat. I promised him that we wouldn't do anymore outside activities the rest of the week. Bob needed A/C! As soon as we got dropped off at our hotel, we headed straight to the casino, and Bob ordered a cold beer. We would stay there the rest of the afternoon.

As we walked around the casino, we had to pass by a roulette table where people were being taught how to play. I had never played roulette before and wanted to watch for a bit. Before long we were both playing and hoping our numbers would come out. I played number 14 for my mom, Coffee, because that was the number she always asked us to play for her. It never won, but we had fun trying. I liked roulette because it was easy, and we just had to sit and sip on a drink while rooting for our number. It was fun, even if we lost money or just broke even.

There weren't many people at the table, so the croupier began to teach us about outside bets and colors. He told us that we could play four corners, which could increase our chances of winning, but if we did win, we would only get a percentage of our money. It was simple enough, and I liked it. The bet was about two dollars that early in the day, if I remember right, and Bob and I played all afternoon and drank for free. It beat being in the sun, he would tell me.

That night, we went to a show called the Blue Man Group. We had never heard of them, but the taxi driver who drove us to the strip recommended them, so we checked it out. I loved their drumming the best and their crazy antics with props and music. It was an exciting show and very entertaining.

We also went to the Jubilee show at the Riviera with sexy show-girls and beautiful costumes, wearing big headdresses with vibrant colors. Las Vegas sure knows how to deliver a good time.

Afterwards, we walked the strip. I felt as though I were in a fairy-tale, surrounded by all the neon lights shining in the night and brightening the sky. It was beautiful the way it was all lit up. No matter where you looked, everything was aglow.

We went to the downtown area to see the Freemont Street Experience, a laser light show projected overhead. We checked out all of the street vendors selling their wares, creating paintings, singing, or trying to lure you into their casino to win your hard-earned money. We were having the time of our lives!

Bob spotted a neon cigar sign in front of a shop and wanted me to take a picture of him under it. Of course, he had to go in and check out all of the cigars as well. He came out bragging about the expensive cigar that he had just bought. He said that he had never paid so much for just one fatty before and thought that the quality must be good because it cost so much. I laughed so hard when he tried that $12 cigar and threw it down because he said it tasted like shit! He had me laughing so hard that I peed my pants a little.

There were many free shows down along the strip scheduled at certain times of the night. We made sure to see the pirate ship show in front of the Treasure Island Hotel, the volcano exploding at the Mirage Hotel, and the statues come to life at Caesar's Palace. It was a fantastic, fun-filled honeymoon!

I had been to Vegas four times before meeting Bob, but being with someone you love makes it so much more romantic. Walking the strip together, hand in hand with all the neon brightness surrounding us was spectacular. I loved the way the lights lit up the night!

There was one Vegas show that I definitely wanted Bob to see—my favorite, Siegfried and Roy, who knew how to create a great spectacle. I had gone to this show on every trip and loved it. It featured white tigers, elephants, and lots of magic with beautiful costumes. Bob couldn't believe his eyes! He kept saying "Wow" under his breath, so I knew I did well booking this for him.

Bob and I wanted to go to a casino on the strip and play some poker or roulette on our last night. After finishing a huge steak dinner, we took a taxi to the strip. We walked along, holding hands, just taking it all in one last time. It was hard to believe that a week had passed already. Bob nudged me, telling me to pick any casino, and we would check it out and play the slots. I can't remember the name of the place that I chose, but the name didn't matter—we just wanted to get inside and play.

On the way in, I spotted a roulette table that was pretty much empty except for a couple of people. There was room for both of us to sit together, so Bob and I each took out a hundred-dollar bill. We had money left because we really hadn't spent that much on gambling that whole week. It was time to "make it or break it," Bob would say.

I cashed in that hundred-dollar bill for one-dollar chips and chose the light green colored ones for myself. I'm not sure which color Bob chose, but soon we would be betting on numbers, having a drink, and just yelling for the ball to drop into the right numbered slot!

It was about 7 p.m., and the bets were now at $5 to play. I stacked my chips into $5 piles and played to my heart's content. When this money was gone, I would be done. I wasn't a big gambler, and neither was Bob. We always limited ourselves each day, and this was the most we had ever put down, but it was okay because it was our last night there. "What the hell," we thought. We were going home with money in our pocket anyways. We always took extra in case of emergencies.

After a little while, I began to feel strange, and my vision was also affected. At first, I didn't quite understand what was happening. I thought maybe it was that my drink was too strong. Soon I came to realize that something unknown was showing me which numbers to play.

As I looked down at the table to place my bet, the black square for number 31 appeared to be raised higher than the other squares. I was being told to place my money down on black 31. I took $5 in green chips and placed one on black 31 to win and the other four on different numbers. You could split up the bet as long as you played a total of $5.

The croupier soon yelled out where the ball had dropped, "Number 31 and we have a winner with this young lady right here. You just won $35!"

He handed me a stack of 35 light green chips. I made stacks of five so that I would always be ready to play the next game. Whatever had happened to me earlier didn't happen every time, just here and there. I was getting lucky at my own guesses and raking in $35 quite often.

My luck started to become noticeable to others who sat to play, and before long people began putting their bets on top of mine. I really didn't understand what was happening, but it was okay. I guess they thought I would be their lucky charm. Again, my eyes got funny, and I could see a numbered square rise. This time it was red 16. I took my $5 in chips and put it all on number 16, this time for a straight bet. I didn't split it up. Three people followed my bet and stacked their chips on top of mine.

The croupier spun the ball, and soon we were all screaming because number 16 had just been hit!

"How much did I win?" I asked the man.

"Its $35 to every dollar you play, so you just won $175," he said.

Bob congratulated me with a big kiss, but I was confused and wondering what the hell was happening to me. "How did I know that number would come out?" I was thinking to myself.

Before long, more people joined our roulette table because they heard so much screaming at ours and wanted to get in on the action.

The table was now packed, and all the colored chips had been taken by those playing. That meant that the table was sold out and no one else could join.

Bob whispered to me, "Babe, these people are here playing whatever you play because you're lucky tonight. They are watching your every move."

I played a random number on a straight bet, and this time my babe followed with everyone else. I chuckled to myself because Bob wanted a piece of the action too. He was not having the same luck as I was with his own numbers. People were calling out that they wanted to follow my bet, but there was no room for them on the number grid and the stacking couldn't go any higher.

The ball went around and around, but this time it didn't stop on our number. We all lost that time, but that one loss didn't stop people from continuing to bet on the same number that I chose.

After a while, I noticed that if Bob didn't follow my lead, I would win. If he did follow my lead, I would lose. There was a connection, and I told him so, "Bob, don't bet on me this time. I want to check on something."

He asked me why. I told him that every time he followed me, I would lose. So he played a different number and I played whatever I felt would win. Again, I could see that the square on number 31 was raised. I liked that number as I was born on that date, so once more I bet a straight shot of five bucks on number 31. People followed my lead, and we hit again! I won another $175, and they pushed the last of my green chips to me along with $25 tokens. People were touching me for good luck and patting my back because they called me their lucky charm.

With all the yelling and screaming going on, onlookers kept stopping by to see what all the commotion was about. It was really getting crowded at our table, and I was in awe of it all. I never saw anything quite like this.

I decided not to play the next game just so that I could stack up my chips. It was getting messy with so many on my little bit of the table. So that's what I did. I was stacking my chips when I heard the croupier yell out that the number 31 had hit, back to back, and now the table was roaring. He gave me $175 in $25 chips. I looked up and told him that it wasn't my money, that I didn't even play this game. He said to me, "You never took your chips off 31 after the last game, so you let it ride, and it hit again!"

By now even Bob was laughing along with the whole table! I forgot to take my chips in and they still won for me. I guess that was my lucky night!

Soon after, the pit boss changed out the croupier to throw off our luck. After a half an hour, he was changed out again, and then every 15 minutes. It didn't matter. We kept winning because Lady Luck was still with us.

There was a professor seated at the table way on the far end from where I was sitting. He had a few drinks too many, but he was still polite. He threw me a hundred-dollar chip and told me to place it on red or black, my choice. When I went to grab it, I was told by the croupier that it was not allowed, and that he would place it wherever I told him too.

That pissed off the professor. He said that it was his money and that he wanted the little lady to place his bets for him. I didn't want to get thrown out, so I let the croupier place it on the color red for me. Of course, a few others followed. That bet was a winner and paid $200. The professor asked me again to name a color. Soon $200 would be $400, and then $800.

I told him then that I wanted him to pull in his chips because I didn't want to bet for him anymore. I didn't want to be the one responsible if he lost. I would never have made a $100 bet for myself, and I didn't want to lose $800 for him. I actually begged him, and he finally agreed. I was happy with just my little $5 bets, and this had started to get out of hand.

Bob gave me a kiss and said he was going to play poker. He said that he would check back with me in a few hours. I told him that he knew where to find me because I was having way too much fun to leave now. I asked him if we could just stay up all night and then sleep on the plane later, and he was okay with that.

He came back to the table at five o'clock in the morning and reminded me that we still had to pack and get to the airport for noon. He saw that my $25 chips were no longer on the table and told me that he was sorry I had lost. I smiled and opened my purse to show him how full it was. He told me that he had lost but was happy that I had won. He joined me back on the table. By now most of the crowd had moved on or gone to bed.

By 7 a.m. it was time to hail a cab and get back to the Rio to finish packing for our flight back home. But first I had to cash in my chips. I exchanged the light green dollar chips with the croupier at the roulette table for $25 chips, which would then be cashed out at the cashier's window.

As I was leaving the table, I watched the black 31 rise again before my eyes. It was too late to place a bet, but I whispered to Bob that black 31 would come out, and sure enough it did!

We left with smiles on our faces, and I had won $1,600 to boot. This paid for all our shows, the hotel, and even both of our flights. A free trip, I would say! I gave the money to Bob and told him to save it for our next trip, whenever that might be.

We got back to our hotel, took showers, and packed up. We headed down for a quick breakfast at the same place we had eaten every morning and said good-bye to all the staff. They had gotten to know us quite well.

We loved it at the Rio. We loved the way they made it look beachy outside by hauling in real beach sand and palm trees. We loved the real yellow roses they had placed in fancy vases throughout the dining area. We loved that they had entertainment going on inside the casino while we were gambling. There were dancers, clowns, confetti, and acrobats overhead while we played at their slots! We loved that they knew our names and greeted us personally every time we walked through the doors. I was happy that we had tried someplace new, away from the strip.

It was time for Mom and my sisters to drive us back to the airport. Quite a few members of my foster family were already waiting there to see us off. It was then that Bob started crying and hugging everyone goodbye. They had all made his week extra special, and I knew that he would love them as much as I did.

When I hugged Mom, I slipped her a $100 bill and gave her many thanks for all that she had done to make this trip extra fun for us! She didn't want to take it, but I told her it was okay because I had won. I told her to keep it quiet, and that it was just for her.

Finally, aboard the plane and waiting to be cleared for takeoff, I let Bob know what had happened to me at the casino. I told him about the way the numbers had just jumped out at me, rising before my eyes. I said that it didn't happen often, but it did happen! I told him that it was a really weird feeling and that I loved playing roulette.

Bob thanked me for a fun week and called me Mrs. Durant. It seemed weird to hear that but, it also sounded so good. Mr. and Mrs. Bob and Gail Durant. It had a nice ring to it. That will be my name forever!

He also told me something that he thought might upset me: "Babe, I hope you don't get mad at me for what I tell you. When I hugged Osbie, I slipped her a $100 bill because I had the best trip ever!"

"It's all good, Babe, now let's get some sleep because you kept me up all night and I am very tired!"

He laughed and held my hand because he knew that I hated planes and wouldn't sleep at all with my travel anxiety. Soon he would be sleeping like a baby. Looking at him, I knew that I had married a good man indeed!

I would have beautiful memories of our honeymoon and the way Spirit had helped me to win a little cash.

Good-bye Las Vegas! We will be back!

CHAPTER 4

Custody Battles

OUR HONEYMOON WAS VERY NICE, but it was time for us to get back to work and face reality. Bills had to be paid and we were still trying to make our house a home, a place that would be comfortable for us.

In the months to follow, Bob began calling me his "wifey," which amused me. It also felt weird for me to introduce Bob as my husband. It had a certain ring to it, but it took a long time before it sank in for both of us!

Our Saturday nights were spent playing poker with Bob's relatives, and we shared many laughs. We did this for several years. Sunday was a time for fishing and household chores, groceries, and the like. We had already established a pattern with our lifestyle because we had lived together for over three years before we got married.

We would have Bob's son and sometimes his two stepbrothers over on weekends, when it was Bob's turn for custody visits. We brought them to the fairs and carnivals whenever we had all three kids. We went ice fishing in the winter, played board games, bowled, and sometimes just sat at home to watch a good movie on the tube. I made it a point to have them all together, when we could, as a family even though they weren't all Bob's children. We always treated them equally.

I remember one day after having been at the agricultural fair for the day, the kids wanted to go to a restaurant for dinner. They had just finished eating cotton candy, French fries, fried pickles, and fried dough. Bob told them that he knew a great little restaurant at B & G's, and he knew that they would love it! When we pulled into our driveway, they asked why we weren't stopping at a restaurant. Bob replied,

"This is a great restaurant called B & G's. It means Bob and Gail's and they serve good food here too!"

It didn't take long for them to catch on after that. Whenever he would talk of B & G's restaurant, they knew that they would be eating at home. I loved how Bob handled the boys that way. They were spoiled to a certain degree.

He always allowed me to have a say in anything that we did and always included me in all conversations. He would even listen to my intuition. By now he knew that there was something different about the way I felt things. He had seen it numerous times and had learned to trust it.

Bob and I made a good home and took good care of it. I would always help with raking the lawn or staining the decks, and with planting bushes, trees, and flowers. We had an above-ground pool installed with an upper and lower deck and loved having all of the kids in our lives over to take a dip in it.

Bob and I always held the family BBQ at our house because the yard was big enough to gather both sides of our families at once. Our house was too small for any indoor gatherings, but outdoors there was enough room for everyone.

There were good times in that pool. Sometimes the kids would have it to themselves, and sometimes it was the grown-ups' turn. There were just so many of us that we had to take turns. That pool is gone now, but I still have many pleasant memories of it.

One day, out of the blue, I got a phone call from an old neighbor who still resided at the tenement building where I used to live. She told me that she had heard from Bob's ex-girlfriend that his son was living in a foster home in Massachusetts. At first, I didn't quite understand what she was telling me. Why hadn't Bob been notified by his son's mom?

She gave me the name of the agency, and I let Bob make the call, seeing that he was the father. Sure enough, his son had been placed in a foster home until further notice. The guardians had physical custody for now. They didn't even know that there was a dad in the picture! They had been told just the opposite, that Bob had nothing to do with his son.

Being the photographer that I am, I had taken many photos of all our adventures with the kids. This was all the proof we needed to show that we were indeed in his life. Those three photo albums showed a very different story to the courts.

I knew in my heart that we had to bring Bob's son home with us, and Bob agreed. Our next few months consisted of hiring a lawyer and repeatedly travelling to the courts in Massachusetts to prove that we were capable of taking care of Bob's son—my stepson. There were background checks taken on both of us. Our house was inspected to make sure it was suitable and that there was a bedroom set up specifically for our son.

After months of waiting and more than $5,000 in legal fees and other expenses, which I helped Bob to pay, we finally had his son home and living with us.

There were adjustments to be made by all. Bob gave up his pool tournaments and meetings at night to help his son with homework and to make sure he was never alone. We would be a threesome every weekend now. He had a family with parents who showed their love for him by getting him out of foster care.

I would be lying if I told you it was easy, but I can tell you that I gave it my best shot. It was a thankless job, without much recognition except for the thanks that meant the most to me, and that came from Bob himself!

My story isn't about Bob's son. It's about what happened while he was living with us. We received a notice that Bob would have to start paying support into the welfare system for one of his son's step-brothers, one of the boys we had always treated as part of our family. I asked Bob if this boy could actually be his son. He said it might be possible, but he wasn't sure. Before he had met me, he was still seeing his ex-girlfriend occasionally.

In my heart, I knew that this child was *not* Bob's—you know, that gut feeling of mine kicking in again. I told him so. There was no way that we would be paying child support until I had the proof in my hands that he was Bob's child for sure. I mean, we already treated him like our own, and that wouldn't change because of this.

"Bob, I have no problem helping to pay for a child that is yours, but first I need proof. I don't see it. His skin is olive and yours is lobster, and my feelings tell me differently. Let's do some blood tests. I'll even help you to pay for them."

This child needed to know if Bob was his father and if not, he deserved to know who his real father was. Plain and simple! If I was wrong, then we would still love him as our own, just as we were already doing.

It would eventually cost us $1,800 for the bloodwork for all three of them: Bob, his ex-girlfriend, and his son's step-brother. The cost of $600 apiece was a small price to pay to learn if he was Bob's son.

I really felt that this was not Bob's biological child, and I couldn't see paying support for the next fifteen years unless he was. Bob and I were just starting our life together and had already put a dent in our savings with the legal fees to get custody of Bob's son, my stepson. Of course, we would seek legal custody if he was proven to be related to Bob.

When word about the blood tests got out to Bob's family, I was chastised. I was told to mind my own business. I thought to myself, "This *is* my business because Bob is now my husband and I am trying to protect him from a responsibility that might not be his." I just knew in my heart of hearts that I was right.

Bob must have believed me also because he went along with the blood testing. He wanted to know the truth too. This whole process took a long time, but eventually we learned the facts. This child was *not* Bob's son, and in the end, the blood testing gave him the opportunity to find out who his dad really was.

Bob was most grateful for my help. He told me, "I am not sure why you suspected this but I'm really happy that you brought it to my attention and questioned it. I appreciate your help moneywise and I will pay you back. Thanks for helping me set the record straight. At least I know the truth now."

That thanks meant a lot to me because it came straight from Bob's heart. He was the only one who acknowledged me and appreciated my help in this matter. His family seemed pleased that the truth had come out, but they never could recognize my efforts, which was okay because Bob had thanked me, and his opinion was all that really mattered to me anyhow.

On another note, Bob's son's older stepbrother always used to call him "Dad." After all of this, we decided that we should be open and tell him the truth. We sat him down and told him that Bob was not his real dad, but that he would always love him as his own. I know that it hurt him to hear those words, and it caused a lot of commotion within the families. This child had the right to know the truth.

After some years had passed, he formed a bond with his real father. I feel that everything really turned out for the best. I am glad that Bob spoke the truth long ago, with a little help from my nudging.

Gut feelings can be really strong and make you stop and take notice. I'm glad that my feelings were working overtime then and that I listened and was in tune to them.

I was so happy that Bob listened too!

Sometimes, if you trust your intuition, the truth will reveal itself. We all have a sixth sense, we all have gut feelings. Pay attention to that voice within, it can make all the difference in what is going on in your life at the time. Don't listen to anyone else's opinion but your own. I learned that lesson early in life, and now I always trust my gut. Learn to trust yours!

CHAPTER 5

Our Love for Animals

BOB AND I HAD A LOVE FOR ANIMALS—DOGS, to be exact! I had three mutts before I met Bob: Tiny was the first, then Punky, and Squiggy. After they all passed to the Rainbow Bridge, I moved to a better apartment, and no dogs were allowed. I had a stretch of twelve years without a dog. It wasn't long after I met Bob that we bought a house with a fenced-in yard and moved in together. Thoughts of getting a dog soon popped into my head.

Fanny, one of my neighbors and also a co-worker, came in one day to say they were trying to find a home for a cocker spaniel. Bob had always wanted a cocker spaniel, so I jumped the gun and said we would take her, sight unseen. The next morning, I said to Bob, "I got us a dog, Honey—it's what you wanted and she's free! She comes with a leash, a bowl, food, and toys. She's a cocker spaniel!"

"Oh yeah?" he replied. "That's good." He asked when we would get her.

"Friday night after I get out from the second shift, they will deliver her," I said.

He was in a hurry to get to work, so rushing out the door he kissed me and told me he loved me. Bob was laid back and easy to please. Our kind of love was about always making the other happy. This time was no different.

Bob was sleeping by time the dog arrived at one in the morning. Upon seeing her, my first thought was *Oh my God, this isn't a cocker spaniel.* It was a puppy, but not what Bob had wanted. I didn't have the heart to say anything to the owners because the minute I lifted her up to cuddle, she licked my face. That was it! I was in love with this beautiful golden retriever/spaniel. I sure hoped Bob would feel the same.

After they left, being a proud new dog owner, I went into the room where Bob was sleeping and put her right on the pillow at the top of his head. She started whining and crying. Bob woke but never lifted his head. He muttered the word "puppy" half asleep and before long he was wide awake playing with his new best friend. She licked him too.

"I'm sorry, Babe, but she's not all cocker spaniel," I told him.

"She's beautiful," was his response. "What will we name her?"

"I picked her out, so you get to name her" I said.

He thought for a bit and after contemplating, he said, "Her name will be April."

"How did you come up with that name, I asked?"

"Simple, he said. We are in the month of April, and we have many showers, so we will call her April Showers Durant!"

I loved that name—it had a ring to it.

Our lives were complete with April, and we loved her very much. She took rides with her daddy and loved to go swimming at Emerald Lake in Hillsborough, NH. We kept a fifth wheel (a camper trailer) on the land until we were ready to build our log home, and it became our home away from home. The minute we would arrive and open the truck door, April would dash for the water. She loved it there.

She also loved to go in our pool at our Beech Street home and climb out by the ladder. I taught her how to take off my socks when I got home at night. She even had the mail lady trained to give her a snack. She was gentle and kind and everyone loved her. She didn't care if the kids sat on her, and she loved playing tug-of-war. She was pretty strong and pulled me off the couch many times. I think she had allergies, as she sneezed a lot. I never did figure out what caused that.

She died at nine years old due to an autoimmune disease. After many blood transfusions, we took her home so we could be together when she passed. We didn't want her staying in a crate at the vet. We wanted her to be with us. We took her to Dairy Queen to let her have an ice cream, and to our amazement she licked most of it. She loved ice cream, and it was the only thing she had eaten in a few days.

The vet said to let her go naturally and for us to sleep in our own bed and not on the floor with her because she would try to please us, so we should just let her be. We went to bed that night knowing she would pass. We told her how much we loved her and what a great girl she was.

I wakened to a stillness in the darkness of our bedroom. I turned on the light, looked down to find her bed empty. I could see she was in our bathroom across the hall. I went to check on her, but she was already gone. Blood was coming from her mouth and she was stiff. I climbed on top of her and bawled my eyes out. When Bob heard me, he came in and we cried together on the floor with our precious little girl.

This was going to be tough for both of us. She was family. Neither one of us made it to work the next day. Some thought it was silly that we stayed home because of a dog. Some people will never understand the love that comes between a human and an animal. It's an unconditional love that you experience and can never forget.

After April died, another special dog entered the equation.

It had been eight months since April passed when I started looking for places to get a dog. I said nothing to Bob and just looked here and there. One day I saw a picture of this little black dog on a local puppy website. That "I didn't do it" face caught my eye. It was small and had curly dark hair. There were no details about this dog, like it was just a spokesdog.

I called to make an appointment because the dog was in Northwood, New Hampshire, and we would have to go a little out of our way. I knew I wanted *this* dog, so I printed out the picture and put it in my pocketbook.

"Bob," I said, "can we go look at another dog this weekend?"

"What do you have in mind?" he said.

I pulled the picture from my purse and showed it to him.

"This dog is in Northwood, and we have an appointment. Look how cute it is!"

Bob just smiled like he knew it was time for another dog. He missed having one around as well, and I knew we wouldn't come home without one. I had to have this dog because I felt like it belonged to us already.

On the drive there, I asked if I could pick out the name this time since he had chosen April's. I said if it was a male dog we would call him Spirit, and if it was a female, we would call her Miss Spirit. It would be Christmas soon, and the name is part of Christmas spirit—get it? Christ-*Miss* Spirit? Since I preferred a female dog, I was really hoping for Miss Spirit.

"Oh yeah, that's cool" he said. "Don't get your hopes up though, that dog might not be there."

"It's got to be there," I told him. When I saw this dog's picture on the website, I knew this would be the one. I could just feel it!

When we arrived at our destination, we were told to go into a room where there are puppies running around all over the place. They had many couches and chairs where you could sit and watch them like they were in a playground. People were there ahead of us, holding onto puppies they wanted, making sure not to let them go so no one else would scoop them up. There were many people there looking for a dog. Suddenly, a little golden puppy comes out from behind the couch, comes up and touches my knee with its nose. The owner pipes up that this dog is very timid and that she chose me.

"This dog is meant for you," he says, as he does his sales pitch.

I didn't want another golden. I didn't want to call her April by accident. I didn't even want to pick her up because if she licked me I was a goner. I wanted the black puppy that my heart had settled on. I looked all over the room, but it was nowhere to be found. My heart sank as I truly felt that dog was going to be ours.

I finally take the picture from my pocketbook and ask the man where this dog is. He tells me that the dog is not for sale. My heart is sinking deeper.

"Can I ask why this puppy is on the site for sale? Because this is the dog we came to look at?"

"Yes ma'am," he says. "She needs surgery. She has a hernia, and it would cost plenty to operate."

"It's a girl! Please may I see her, I am willing to pay for the surgery!"

"She's really not for sale ma'am, but I can fetch her for you," he said.

I know Bob sees that I am determined, and I tell him, "I'll work overtime and I'll pay for her surgery. I have to have her!"

Bob must have thought I was crazy. I hadn't even seen her yet, and I was already in love with her picture!

He reminded me what the man said about her not being for sale. When he brought her out and put her down over the pen, I saw that she had four white paws, and I was excited because I remembered that this is good luck in the home. She had spots of white on her chest; she was a black-and-white golden/English setter. I scuffed her up, and she was playful and quite rambunctious—really high spirited. I knew the name "Spirit" would fit her well.

"Sir," I said, "we came just for her. Please let us take her home, and we will make sure she has her needs met!"

I think that was music to his ears. He let us have her for a hundred dollars less, and we left with this beautiful mutt that we had come for. I held her in my arms all the way home. When we got out of the truck, Bob put Miss Spirit in his shirt and I took my first picture ever of her. We both loved her already.

Photo by Gail Durant

When we brought her into the house, she was sniffing everywhere. I kept a keen eye on her, so she wouldn't make a mistake in the house. That's what Bob called it—a mistake! As I followed her around, she looked inside the bathroom but wouldn't go in. She froze. She stood just outside the doorway, but her sniffer was in and smelling away at something. She stood there for a long time. I asked Bob if she might know that April had passed there so long ago.

"How can she smell that?" I am thinking to myself. "I bleached those floors!"

That precise moment, I knew I had something special. She couldn't go in that room for months. Good thing, because that psycho puppy side of her wouldn't leave my pants, my ankles, or my slippers alone, and her eyes would roll back in her head as she attacked. She was a rough, playful tiger. *Oh my God,* I thought, *I think I made a mistake!*

If I wanted peace time, I had to go in that bathroom because it was the only place she would leave me alone.

Miss Spirit had many names beside "psycho puppy." Bob would call her "Shitty Ritty," as her training took way longer than it should have. You could take her out for a couple of hours to go potty, and she would go immediately as soon as you stepped back inside the house. That was the first time ever I had to crate a dog. It was okay, because it worked quickly, and soon she became that loveable, sweet little girl we grew to love more and more with each day. She never heard those names from us again, and she didn't need the surgery either, as she outgrew the hernia.

Miss Spirit or Spirit as we would later call her, loved to go fishing at Emerald Lake. She would go back and forth and then stand still and pounce. She never did catch a fish, yet she never stopped trying. She also loved going out fishing on the boat with her daddy and me. I could also take her in my kayak and have her sit between my knees. I didn't go far from shore because if she saw the geese, she was going in after them with me behind her. She was my ears if the doorbell rang. She would always let me know when my mail got delivered.

During this time, we got another dog we called Gizmo. He was a Lhasa Apso. He lasted one month with us. He was not very friendly with children and almost nipped one of the kids in the face. He went back where he came from because we were afraid that someone would get hurt and that wasn't a chance we wanted to take.

One night after work I was watching television and sitting on the couch with my arm draped over the edge of the rest. It's after midnight and Bob and Miss Spirit are sleeping in our bedroom. I felt a nudge on my hand and really thought my dog had gotten up to say hello to me. I leaned over to pat her and said, "Hi Spirit," but she wasn't there!

I could feel movement coming around to where my legs were, and I got a cold chill. I felt the energy was low as I followed it with my eyes, and it went up on the couch close to the window. Just then my flood lights outside came on. At that moment, I knew April had come by to greet me. She and Miss Spirit always loved looking out that window. It was their favorite perch, and I knew she had just visited me for the first time.

This wasn't the last time April came to visit.

The second time was a Saturday, and I had gone in to work for five hours. I was a little tired, as I had worked the second shift before going back to work in the early morning. I felt that I needed a nap when I got home. When I got in, Bob and Miss Spirit were watching television on the loveseat together. I told him I was going in the bedroom to take a snooze and to wake me up in a couple of hours.

I went into our room and laid on top of the comforter, grabbed a blanket, and started to drift off to sleep. I don't know how much time had passed by before I felt movement and something walking up the side of me on the bed. Slowly and quietly, I could feel each paw as it moved up closer and closer. I thought Spirit had come to lie next to me. Without looking, I patted the bed for her to lay down behind me.

"Lay down Spirit, Mommy's tired!" I said, and she did just that.

I felt no more movement as she just plopped down by my side. It wasn't long afterwards when I heard a few sneezes.

"That kind of sounded like April's sneeze," I thought as I fully lifted my head and looked to the side. But no dog was there at all! I thought I was dreaming and laid my head back down. Again, I felt a dog crawling up to get closer to my head, slowly inching its way up. I opened my eyes wide and waited, and April sneezed a few more times in my ear! I sat up and again nothing was there. I grabbed my blanket, got out of bed, and went into the living room, really annoyed because I am totally exhausted!

"April won't let me sleep" I told Bob, "She keeps sneezing in my ear!"

I laid down on the big couch trying to get comfortable and Bob said, "I knew something was going on in the bedroom because Spirit stood up on the loveseat and kept looking down the hallway. Her tail was pointed, and I asked her, "What is it, girl?""

At that instant, Spirit jumped down from the loveseat and took off to the bedroom. That piqued my curiosity, and once again I went to see what she was up to. When I got to my bedroom door, I was amazed by what she was doing, and I ran back to tell Bob to come and take a look.

"Come and see this, babe, hurry!"

He witnessed the same thing I did that day, with Spirit sniffing up and down my side of the bed frantically. Up and down, up and down, my side of the bed, not Bob's!

"I told you—April was here, and Spirit knows it!"

We watched her for the next five minutes in awe. Bob wasn't surprised, because he knew me pretty well by now and was used to my sharing these kinds of surprising experiences with him.

"You are right again, babe, there was definitely something here!" he said.

I don't think I ever took a nap that day. Who could sleep with all that commotion? I always knew Spirit was special. I had that name picked out way before we brought her home, before I even met her! It's something I just knew! She sensed *spirit* energies too, just like her mommy. Special indeed!

CHAPTER 6

Mother-of-the-Year Contest

BEFORE I MET BOB, there was a Mother's Day Contest running with the Union Leader, our local town paper. I had rented an apartment and paid for delivery of the newspaper for the first time. This contest grabbed my attention while I was flipping through the pages. I stopped immediately to read the rules which were simple. They wanted a story that would explain why your mother should be named "Mother of the Year-1981." I was a mere twenty-six years old at the time.

A little voice inside of me told me to enter because I would have the winning story about my mother. I knew that I had to at least try.

"What could it hurt?" I thought to myself. "Someone's got to win, so it may as well be me."

I was going by the little sixth sense I was feeling on that day and knew I would soon be writing.

I remember calling my mother to let her know that I wanted to enter "The Mother of the Year Contest" and that she would be their next winner. She just laughed and said, "Yeah okay, whatever you say!"

"Mom, there's a prize of fifty dollars and a plaque that will be presented when you win. Also, our family picture will be in the *Sunday News*."

My mother was a tiny, nervous, and timid woman. I wanted to make sure that she could handle all the excitement when she won.

"Mom, I have a feeling that I can win it for you, but you will have to meet this man as he shakes your hand and gives you the money prize. Can I enter it for you? Do you think you are up for it?"

She told me that it was okay to enter because she wouldn't have to speak in front of anyone or go anywhere, and that she wasn't going to win anyways.

"What could you possibly write that would make me win?" she asked.

She had agreed to it only because she thought it was impossible for a stay-at-home mom, bringing up her own twelve children, who didn't offer anything to the community, to win the title "Mother of the Year!"

I was going to try my hardest but had no clue how I would start and what I could write that would stand out to the judges.

The next day, I was off to work on the day shift at E & R Laundry and Dry Cleaners. There were about fifteen of us co-workers who would sort clothing for Catholic boarding school kids from all over New England. The heavy laundry bags came with slips that told us what was inside and who they belonged to. We had to make sure that their names were on every item and then throw them down different chutes for washing. We would count and check off to make sure the slips matched what was inside their laundry bag.

At lunch time that same day, I sat and ate my sandwich quickly because I wanted to get started writing my story. Our lunch table was set-up in the corner of the work room and only had seating for five. Instead, I sat on top of my bin, grabbed a laundry slip and began writing on it.

I told all my co-workers that I was going to win the "Mother of the Year Contest" for my mother, and they laughed because I was writing it on the back of a laundry slip. I assured them that I would copy it over on white-lined paper when it was done. Some wished me luck, and some muttered behind my back, making a joke of it. I didn't care. I was never a follower. I strongly believed that they would all see in due time!

I don't know where it all came from, but I wrote freely from my heart. My hands were moving quickly to keep up with all that my mind was telling me to write. The words were coming to life and flowing easily. I knew I had a catchy first line that would make the judges want to read more.

That night, I reread it and made a few changes before I copied it to white-lined paper and sent it off to the *Union Leader*. Then it would be a waiting game. Soon I would know if my sixth sense was right.

One day, after coming home from work, I found a note taped to my door, which I still have to this day. It was written by a *Union Leader* staffer who said that they had waited for a while, because they wanted to deliver the good news in person but I was still at work and they couldn't wait any longer. Since my number was unlisted, they said I should get in touch with them regarding the "Mother of the Year Contest." The note also said that if there was no one in the office, to please leave my name and phone number with the switchboard operator.

I couldn't contain my excitement! My mother had just won, and I was sure of it! I didn't even call the office at the paper, because I wanted to call my mother first to let her know that she had won. I know that I was more excited than she was. I think she was in shock when I told her the news.

"Mom, I got a note from the Union Leader, and I know you won the contest!"

I read her the whole note and told her that she was going to be in the paper because of the story I had written.

"I told you my sixth sense was right!"

"Gail" she asked, "did they tell you that?"

"No, Mom, but why else would they leave that note on my front door?"

"You're getting way ahead of yourself!" she said.

"I'll call them now and let you know what they say!"

I made the call. The switchboard operator asked me to hold while she transferred me. It was then that a very nice lady came on to tell me that my story had won. Out of all the entries, this was the one that had caught the judges' eyes!

I knew it! I told her how I knew that my mother would win! She assured me that it was the way I had written about my mother that helped her to win!

My mother was so nervous on the day of the presentation that she washed her hair with bubble bath instead of shampoo!

The editor-in-chief presented the gifts and took a picture with my mother. They also took a family picture, which was posted in the news.

When the paper came out, we were all excited. I was just as excited to be featured in the newspaper with my siblings!

Here are a few paragraphs from that story:

> *From the moment Gail Adams submitted the name of her mother, Mrs. Doris Irene Adams, of Manchester, in* The Union Leader and New Hampshire Sunday News *"Mother of the Year Contest," she felt she had a winner!*
>
> *"Call it a sixth sense if you want, but I just knew she would get it and I told her she would win!" Gail told elated family members who gathered Saturday to see their mother receive a $50 check and the Mother of the Year Plaque.*
>
> *The presentation was made at the family's Hayward Street home, in the presence of nine of her twelve children and two grandchildren. "She's been shaking ever since they called last week and told her she had won" Gail said.*

Here is the story, which I wrote on a whim that afternoon on lunch break. I couldn't wait to let all my co-workers know that writing on a laundry slip has its rewards!

I know that my mother was proud that day. Winning this for her showed how much I loved her!

In the weeks to follow, she would receive a letter of congratulations, affixed with the embossed seal of the State of New Hampshire, from the Speaker of the House. I have kept it all these years in my book of mementos.

But for me there is one treasure, a commemorative plaque, which I keep

Photo by Gail Durant

displayed on my wall as a reminder that you have to "trust your gut" when it speaks to you.

On that day, it was my sixth sense. I listened to it and I am so glad that I did, because you can't win if you don't at least try.

Somebody's got to win! Why not you?

◆ Our Mom, 'Coffee' ◆

What is it that: Is 4 feet 11 inches and weighs 87 pounds?

Is it a bird? A plane? Superman? Of course not! It's our Super Mom! And here are 12 reasons why she should be named "Mother of the Year": Linda, Diane, Michael, Gail, Donna, John, Daniel, Tami, David, Ann Marie, Nancy and Kelley.

There's one main ingredient that our mother used on us while growing up — lots of love, but mostly courage because that's what it took for her to keep up with us. Our father left 12 years ago, something we'll probably never understand, but we love our mother, as she stood by our side and watched us all grow one by one. She took the happy times with the sad but always came out a winner.

Most of us are out on our own but she makes it a point to keep in touch to see how we all are. That sometimes is a phone call every night of the week, but at least we know she cares.

If her children aren't enough, her home is welcome to the neighborhood kids who also call her "Mom."

She's a tough cookie when it comes to cards or bingo — and can beat anyone at a game of rummy.

She is especially a good cook.

Of course, our favorite is an easy recipe — homemade tomato rice soup. We love it.

Of course, she has hobbies. She loves to sing but most of all she collects salt and pepper shakers — these she can never get enough of.

Holiday time is fun time for us because it gets us all together again — I think Christmas time is our favorite. We get together and sing Christmas carols, but the best part is countdown time. That last important minute before midnight, before we open our gifts. She makes sure it's right on the button. There's so much glow on her face just watching us. There's a certain proud look and she deserves it.

There's an old saying "cheaper by the dozen." This is something she does not believe in. She always said a dozen eggs wouldn't feed 12 children. She's right!

She also has a knack of knowing when you're feeling down, and does her best to get you back smiling.

Even if our mother doesn't win, we all want her to know, to us, she's the best there is and "We Love Her Very Much."

GAIL ADAMS
Manchester

Photo by Gail Durant

CHAPTER 7

Mom Coffee to the Rescue

FATHER'S DAY, JUNE 21ST, 1998. My biological mother had just passed four days earlier, on June 17, and Bob and I were taking care of the arrangements. We had already held the wake at McHugh Funeral Home, a showing for family friends, and now we were waiting on her cremation in order to hold the funeral mass on the following Saturday.

Bob wanted to give me some downtime in order to cope with her loss. The night before, he asked me if I wanted to go fishing early the next morning and then afterwards to go and look at a cabin that he had seen in the newspaper for sale.

I instantly said yes—after all it was Father's Day, and he needed the quiet also!

We headed out at about 4 a.m. to do some fishing. I don't remember where we went, but it was somewhere around the Littleton, New Hampshire, area. The sun was just rising as we put our crawdad boat in the water. At the time, this boat was all we had, and it was easy to handle. It fit perfectly in the back of the truck.

We had the place to ourselves. It was still pretty cold before the sun came up, so I always dressed warmly. I brought a hat, my redneck plaid jacket, a blanket, and some gloves, along with a cup of tea. Bob would wear his brimmed suede fishing hat and flannel shirt. He would carry a Thermos® of coffee and smoke a cigar while enjoying the calm of the morning. I always had my camera attached to my hip in case we caught the Big Kahuna and needed proof of our catch before releasing.

An hour had gone by, and we still hadn't even gotten a bite! I was thinking about my mother now and how she always loved the color yellow. I told Bob that I would ask Mom to send me a sunfish because they had a little bit of yellow in their coloring. We always made a game of it, saying that whoever caught the first fish would have a lucky day of fishing, but the opposite always seemed to happen. Sometimes that first fish would be the only fish.

I looked to the heavens and spoke to Mom out loud; "Mom, if you can hear me, let a sunfish bite my worm, because we aren't having any luck."

Bob chuckled and asked me if I thought that was really going to work. I answered, "We shall soon find out!"

He puffed on his cigar, and before long I had a nibble. I waited for the right moment and then hooked it. As I reeled it in, he started laughing because I had hooked onto a fat sunfish. I was so excited, and as I told Bob, it was not because I was the first to catch a fish, but because my mother had heard me!

"Oh yeah," he said. "So you think your mother had something to do with it huh?"

I told him "Absolutely! Not a doubt in my mind! She was definitely here. It's exactly what I asked for!"

Again, he just chuckled.

We fished until about 11 a.m. but we never got another bite. It was a long morning without one, but we passed the time peacefully with Bob smoking his fatty and me taking pictures of the loons and the nearby camps. In the end, at least I had the photo of myself holding up my sunfish. I had won this round, and Mom had given me a sign, so I was happy!

Soon we would be off to get something to eat and to try and find a cabin Bob had seen in the paper for sale. We did that often, looking at places for sale or land to build on wherever we went. We knew that someday we would have a second home, and hopefully it would be on the water.

We didn't have a GPS, but Bob was good with directions, and we found the road easily. It was a quiet area, but for June it looked really deserted, with no people or cars in sight. We had to go down this road, muddy from the recent rains, and the mud was quite deep. We saw a few camps along the road, but not one cabin looked as though it had been opened for the season yet. I found that strange! Without paving, the road was muddy as hell!

I finally asked Bob why no one had opened their places yet, because many do that by Memorial Day. He said that by the looks of the road, they probably had to wait until after the rains. It was all we could do not to get stuck, and then before you know it, we did!

It was a nice quiet day, and I was hoping we could get out of this mess quickly. I got out and tried to guide him as he rocked the truck back and forth.

This is a lesson you don't forget: Don't stand too close to a spinning muddy tire! It wasn't long before my clothes were covered in mud, and my white sneakers weren't white anymore, as I too got stuck.

The more Bob tried, the deeper the tires went into the mud. I told him to stop because we weren't getting anywhere. When he took one look at me, he couldn't stop laughing.

"Sorry, babe" I could hear amongst the snickers.

Well those chuckles didn't last long as he too had to get out of the truck and soon he was deep in the mud as well! He came back with some cardboard that he found in the back of the truck. He put it under the back tire to give it some traction, but it didn't work. The longer he tried, the deeper the tires sank. It was getting worse.

Soon we were walking, trying to find a business that was open and maybe get some help. We had walked for a while, but our surroundings seemed deserted. It was hard to call anyone because we didn't know the names of any of the businesses in town. We also assumed that they might all be closed on Sundays, and especially that day, because it was Father's Day.

I was starting to get worried about having to sleep in our truck for the night. This wasn't funny anymore. We walked back to the truck, and Bob was soon down in the mud again, trying to dig so that the tires could grasp his cardboard. I could hear the swear words every now and again. Cursing didn't help us either.

Two hours turned into three, and I finally told him that I was going to pray to my mother and to God, hoping that they would help us.

"Oh yeah, so you think your mother's going to get us out of this situation?" he asked me, sounding a little peeved.

"I don't know, but it doesn't hurt to pray!" I told him.

I made the sign of the cross and said an Our Father along with the Hail Mary prayer. Then I did my spiel, speaking very loudly to Mom and praying to God.

"Mom, if you are watching us, can you please help? We are stuck, and I know that you can hear me. I am not sure how you can help, but please, if there really is a Heaven, send me a sign."

I always believed that there was a Heaven, but here was a chance to prove it!

I could hear Bob mumbling under his breath about me and God, saying, "Like anyone can hear you, let alone help us!"

I wanted to laugh, not only at what he just said but also because of the way he looked. He was just as muddy as I was, except that he was more so since he was laying on the ground, still trying to dig out the two front tires. I really wanted to go and get my camera and take a picture of the mess we were in, but I decided against it and just kept on praying!

We seemed to be out in the boonies, with cabins few and far between. I couldn't imagine anyone else coming down this road today. I began talking now with God directly, asking him to send us some assistance.

"Please come and help get us out of this mess we are in God. I just lost my mother and she's in Heaven with you and we just wanted a quiet day," I said.

After about five minutes, I saw a truck coming down the road toward us. Three guys got out and asked if we needed help. Oh my God, I was so happy to see them!

I asked if they had any chains to pull us out, and to my surprise, they did! Within minutes, we were pulled free of the rut we were in. We were saved! Muddy and dirty but saved!

Out of curiosity, I asked a burning question; "What brought you out here, on this road in the boonies?"

One fella said they were coming to look at a property they had seen for sale in the paper that morning! Guess what? It was the same one that had caught Bob's eye. Only thing is, we never made it, and at this point, we didn't care.

We shook hands and thanked them and wished them luck with trying to get through and see it with all the mud. We hoped that they wouldn't get stuck like we did, and we finally headed home.

We were content to be on our way, and I was happy that someone above had heard me praying.

"Well Bob," I said to him, "now do you believe that when I pray and talk to God and Mom that someone does listen to me? Mothers always watch over their children, and Mom was doing just that today. She sent that truck our way with God's help! Do you finally believe me?"

With a muddy face and a sigh of relief, he said again, "Something out there listens to you, babe, and that's all I've got to say, but thank you for praying and believing, one of us has too!"

He turned on the radio and listened to his country music all the way home. I could see him finally relaxing. He was still handsome, mud and all.

My thoughts were now on our traditional Sunday Jacuzzi night, and tonight it was really calling our name. This was a Father's Day we would never forget!

As I finish this chapter, I glance at the time on my computer. It's 6:17 p.m.!

I smile now because I know that my mother is watching over me as I write about her and God helping us!

June 17 was the date of her passing. Coincidence or not? I like to think of it as a love connection from Heaven; that she is still watching over me! My mom is with me, right now at this very moment, as I end my story.

That's my take on it, and I'm sticking to it!

CHAPTER 8

The White Dove

WHEN MY MOTHER PASSED, it took a few months before she made her presence known to me, but she did so in a very big way. During fall 1998, I was having a lot of pain from uterine fibroids. Tests showed that they resembled a cluster of grapes and that I needed surgery.

I remember telling my mother when she was in the hospital that I needed a hysterectomy. She knew that I had a lot of pain with my menstrual cycle and was happy to hear that surgery would rectify the problem.

What I didn't know at the time was that she wouldn't be coming out of the hospital to go home ever again. She had been in the Intensive Care Unit for many, many weeks due to pneumonia but spiraled downward after learning that she had cancer. She died peacefully with family at her side. She had touched so many lives, and her wake and funeral showed us all just how much she was loved and respected. She had friends from all walks of life.

What I remember most about my mother is the way she loved feeding everyone, including the birds, whom she always shared our bread with. I chuckle now to myself because I follow in her footsteps, feeding everyone, including the birds.

She used to get mad at me if I took what I considered to be the best part of the bread, which we called the crust, to make a sandwich. Once, when I was visiting, I grabbed the crust again.

"Leave the crust for my birds!" she yelled.

"Mom, give them my good piece. I'll trade with them!" I told her.

She never understood that logic or why anyone would want the crust.

During another visit, she told me that she had seen a white dove in the yard with all the other birds she usually fed, which were mostly pigeons. I didn't know that we had doves in the area, and I think it was the only time she ever saw one. At least, she never spoke of it again.

It had been about three months since my mom passed. It was time to get my suitcase packed, as I was told that I would have a three-day hospital stay after my procedure. I was scared about the surgery but knew that I would be okay.

Afterwards, I was wheeled into the room where I would stay for the duration of my recovery. I was very tired and all I wanted to do was sleep. I was really out of it, and I don't remember feeling any pain. A nurse came in to check on me asked how I was doing as she took the needle out of my wrist and bandaged me up. I told her that I was alright by nodding my head because I was so exhausted and just wanted her to leave me alone.

I am not sure what happened next, but this is what I remember; I opened my eyes to a lot of commotion. Two nurses were holding me up, one standing on each side of me. There was another nurse changing out the bloodied sheets from the bed where I had just slept. I remember that I was apologizing over and over for making such a mess. They assured me that everything was okay and that it wasn't my fault. I remember how tired I felt and wondering what had just happened.

Once the sheets were changed, I was back in bed and off again to sleep. Hours later a nurse came in to get me up walking so that I would be able leave in a few days.

She told me that she was the one who had asked if I was okay and then left my room earlier. She also said that something had kept nudging her to come back and check up on me again. She said it was so strong that she knew she had to double-check to make sure that I was okay.

When she came back into the room, she noticed blood on my pillow. My vein was gushing from where she had just removed the needle, even though it was bandaged. Because I had slept with my hands tucked under the pillow, with my head adding more pressure, it caused me to bleed even more so. She was happy that she had come back to check on me. She couldn't believe how strong the presence was that had pushed her to return to my room. I thanked her for listening to her inner voice because who knows what the result would have been had she not done so.

She got me up to go to the bathroom and then took me for a walk down the hallway holding on to me.

"You need to get more exercise, so you can get out of here," she told me.

I was really not in any mood for walking, but if I wanted to heal fast, I knew I had to move.

At the end of the hallway there was a huge window. She looked out and said that there were a lot of birds on the rooftop below, mostly pigeons, except for one white dove that was in the middle of them all.

That definitely got my attention because it reminded me of the story my mother had told me. I wanted to take a look for myself, and even though I didn't have my glasses with me I could still see that speck of white in the middle of all the birds and I almost cried. I knew at that moment that my mother had been *that* nudge, the one the nurse had felt causing her to come back and check up on me.

We started walking back toward my room, and I told her the story of my mother feeding the birds and how she had seen the white dove. The nurse was all ears. It helped me to know that my mother was definitely by my side and looking out for me on that day.

This was the biggest sign I've received from my mother to this day, but she has reminded me of her presence in this same way another time since then. In the twenty-five years I've lived at this little cape in Manchester, I've seen a white dove just once from my kitchen window, sitting on the rooftop of the addition to our bathroom. The bird turned and looked my way for a split second before taking off quickly, making me wonder if I was seeing things because it happened so fast.

I knew in my heart that it was a sign from my mom, who was still checking up on her kids. What else could I think?

Just as the dove represents peace, my mother is at peace now.

When I looked up the symbolism of the white dove and read through some of the different interpretations, I was surprised to learn of the connection to motherhood and to Mother Mary in particular. I was thinking of this as I finished this chapter about my mother and the white dove. My entire book has been inspired by a visit from Mother Mary in my dreams. This interpretation connected directly to my story. How can one not appreciate that sign?

Recently, I received two prayer cards in the mail, in the same envelope. One had a coin attached to it. This gift validated that my mother is still watching over me and happy that I've kept her stories alive. It also proves that my spiritual guides are sending me signs to let me know that I am on the right path.

One prayer card was Pope Francis holding a white dove in his hand.

The second card is a prayer card, which had the coin attached to it and depicts an angel with outstretched wings. The prayer is called *Angel of God*. What struck me most is the saying at the bottom of this little card., which reads: Keep this guardian angel as a reminder of the children you help.

"I know than I am indeed on the right path because helping children is precisely what Mother Mary asked of me."

The Universe is quite mysterious, but I already knew that!

CHAPTER 9

Ma Says Hello

————————

Bob and I always had many kids in our lives, and we loved them all! If we counted both sides of our families, children, grandchildren, and those we called our own, they would number close to thirty.

It made us happy when they would stop by to say hello. One day, my niece Tasha had come by to pick up a picture of Jesus that I had wanted to give her. On this image, there were four black dots near the nose. If you stared at the dots for a full minute and then looked at a white wall, the image of Jesus would float in front of your eyes. It was the neatest thing to show people, and she had come by to pick up the copy that I had printed up for her.

When she arrived, we talked for a bit in the kitchen before I brought her through my bedroom into the office to get the picture from my writing desk. She seemed rather quiet on this day, but I thought maybe she was just tired. I was going through my desk drawers, trying to find the picture of Jesus, but to no avail. I couldn't seem to locate it, but I really wanted her to see it, so I kept looking.

"Tasha," I said to her, "now that you're here I can't find what I wanted to give to you!"

I decided to look in the top middle drawer and moved things around inside to see if it was there. Suddenly this one little picture of my mother, Tasha's grandmother, came sliding out from among all the paperwork. At that moment, I heard a voice in my mind, say loud and clear, "Give this picture to her, now!"

So I did as I was told.

She was sitting on my bed when I handed her the photograph. I told her that spirit had just told me to give her this, but I didn't know why.

She took one look at the photo, yelled "Oh my God," and ran out the door, with me trailing behind her, asking what was wrong.

I never did get an answer because she was in such a big hurry to get the hell out of my house. Before long she was pulling out of my driveway.

I was left standing there thinking, "What the hell just happened?"

Not long after, I received an e-mail from her, once she had calmed down, explaining why she took off so fast after I had handed her the picture of my mother that morning. She spoke of feeling a "rush of happiness" going through her body as she looked at a picture of my mother on the mirror, to the point that she could have cried!

My mother, Tasha's grandmother, had passed away in 1998. She had a huge impact on all her grandkids and played a big role in their lives. She loved them all and they loved her.

Here is her original e-mail to me, typos and all.

Subj: (no subject)

Date   9/10/2008 7:52:56 PM Central Daylight Time

From: Tasha

To: Gail

Aright so here's the story that I just drove home to share with you . . . .

First of all, a lot of the things I do that remind me of grandma. I believe is inspired thought bc she is around me . . . .

Such as . . . The hand with the rose, my license plate. YLWROSE. I have a bracelet with a coffee charm on it. I have a ring that says coffee. . . I even have paper roses on a cd that I listen to everyday in my car.

Anyway, earlier today . . . I saw the hand with the rose so of course I thought of grandma . . . however I was thinking to myself . . . I never actually felt her actual presence around me, or any physical signs . . . Then I was thinking she wouldn't unless I was ready as you always say . . . I asked for somethinggggggg . . . some sign . . . I didn't know what But I knew it would be hard to believe a door would shut or something

So yeah, At your house when we were in the room I happened to glance at that picture you had on your mirror thing . . . and immediately I felt like a rush of happiness throughout my body to the point where I could've cried and it made me happy . . . I was in AWWWW staring bc it was something about her smile. IT was weird I felt like I had a connection in the moment that I was staring . . . then I turned away . . . .

Then I looked again, same feeling. And I started thinking to myself how I really miss her and wish that she was still alive today and I really was just caught up in the moment.

As you were rambling around looking for the jesus pic . . . then you say you can't find it. We wrap up conversation . . . getting ready to head out.

I glance over again and I thought to myself, I'm not even sure I have any pictures of her smiling like that and I should look for one.

Then I look back at you and immediately you walk up to me and say here put this in your wallet . . . and it was her pic, with the same happy smile very similar. It was soooo weird bc of my prior thoughts in my head earlier in the day. . . I know you knew because you had that same Smiling Smirk you always have on your face.

So I tell Sharon about it all, and called chris and told him about it and how I felt like that was her way of saying Hello, because if it went through you it wouldn't freak me out . . . and clearly you picked up on it . . . and so I drop Sharon off . . . get off the phone . . . pull over to the side of the road to get my paper roses cd and realize it's in chris's car . . .SO I take the pic out of my pocket . . to put it on my dashboard thing . . . and I look at the pic one more time . . . and I DIDN'T NOTICE BEFORE but the bottom left corner it says . . .

"ma says hello". I just frighin smiled and laughed . . . gOoOooOOo figure!!

I really don't know what to say about it. Weird in a good way . . . good feelings . . . don't even know how to explain it . . .

But I felt like that was her way of saying hello . . . that was her sign. . . through you . . .

Between the thoughts I had today, and then that moment i felt at your house and then you with the pic yeah . . .

Thank you!!

Anyways I'd thought I'd share the whole story with ya as to why I was like

wOoOoooooooooooowwwwwwwwwwwwww . . . . that's soOoOo weird . . . .

I love you!!

Tasha

How can I not love Spirit? I knew after receiving Tasha's e-mail that it was my mother who had made that picture slide out from under all of the paperwork in my desk drawer. It was she who had spoken to me in that powerful way!

How can one be afraid of someone they love so much? I know that Tasha had finally experienced spirit for herself that day, as she explained in her e-mail.

How could either of us have known that in that same moment, I too was receiving a message from my mother? To me it was clear: I just did as I was told.

I can't explain how I hear voices sometimes, but I sure love the reactions I get when I relay a message! Makes me laugh too, each time I picture her running out of my house that day. You'd think she had seen a ghost!

When I look back on it now, I wanted Tasha to see Jesus float, but I couldn't find that paper. Instead she received a more personal message, one that she had asked for herself on this particular day. It was nice that she got her answer right away!

Photo by Gail Durant

MA SAYS HELLO!

Her Grandmother's soul was present with us that day, letting us both know how much she still loves us. Tasha got everything she asked for, a smile, a sign, and a big hello! My mother had found a way to give her that message, through me.

How awesome is that?

CHAPTER 10

Ten-Year Anniversary

ACCORDING TO THE COURT SYSTEM, Bob's son could return home to live with his mother at fourteen years of age if he chose to. When both parents agreed, he did just that!

We had him under our wing for over five years. It was hard for him to follow rules, keep his room cleaned, do his homework, and be in the house by dark. Our life had stability and discipline, and he hated that! He had a lot of freedom before he came to live with us, so he didn't like rules. He also told me many times that I was *not* his mother and that he didn't have to listen to me. That began to put a huge strain on our marriage.

The result was that he got to go back home as he wanted. We prayed that things would change for him for the better. I just hoped that in those years when he was with us, he learned a few things from his dad and me. I was grateful that my work at Sylvania had an Employee Assistance Program, which Bob and I utilized to the max! We went to family, behavioral, and drug counseling and followed exactly what we were told to do.

I can only hope that Bob's son's life has great meaning today. I can truly say that I tried my best and that it was I who had pushed for him to come to our home when he was first placed in foster care to begin with. Bob agreed!

I hope that he sees how we both tried to get him on the right track. In all, I invested over twenty-two years to teach my son the fundamentals of life. I grew tired as my efforts fell to the wayside. I gave love and respect but didn't receive it back. I finally forgave myself for letting him go. I can only wish him and his stepbrothers the best in their life, and I truly mean it.

Bob and I didn't see his son and the other stepbrothers for quite some time after that because they all moved out of state. It was now time for us to focus on our life together, and we did just that.

Bob's business was growing, and we started traveling whenever he could get time off as well as during my company's planned annual shutdown in July. We would vacation with many different friends and enjoyed each trip to the fullest.

I hated to fly, but I did it for Bob. I used to tell my family doctor that I needed two valiums, one for the plane ride up and one for the trip back. In return, I promised him a postcard each trip, and I delivered.

Bob always had to hold my hand during takeoffs and landings. He would laugh when I prayed to God hoping that the plane wouldn't crash, but if it was going to crash, I prayed that it would happen on the way home so that we could at least say that we had enjoyed a great trip.

I started seeing the world through Bob's eyes, especially his love for nature and God's creatures. He also got me to love fishing because it meant that we could spend more time together. Before long, we bought a small fishing boat, and soon I became this little redneck who wanted to be at her husband's side, no matter where we went.

My friends couldn't believe that I would get up so early to go fishing. I enjoyed being out in the open water or even in the woods for that matter. There was only one thing that I refused to do: sit up in a tree to film Bob on a hunt. I worried too much about a bear climbing up after me, so he would go it alone. He enjoyed the wee hours of hunting and I would enjoy the extra hours of sleep until he got home. I became a good cook, using the meat that was harvested.

Life was changing, and we were growing more and more in love together. We shared many laughs, and Bob could make me smile at the drop of a hat. I could do the same for him. He was goofy and silly, and I loved that side of him. I loved hearing him laugh. We were perfect for one another.

I had always heard that marriage was hard work, but I didn't see it that way. When you love someone so much, you are always looking for ways to make that person happy, and vice versa. We became a team and talked about everything. One didn't do anything without the other knowing. I felt that our marriage was easy because our goals were the same and the love was strong.

I am not saying we didn't go through life's ups and downs, because all married couples do. My husband knew that drinking had played a big part in my life when I was growing up, and he knew how it had affected me. He began curtailing his drinking to please me.

I used to tell him about all the safety talks we would have at Sylvania, and I would bring safety into our home life. One talk I remembered, warned against the dangers of drinking at lunchtime and then coming back to operate machinery.

"Bob, don't have a beer sitting between your legs coming home from a hard day at work. If you get stopped, that's your license being taken away. We cannot afford to have that happen. That's your livelihood and it certainly would mess up your hunting and fishing. Have the beer after you get home. Drinking and driving is not worth it!"

He told me that I was right and started changing his ways to please me and to better himself. We became one as we grew together. We just loved being in each other's company.

When I first met Bob, he was twenty-eight years old. I was wise in my years and older than him, but somehow, we were meant to be together and we learned from one another. We taught each other!

Bob always showed up at my work once a week just to bring me supper and to spend some time with me. He would either make it himself or just wing it from a fast-food place. He started coming every Wednesday night but then changed it to Fridays after a while. It continued that way for nineteen years, until I retired from Sylvania!

If his truck was in the shop, he would ride one of the kid's bicycles over to bring me my supper. I told him he didn't have to do that, but he said that he missed me and wanted to see me, and that was that!

I used to think it was funny that he seemed to read my mind when it came to food. I would be thinking how I could really go for a D'Angelo's® chicken wrap, and he would suddenly show up with one out of the blue. Whatever I had a craving for, he would show up with, without me ever having told him: Kentucky Fried Chicken®, Boston Chicken®, alfredo and ziti broccoli, or steak tips from Giovanni's®. I'm not sure if I was mentally using telepathy on him, but it sure seemed that way!

I asked him many times how he knew what I was craving that night. He told me that he could read my mind! It happened way too many times to be a coincidence, and after a while we just went with the flow. That will always be a mystery to me.

One night he showed up with a home-cooked meal of meatloaf and gravy with mashed potatoes. I can assure you that I wasn't thinking of this for supper, but I loved meatloaf, so it was all good. He handed me a container with my food and then gave me a fork. There was something on the fork, so I just flung it off.

"Hey! Hey! Hey!" He yelled! What did you do that for?"

"There was something that was on my fork, so I flung it off."

"Well, you better start looking for it because it was a surprise" he said.

Not even Spirit could have told me about this night ever!

I asked him what I was looking for, but he wouldn't tell me. He just said to find it. I only had half an hour for supper, and it took a good twenty minutes to finally find what I was supposed to be looking for.

He had placed a three-stone ring on that fork, with the diamonds facing downward. I didn't realize what it was when I flung it because it was white gold and matched the fork. I never expected a gift during one of our hurried visits.

I didn't get to eat my meatloaf for supper. I was too busy crying. It was almost our tenth wedding anniversary, and he wanted me to have this ring, which was known as a forever diamond. He told me that the three stones represented the past, the present, and the future. He also said that it reminded him of me, his fortunetelling wife, because when I read people's cards, it was always about their past, present, and future.

I had no idea he was going to give me a ring that night. It felt like *déjà vu*, just like the night he proposed. Spirit didn't let the cat out of the bag that night either, and I never sensed it. That was one special night that I will never forget!

That was my babe, a romantic for sure! A homemade dinner and a ring, all in under thirty minutes! I hugged him and let him know how much I loved him and how much he truly meant to me.

I wanted to take the rest of the night off, but they needed me inside. I brought my meatloaf with me to eat at the next break. I was on cloud nine all the way back to my work station. I couldn't wait to show the girls who I was working with, what Bob had brought me. With the biggest smile on my face and tears in my eyes, I raised my hand to showcase the shiniest sparkles ever!

They all told me how lucky I was to have found Bob, but I knew that right along. From the moment we first started dating, I knew he was the one for me.

Bob was waiting up for me when I got home. The Jacuzzi was filled, and champagne was waiting in fluted glasses by candlelight.

I don't have to tell you what happened after that—I can only say that I didn't come down from cloud nine for quite some time!

I indeed had a better gem in him than I had on my finger. I loved him more than life itself!

Our life was peaceful and quiet and full of adventure, but soon my curiosity with Spirit would add another dimension to our lives which would come a-knocking.

Table knocking that is!

It was something I have never heard of but, it would soon become a new pastime among my many spiritual endeavors!

CHAPTER 11

Drumming with Sharon

BEING MARRIED TO BOB WAS EASY. He was the kind of man who wanted to make his wife happy. We were good for one another because that was also my main goal, to make him happy! It balanced us out. It's really no wonder that at the young age of fifty-six, when I told Bob that I wanted a drum set with lessons and that I would pay for it all, he would make sure it came about.

I'll never forget his response.

"A drum set?" he said with a smile, and then asked why.

"Bob," I said, "all of the times when I used to go clubbing and dancing, even before I met you, my eyes were always on the drummer's hands!"

I loved to watch their every move and follow the way their hands matched the beat of music filling the room.

Jameson's Club was my favorite dance place, and it was so close to home that I could walk there. Every Saturday night my best friend Helen and I would go early to set up five tables together and reserve space for all our buddies. We had a gang of friends that we sat with week after week, and we loved our dancing family.

This place had live bands all the time. They knew me quite well, since I always jumped up on the stage with my mean tambourine to bring the songs to life. I would get the crowd going, and the band members loved it. Eventually, they told me not to ask anymore, to just come up if the song felt right for me. I liked a fast beat and loved being up there. I was very confident that I could keep up with their pace.

One Halloween, which was also my birthday, Helen had a cake made for me. It was so huge that it had to be wheeled in. The DJ had the whole club stand up and sing "Happy Birthday" to me, and that made me cry. I was so shocked when they sang and clapped as I sat in awe of it all. I had no idea that I had made an impression on that many people. It was one of the best nights ever, one I will never forget! Jameson's was a stomping ground for us, and I made many new friends there!

Now let's get back to that drum set. We had a friend, Bob, who was our Emerald Lake Village District, Commissioner, and Chairman of the Board in Hillsborough, New Hampshire. He had a few drum kits, and when he found out that I wanted to try my hand at playing, he offered to lend me one of his. He set it up for me in our Manchester home and said, "If you decide you don't like it, you won't waste any money buying one for nothing!"

After it was all set up, it was time to get some lessons. My niece Tasha had a friend named Sharon who played percussion and could use the extra money teaching me. I liked the idea of a woman showing me the ropes.

It wasn't long after I met Sharon that I felt comfortable with her style of instruction, so I hired her for monthly instruction. She would come by to give me lessons before I had to head to work on the second shift. I made sure to feed her lunch and always had a dessert for her to eat. She loved my chocolate cake. I was having a ball, and she loved my company as well. She would even tell me so. I would make her laugh because my beat was so different from all the others.

After only a few lessons with Sharon, I knew that I loved drumming and that it was time for me to get a set of my own. It would have to happen soon because I needed something to practice on. I thanked Bob (the commissioner) for lending me his when he came to pick his drums up.

One weekend we parked our truck on Elm Street and walked to some of the music stores that sold every kind of musical instrument imaginable. In my heart I knew I was buying a drum set. Bob didn't mind—he always aimed to please.

We shopped in a few places, but Music & Arts got my business that day. They had a few drum kits set up and asked me to try one out. I was feeling kind of self-conscious because I had no idea what to do. I hit the drums and snare a bit, but I felt awkward. I bought a Maypex drum kit on the spot, so there was no need to look anymore foolish.

I asked the salesperson what else I needed, and he showed me some extras. Of course, I had to buy the miniature tambourine that fits the kit. That was a given! I also had to have the cowbell, because it sounded good. I let them know that I was fifty-six years old and wanted to learn. I am sure they all snickered when I left the store that day. I just had to find out for myself if I could play to a beat or not and whether I could make it sound good. It really didn't matter, because it was fun trying.

Now I was good to go! I could tell that Sharon, my new young friend, adored me. She would laugh when my beat didn't match her hand clapping, which was always the opposite of what I heard when the tune played from the CD player. That was how she tried to teach me. She would clap when I was supposed to kick the foot pedal. I couldn't get it. Finally, I told her to sit and play and let me put my hands over hers so I could get the feel of it!

As I stood behind her, I cupped my hands over hers while I played along to a Creedence Clearwater Revival's "Bad Moon Rising." I would close my eyes and feel the music through Sharon. I told her that the song was too slow for me. She just laughed and told me that I wasn't ready for anything faster just yet. She told me that this song would get me started.

I would practice everything I had learned after each session. By the end of the week, I had it down and I couldn't wait to show her what I had learned the next time she came by.

Tasha would stop by sometimes, and I would show her my progress. I asked her to record a video after just three lessons as I tried to drum to the song *Mamma Mia*. Before long she was uploading it to YouTube and we would have a laugh watching my efforts.

Our crazy antics can be seen online at https://www.youtube.com /watch?v=4IUrOzRtalc. At least I could keep a drumbeat with my instructor! That video, dated May 7, 2009, was my third lesson. Sharon was trying not to laugh at how ridiculous I was. But I am so happy that it sounded swell, at least to me!

There is another video of me finally doing a solo at https://www. youtube.com/watch?v=fPLAjZo_O5w. The date is August 30, 2009, and I played *Super Trouper*, by Abba, unaccompanied. I was very proud of myself after only seven lessons. Like I said, I drum to the sound of a different beat, but it works for me. I shake my tambourine for a bit as well. Seven lessons! I was so proud!

My babe loved to watch me play when I sounded like I knew what I was doing! Sometimes he would lean into the doorway just to watch me drum with my headphones on, closing my eyes to feel the music. When I would finally look up, he would have that big shit-eating grin, as always. I could tell he was proud of me and happy to watch me play. It always showed on his face. I found it cool that he would stop smoking his fatty down in the man-cave when he heard the drums, especially after I had learned the whole song.

I think he loved watching my boobs bounce more, as it wouldn't be long after that we were both in the bedroom!

Yeah right, I like that answer!

I showcased Sharon E. Martin, my drum instructor here for a good reason. In April 2010, I got a frantic phone call from my niece Tasha that Sharon had passed. As we were both on the phone crying, I told Tasha that I was sorry for her losing a friend, and she blurted out between the tears, "She was your friend too, Auntie!"

She certainly was, and I knew I would miss her too!

Her family held a celebration to honor Sharon soon after, and I played the meanest tambourine to the fastest song the DJ could muster up. I stood on a huge stool at the end of the bar and rattled the bells of my Ludwig® for Sharon, with everyone clapping along. I got them all going, and it was extremely loud, as everyone surrounded me. For one moment, people were really happy! People were telling my babe how good I was, and I heard him say, "That's my wifey! She can always get a crowd going!"

I loved that it never bothered him when I got up on a stage and did my thing. He was quite used to me!

Sharon was all around me that night, sending me so many messages for people as they came around. Some of the messages were very strong. Even I was surprised and wondered why it was happening so much in one night! I had never experienced this before. I normally don't receive messages that often—it comes on a whim. I was glad that I was able to help so many to forget the pain of losing Sharon that night, if only just for a moment.

This was a celebration of her life, and I wanted them to feel that, to celebrate her.

It was fun reading people, and wild for me because Sharon had found a way to let them all to know that she would always be around. I could feel her energy very strongly in that room!

That was not the only night that Sharon showed up for me. She will appear later in this book, in the chapter on table knocking. (For many years, folks who did table risings called it table tipping. I had my own way of doing things and I liked the name "table knocking" better. I did things my way because I found what worked for me!)

People come into our lives for a short time. Some stay longer, and many are with us forever. For me, I know that I was meant to be in her life. I watch those YouTube videos now and I can see how I made her smile. God put her in my path because she needed me, not because I needed drum lessons. While she had come to teach an older lady new tricks with sticks, I also had something to teach her.

We both drummed to a different beat. After watching me play, she would sit and try to play it the way I just did. She liked what she heard and tried to copy me. I used to tease her and would ask her who the teacher was. She would always smile and tell me that she had just learned something from me! I would sit back and laugh because I was becoming the teacher watching my student. I still didn't understand what the hell I had just done that she liked! We were magical together.

Heaven received a great percussionist, and I tell her family when they hear the thunder roar, that it's Sharon, still playing what she loved best!

Bob the commissioner was my next instructor. He lived in Hillsborough, and after we moved there for good, I talked him into giving me lessons.

Now if only he can put up with my drumming to a different beat! Time will tell, time will tell!

CHAPTER 12

My Love for the Spiritual World

I AM NOT SURE WHEN I FIRST REALIZED my love for the spiritual world. I do remember that when I was younger and living in the projects, I hated the closet because there was no door on it. I always saw images of faces on the clothes hanging up when I went to bed at night. It scared the crap out of me to the point that I would put the blankets over my head when I tried to fall asleep, but that wouldn't last long because then I couldn't breathe. The covers would come off, and I would see dark shadows always from the corner of my eye.

I fondly remember the time when I asked my brother Michael if he wanted to have a séance with me. I had an idea that would scare the heck out all of those who would participate.

Putting our heads together, we came up with several ideas to rig the bedroom. We set an alarm clock to go off at a certain time. We connected a string to the shade with a hanging loop that caused it to go up the moment you tugged on the string. Michael attached a glove to the end of a stick. When it was dark, he would use it to tap someone while they had their eyes closed, to scare the crap out of them. He set up a remote control to make the lights turn off and on, and he kept it hidden in his pocket. He was good at things like that. He also showed me how to rub the sulfur off a book of matches. When you sprinkled that dust inside a candle and the fire hit the sulfur, the flame would flicker and smell. Rigging a séance was going to be fun. Our poor victims had no idea what was about to hit them!

We were good to go and just needed to find some siblings that we could scare. A few came in along with some of our friends to play séance with us. I don't remember everyone that was there so long ago, but certainly our brother, Johnny and our sister, Donna. She was the one we scared the most!

We told everyone that we were going to conjure up our sister Brenda's spirit. She had passed as an infant. I was the lead person who would bring her spirit into the room. I made them all sit in a circle and told them to close their eyes. I asked them to chant for our baby sister to come forward.

We chanted: "Brenda, if you're here, give us a sign. Make something happen in the room, anything. Brenda, let us know that you're here, do something."

The bedroom was dark except for our burning candle. We needed it that way so that we could pull off the stick glove trick, touching someone close on the shoulder. That would make anyone jump and would be sure to get a few people going. Michael was sneaky and didn't get caught. Being the lead, I would say they were just making things up, even though I knew darn well what Michael had just done!

After a few minutes, I asked Brenda again to do something to let us know if she was in the room. Michael pulled on the string for the shade that ran under the bed, but it didn't work. The alarm clock did go off as planned and made some people jump to the sound. Michael made the lights go on and off with his remote and the candle did its part, flickering with the burning of sulfur. We told them that ghosts stink and that's what the smell was, trying to contain our laughter.

It wasn't long before Donna was screaming and crying, running down the stairs telling our mother that Brenda's spirit had showed up!

We knew that we were both in deep shit, but my brother and I couldn't stop laughing. By now everyone was out of the room and running down the stairs like a herd of elephants. We could hear our mother yelling from below, telling us that we were in big trouble.

"Just wait until your father gets home!"

Suddenly, the shade snapped up fast from the tension spring and spun. We both looked at each other and ran downstairs screaming our bloody heads off, knowing that Brenda's spirit had finally showed up. My mother was so mad, but after seeing us so scared, she decided not to tell our father. Lucky for us we missed the belt that night!

I remember that when I first bought a Ouija Board, it scared the crap out of me. I didn't have it long because I never felt right playing with it and did not enjoy trying it out. I tossed it in the garbage. I didn't care that it glowed in the dark. I knew that it was something I shouldn't be playing with. I never touched one again.

If I look on my bookcase now, all I see are spiritual books. I don't have any romance novels, horror stories, fiction, or the like.

The first spiritual book I bought was by Jeanne Dixon when I was twenty-two. It was about her famous prophecies regarding current personalities and events. I read books about orbs, famous psychics and mediums, ghosts, the sixth sense, and how to tap into your inner soul. I bought games with runes, tarot cards, and the I Ching. I got books by some famous psychics who have been in the media, television, and in the newspapers. I loved it all.

One book stands out to me, one that I used for over thirty years when doing card readings and fortunetelling: the *Gong Hee Fot Choy*. My sister Diana brought this book to my attention after buying one for herself. Another sister, Linda, showed me what a regular deck of cards represented when placed on the thirty-two house sheet that comes with the book. This chart is used to explain one's life, past, present, and future.

I practiced first on family, then friends, and finally on friends of friends (who were strangers to me), until I felt comfortable enough to do personal readings using my own method. In all those years, I only charged five people for a reading. I had a hard time taking folks' money, so I just stopped. Bob always said that I wouldn't make any money because I always wanted to help people out. I enjoyed sharing my talents, especially when I saw the personal effect it had on those I read.

Some of my peers called me a "light keeper," helping others for free. Others called me a "lighthouse for the Lord." This was something I enjoyed immensely!

It would usually take me more than two hours to read a person. They would type what I would tell them as they sat at my personal computer while I read the cards before me out loud. That way they could have an individual print out of the reading to keep. It was good for a year. I would tell them to put it in their underwear drawer and to look back on it once in a while to see what had already come true for them. You can bet they listened. No one ever called me saying that they had lost their copy and needed a new one. Underwear drawers come in handy. I always signed and dated each reading.

I used thirty-two cards from a brand-new deck that had to be provided by the person whose fortune I was reading. I only used the sevens up to the Aces. They were shuffled by the person and spread out in order on the thirty-two house sheet. I would also make sure that I had wine on hand. It would calm me to have one drink, and then I'd be relaxed enough to receive messages. Card reading was fun, and I enjoyed it when people would leave here with happy tears, telling me that I helped them! I loved helping people out and their hugs were so genuine when they left, it made me feel good. My babe saw that it gave me enjoyment, helping others, and he didn't mind all the readings I did during those years, as long as I made time for him. He knew there was something special about me and that I didn't flaunt it. He used to say I was very caring, using my time and energy to help so many. I would schedule readings during the day, before I went to work, so that it wouldn't interfere with our time together. I sometimes did readings on the weekend, however, and Bob would get to meet my clients. Some would tell him as they were leaving that I was very good. He always responded, "That's my wifey!"

All my life I have been curious about the other side, and soon I would be dabbling in something new, table tipping. It's something I knew nothing about, but it sure did pique my interest!

A woman that I worked with approached me one day because she had heard through the grapevine that I liked spiritual things. She asked if I would like to join in a table-tipping party at her house the next day, before work. Curiosity got the best of me, and I asked her what that was.

"It's when spirit comes and raises a table to answer yes or no questions," she answered.

"What, a table rises, like a kitchen table?" I asked in disbelief.

She told me it was a special table and that I would have to come and see for myself. She wanted things kept quiet at work, because only a handful of people knew about table tipping. You can bet I was going. I had no idea what the hell she was talking about.

The next morning, when I told Bob that I was going to a table tipping before work, he said, "Oh yeah, have fun, babe!" No questions asked.

I made sure that my camcorder was charged because I wanted to capture the experience on video.

A friend picked me up and we drove to the event. I couldn't wait! Once we had all greeted one another, my friend told three people to sit at the table with her. They all had to touch hands, pinky to pinky, with the people on either side of them. Their own thumbs had to be touching one another, with palms facing down. I told her that I was going to record a video, if she didn't mind, and that I would just watch for now. The table reminded me of a small card table back in the day. I was told that it had to have wooden legs, or it wouldn't work. She said we all had to chant with her, even those not at the table. So we all chanted, in rhythm: "Rise table rise, rise table rise, rise table rise!"

It's a good thing that I wasn't sitting at the table, because I could hardly contain my laughter. I hid behind my camcorder and muffled my sounds. Soon someone else began laughing out loud and then we were all laughing. The master told us it was okay because she laughed her first time too. I cannot tell you how many times we had to stop chanting just to get our composure back from laughing, but soon the table began to twitch just a bit. Things weren't funny anymore. Our curiosity had us at full attention.

For some reason, the lead said she was having a hard time getting spirit to raise the table, but she didn't know why. We had to keep on chanting and chanting, but still nothing was happening.

"Rise table rise, rise table rise, rise table rise!"

Believe me, this went on for some time, and no one was giggling. They were serious because they wanted to see it rise!

Just then, my own spirit guide began telling me that I should remove the negative one, the skeptic, from the table. As they kept chanting, I saw a vase with pussy willows to my left, and the pussy willows were moving. They would twirl a little for me around in a circle, and I found it amazing. I looked to see if anyone else noticed, but all eyes were on the table. Soon, I heard that voice again.

"Get the skeptic off the table and it will work! Change the person out. Put her in the chair in the far back. She's holding you back!"

I knew who had to be pulled out immediately. This was not my party, so I wasn't sure if I should say anything, but I really wanted to see the table rise, so I stopped everything.

"Umm, may I make a suggestion that I just heard from Spirit?" I asked.

All eyes were on me, and I felt foolish, but the leader said it was okay to make a suggestion. I didn't say that there was a skeptic in the room. I told them instead that I needed to change people around, if that was okay with everyone. They all agreed. I moved the disbeliever to the back chair as I was told and got her off the table. Then I asked who wanted to take her place and moved the others at the table around as well. I told them they would be good to go now—as if I knew what I was doing.

"This better work!" I said to myself.

The chanting started up again with everyone participating, and within three minutes the table started lifting off two legs. Up and down, up and down, without the legs touching the floor. Wow! The other newcomers were in awe, just as I was.

The lead told people, one by one, to ask a question out loud or to think of a question in their mind. It had to be a yes-or-no question. If the table lifted up and down just once, the answer was "yes." If it lifted up and down two times, the answer was "no." If it lifted three times, the answer was a "maybe" or "I don't know."

We started having a blast, asking silly questions about work and our personal lives. Each person got to ask a question and after getting their response, we would move on to the next person. Everyone also got a turn sitting at the table, once the spirits and the lead got the table to respond.

Once, we even removed the lead from the table so we would know for sure that it wasn't her doing something to the four-legged beast that was moving in front of our eyes.

I would receive messages for some at the table and would let them know as I got them. It surprised even me that I was making sense to them. We were enjoying ourselves and laughing so much that no one wanted to go to work that afternoon.

Reluctantly though, we all did go to work that night. Although the table tipping was supposed to be hush hush, word quickly spread all around the second shift, and many came by to ask questions. I told them to go and ask the lead. It wasn't my party, but it sure left an impression on me. I was intrigued and wanted my own table—I had to have my own parties!

The next morning, when the alarm clock went off for Bob to get up for work, I hit the button and sat up right away. He didn't even have time to ask me how the table-rising party went because I was already talking about the great time we had. I told him how the table rose, and that I wanted one of my own.

I described the table to him, saying that it had to have wooden legs. I told him that it was small, that only four people could sit there at a time. I told him how we had chanted, how the two front legs had lifted, and how it moved as it answered our questions. I was so excited and rambling on so much that he didn't understand what the hell I was talking about.

I do know however that he poked fun with the "rise table rise" chant. Before long, his buddies would chant it when they saw me.

"I'll show you," I told Bob. "Wait until I get my own table!"

We went out looking for a table that weekend but didn't find one at all. We hit the thrift stores, yard sales, flea markets, all to no avail. I was disappointed, but I knew that I would find one soon enough and have my own. The anticipation never left me.

One night, the same lead was having another party and invited Bob and me. It was a Saturday night, so we could both attend. I wanted Bob to come and see for himself, but he had no intention of sitting at the table and told me so. He would just watch and have a couple of drinks.

As it turned out, one of the participants couldn't make it, and I pleaded with Bob to sit in or we wouldn't be able to do it.

"We need four people," I told him.

Bob obliged, being the great guy he is, just to please me.

Oh boy. Can you picture my babe with a few drinks in him, sitting at the table and chanting? He would give me those glances like he really didn't want to be there, and I would whisper that I loved him and blow him a kiss.

It wasn't long before the two front legs began lifting. I watched him with his hands on the table, touching others, pinky to pinky, but trying to look under at the same time to see if there were cables or something. The lead told him to lift his hands off the table a little, and it kept moving. Bob wasn't having any of that. He stopped everything and told them that he wanted a different seat. I laughed because not long before, I had done just the same, stopping everything to move.

He was in awe of it all, and soon I could tell that he was getting into the fun of it because he wasn't giving me those glances anymore.

When we got home he told me, "Something listens to you, babe. Something out in the universe listens to you! I know this will be surprising to you, but I felt something in the room tonight and I totally believe! Something made that table rise!"

I heard him chanting "rise table rise" before he fell asleep.

The next morning when we woke up, after he had time for the drinks to wear off, he told me, "I know what I saw and felt last night, babe, but I would never ever tell any of my family or friends that I even sat at the table, because they would think that I was off my rocker! I know something hears you, but if you tell anyone what I said or that I chanted, I will totally deny it!"

"It's okay Bob," I tell him. "I've been off my rocker for a long time now, and it will be our little secret!"

I was happy that Bob understood me and that he didn't mind one bit how crazy his wifey was. He loved me that much, and he would prove it soon enough!

Sometime later, on a Saturday he came home from a job and told me that I should be extra good to him today. I looked at him puzzled and confused.

"Aren't I good to you always?" I asked.

"Oh yeah baby, but you will be extra special for me after I show you something!" he said with that shit-eating grin again!

"Okay Bob, what did you do now?" I asked.

He told me to close my eyes as he went out onto the porch adjacent to the kitchen.

"Keep those eyes closed until I tell you to open them!" he yelled.

Spirit didn't even let the surprise out of the bag. I had no clue what the hell he was doing out on the porch.

"Open your eyes!" he said with excitement when he returned.

When I opened, I saw this beauty of a wooden card table in front of him.

I screamed and yelled. I jumped up and down and kept hugging him.

"Where did you get this, and how much do I owe you?" I asked him in excitement.

"I was working in an attic today when I saw this. I told the owner that you had been looking for one of these and asked if I could buy it. He told me to take it and said that it had been lying around for fifteen years and no one asked about it until today.

"It's a gift to your wife from me!" the homeowner had told Bob.

"Oh my God! Thanks, babe," I exclaimed.

Bob told me it was going to cost me. It wasn't our regular Sunday night date in the Jacuzzi, but instead, it was a Saturday afternoon delight. I can still see that grin to this day, but this time it was a huge smile! Got to love that man of mine! I owed him big time, and I sure did pay off my debt that afternoon!

This is a picture of that first table that Bob brought home to me. I called it Starburst!
Photo by Gail Durant

It wouldn't be long afterwards that I would find a second table. This one had metal trim all around the edges and metal brackets on the corners. It also had metal legs. I had been told that the table had to have wooden legs to work for table tipping, but in time I would learn that it just wasn't true for me.

This one I would call E.T. He was a good extra-terrestrial. He had his eyes and skin.

Photo by Gail Durant

I was really looking forward to having my own parties, with my own personal way of doing things, using my own tables. I didn't want to be a copycat. I would be the master of my tables and do things my way. I would find what worked for me.

Once I began dabbling into table tipping, I changed the rules as well as the title. I began calling it "table knocking." Yes, the table tipped, and we got our answers, but for me, there was always a message after someone knocked, and you let people in. For me it was Spirit that I would let in.

It wouldn't be long before I was having my own table-knocking parties after dark. I did it for free, as it was always my nature to do so and because I needed practice. Lots and lots of practice.

I had no idea what I was in store for and who my victims were going to be—only this time, there would be no rigging!

CHAPTER 13

Table Knocking

—————————

I SOON BEGAN HAVING MY OWN TABLE-KNOCKING PARTIES, initially inviting friends from work. I was excited to finally see what I could experience with my own tables!

I always believed in asking for the light of God to surround me and to keep any evil out. That was always part of the ritual I performed *before* we started any process with table knocking. Whoever came to my house had to go through this ritual with me if they wanted to participate. To me it was a way of asking for God's protection so that nothing bad would happen. I had no clue what I was doing at first, but I tried things along the way that would make me feel better. Guests either followed my lead or they couldn't stay. I wanted everyone protected.

Those who came to my parties each had to choose a meaningful talisman to carry with them to keep any evil away. Some held crosses representing God's protection, one held a rock representing the earth, and some held small bottles of Holy Water. If I ran out, I would just use bottled water that I asked God to bless for me. I had small cones of sandalwood incense burning, which someone would hold. This represented wind and air. When we would walk to close the portals, the smoke from the cones would follow. I had sea salt to represent the salts of the earth and used it to bless the tables. I had candles for some to hold, representing the light of God.

An open doorway is a *portal*. The number of portals we had to close depended on which room I used for the table knocking. If we gathered in the basement that meant we had to close three portals because there were three doorways to get to the room we were using.

There were three thresholds to cross over with each of us carrying a talisman.

Every person would have to stand in the threshold and repeat after me: "God protect us with your white light to keep evil spirits away. Watch over all of us and let our loved ones come through with your guidance."

I would go first with the cross in my hands to show the newcomers what to do and then ask God to protect us all from evil. I would tell Him that we were all here for an experience and wanted our loved ones to show up. I would follow up with the sign of the cross before stepping over each threshold, and each person had to do the same. I made sure they blessed themselves because it made me feel better knowing they had that protection.

You could always count on the chuckling and the laughter as each took a turn doing as I had done before them. If they said it wrong they would have to repeat. I made sure each individual repeated my words verbatim to be sure they were protected. Those who held the holy water would sprinkle a little across the threshold as they stepped over. As each did the sign of the cross, they would do so using whatever talisman they had chosen. I always chose the cross with Jesus on it as my talisman.

I had sage burning in the room to cleanse all negativity. I had a round thermometer on the shelf to keep track of the temperature during the night, to see if it went up or down. I always used a compass for direction because I had to stand in the north to receive, but I was not good with direction at all. Only I could stand in the north and I wanted to make sure none blocked the space between me and the table so that the connection would not be broken.

I would be the master of my tables. They each had a name. That night we would be using the table I called Starburst first. I had my camcorder set up on a tripod in the corner to catch anything that would happen, and I also had my digital camera on hand. I would tell people where to point their own cameras whenever I felt an energy in the room. There would be no smoking at all because I didn't want the smoke to interfere with our pictures or videos.

I like to do table knocking mostly after dark. The dark has an ambience to it and can make it a little spooky. Some of my parties started at 10 p.m. and would last to the wee hours of the morning. I made sure to let everyone know that this was for fun and laughter and not to be taken too seriously.

It would be a fun night. If they received messages, more power to them and if the table would answer their questions. I also wanted everyone to just relax and enjoy themselves. If anything, a table rising is meant to be an experience all on its own.

First, I had to do a cleansing of the table. I would gently rub some sea salt onto the top of it and swish it all around. That was a must according to the lead who had taught me not so long ago. I would also tell Starburst that I was the master of the table and that he should only let the good spirits in. The rest of the sea salt I would swipe onto the floor around the table to help clear negativity.

I told those in the room that I would sit at the table to get it started. Once I knew it was strong enough to take on questions, I would have another take my place without letting go of pinky to pinky. They would reach over my hand and I would slide out from the seat for them to slide in. Soon they would know all too well the chant "Rise table rise, rise table rise, rise table rise!"

Slowly Starburst would rise up and down with everyone looking on in awe as the two front legs lifted from the floor. If the legs touched the floor, then we would have to start all over again. Soon, the movement would grow stronger, and sometimes the table would also twitch from side to side as it raised.

It was time for those sitting at the table to ask their questions. It was so much fun for everyone. They all had a chance to sit, get the feel of the table, and see how it worked. You had to call the table by its name and again ask a yes-or-no question. It worked well that way!

There was be a lot of laughter at the questions being asked. Some were important to the sitter, such as:

"Starburst, will I get that new job position I put in for?"

"Starburst, will I ever get married?"

"Starburst, will my kid get a job and move out of the house?"

Some questions that were too personal would be thought about, not asked out loud. The questioner would say: "One is for "yes" and two is for "no!"

That would indicate that their question was ready to be answered, and Starburst did his part.

I would watch through my camcorder, recording the action. I could see orbs floating in the darkness and would tell everyone as they appeared. Sometimes it would get cold, and I'd let them know that the temperature had dropped a few degrees, meaning that Spirit was in the room. I told them who I thought was here based on what messages and visions I was receiving, and many recognized their loved ones based on my descriptions.

I would get tired, so sometimes I would just sit and watch for a while. I wasn't really needed once I got Starburst to respond. I was having fun watching and laughing like the others. That was my enjoyment—watching others!

Trying to get a table going took a lot of energy from me. So did relaying messages. I didn't get them often, but when I did I would let people know what I was receiving.

Sometimes Starburst would shimmy and shake sideways. Other times I would stand in front of the table and ask Spirit to lift it up while the sitters would push down so they could feel the energy, the push back of resistance. They would gasp and be in awe of it all, wondering how that could happen. They would gently push down, and Spirit would gently push up, without letting the legs touch the floor. You could feel that resistance for sure! I would make certain that all experienced it at least once!

There was actually one night where we couldn't push the table down at all, and it really baffled me because I was sitting at this table when it happened. I told everyone that this had never happened to me before. We tried to gently push the table down, but it wouldn't budge. "Wow," I wondered, "what do I do now?"

It was at that moment when my babe opened the door with our dog by his side. We all screamed and jumped, and Starburst slammed down to the floor from its position. Bob was laughing as we all jumped out of our seats. We told him what had happened, and he just smiled and wanted to make sure we were all okay.

I was kind of glad he came in because I didn't know what my next move would have been. That never happened again while I was sitting at the table.

I didn't like sitting with people under the age of twenty-one, but sometimes I would give in to their pleas.

One night I had family over—some nieces and nephews, all of them young. It was a blast, and they all enjoyed it immensely. One nephew was kind of skeptical and thought that I had magnets on the table to make it move, but there was no rigging there! When dawn arrived, no one wanted to sleep alone because they were a little scared, so they all camped out in my tiny living room.

I could hear them talking for hours from my bedroom as Bob snored through it all. In the morning, we watched the video and saw the orbs zoom by as the table lifted. It was a night they wouldn't forget, and they still talk about it to this day.

Every now and again, during a table knocking, I would tell people that Spirit was present and that they should take a picture in the direction I was pointing to. Whoever brought their camera would start clicking away. It was neat to see what they could capture through their camera lens.

Some of the photos would have smoke rings that would surround my head as I was filming. That would baffle me because no one was allowed to puff on cigarettes in the room. I also have many pictures with orbs.

Unexpected things would happen and make the evening most enjoyable and a little scary, but in a fun way, as at my last party to date.

I let the word out to my niece Tasha that I would be having another party and told her that she could ask some of her friends to come. She invited Brianna, the wife of my former drum instructor, whom I had met during one of my lessons. She also invited three other friends. I asked my baby sister Kelley to come with Anna, a friend of hers. My neighbor Denise came with her daughter, Nicole and some of their relatives. One of Bob's cousins, Melissa, also showed up and couldn't wait to sit at the table. I think this night there was at least ten to twelve people who wanted to sit.

This was the night the spirit of my drum instructor, Sharon, showed up full force. It was so strong that she took charge of the entire room, making it hard for others to come through because she took over. It was out of my control. I didn't know that my niece had brought four of Sharon's close friends and that all they wanted was to hear from Sharon. Their energies made that happen!

I had asked everyone to bring a snack or dessert for our breaks. I told them all that it would be fun and would be an experience that they would never forget. Little did I know that I would experience things that night that I had never felt before either!

I let them know the rules once we had all met one another. I didn't mind if they drank as long as no one got drunk. There was to be no smoking in the room whatsoever.

Together we performed the rituals of closing the portals and cleansing the table to rid it of negative energy with the sea salt. After asking for God's protection and doing the sign of the cross, we got down to business. I sat at the table to get it going and then had someone take my spot as I stood in the north to receive.

I was chanting with everyone, and again you could hear the laughter. Soon the table would pique everyone's interest when the two front legs started to tip up slowly. The room got quiet fast as they all watched in awe of its rising. Everyone was having a turn at the table and feeling the resistance with Spirit.

At first, I received just a few messages. Then suddenly my round thermometer, which was on the shelf, started to roll across it as if someone were pushing it. That caught everyone's attention in the room, and I just laughed. I blamed it on movement from traffic outside because I live on a busy street. A big truck had probably gone by and shook my house to make it roll. Nothing much was happening with Starburst after our break, so we decided to switch tables.

It was dark in the room except for some lit candles, but we could see that E.T. (my second table) was ready to answer questions because it started rising pretty quickly. When it got stronger, I had someone take over my spot at the table and went to the north side to receive whatever spirit would show up.

First, I told my husband's cousin, Melissa, that her uncle was here and that he might tap her on the shoulder. He did just that. Then she got a little kick on her leg and started to blame people at the table for touching her. I laughed and told her that there was no way that their legs could reach that far across the table to do so.

Soon the table started answering yes-or-no questions and people were getting into it. I was taking photos and recording what was going on in the room. Soon I felt a man slightly nudge me on the shoulder, and it scared me enough to make me run to the front of the room. People were asking me if they should be scared and I told them, "If you see me running out of the room and up the stairs, follow me because I am scared at that point!"

They all laughed and got back to their questions. While questions were being asked, I asked people not at the table to take a picture here or there.

It was soon time for another break. You could hear people's excited chatter about wanting to get back to the table. It was fun listening to that. People were making friends with each other and having a good time.

As we went downstairs and got back into our positions, my glass ashtray suddenly split perfectly in two and half of it fell to the floor from the top of the bookshelf. The sage that was burning in it at the time fell as well, and the embers were burning into my carpet. A few of us quickly jumped up and stomped out the flames. Thank goodness the guests were so eager to get back to the table, because otherwise we would still have been upstairs eating and not downstairs to put out the embers. That would not have been good.

I learned that night that sage burns very hot, and that you should always use something other than glass when burning it. Some in the room thought that spirit was responsible, but I assured them that it was just the heat of the sage that broke the ashtray in two, not spirit!

It was time to get the table going again, and as we started, I put my compass down to set the table back into position facing north. For some reason, though, my compass was not working. As I set it down, the pin was suddenly spinning around and around! It was out of control! I told everyone to look. They couldn't believe what they were seeing, and neither could I. No matter where I put the compass, it would just spin like a strong magnetic force was in the room. It was crazy!

Suddenly, my kid sister Kelley got up, picked up the table, and turned it around, and put it back down in place. Just like that, the pin stopped spinning.

"What the hell just happened?" I asked Kelley.

Kelley said that something had told her to get up and turn the table around, so she listened and did just that! At that moment I learned that she could get messages here and there also. I never saw anything like that before—it was very exciting to me and to everyone else in the room. I really don't know what happened, but we were good to go!

Now it was time to gain control and get E.T. to start moving again, answering questions. Once we got the table going with our chanting, I went to the north to receive. After a while I told them that I was getting very hot, and I asked someone to check the temperature on the gauge. They told me what it said, and I told them to take pictures in my direction. Here is the picture that Nicole took at this time. Spirit was going into me to receive.

Photo by Nicole Jones

I could definitely feel a presence. I received Spirit and transmitted a few messages, but it seemed that the energy of the five women who had come hoping to hear from Sharon had helped to bring her forward. The table was going crazy, and their answers were being given. The table was going up and down really fast, and it her spirit was loud! I know it was her because I wasn't getting anything for others in the room, only those who were there for Sharon.

My camera was on a table tray when suddenly it slid across for no reason and stopped. Kelley saw this and looked at me funny. I had no explanation and told her so! I picked up the camera to take a picture but couldn't because the batteries were dead even though they had been fully charged when we started the evening!

I was amazed by what was going on in the room, and I just let it flow. Sharon was powerful on this night and wanted us to see that. I began receiving and transmitting a few messages from her, and people were laughing, telling me that I was correct. I asked those not at the table to take pictures in my direction. I tried to get Spirit to lift the table while the sitters were trying to gently push down so that they could feel the resistance also! They were amazed by it all, but I was the most surprised when I saw the picture that captured the moment.

Photo by Nicole Jones

Musical notes! The table was rising, and musical notes showed up in the picture! How awesome was this for all that asked for Sharon, my drum instructor, to show herself on this night? You can't get any clearer that that! The proof is in the pictures!

I was all excited when I went to bed that night after everyone left! So many fun things happened, beyond my belief! I woke Bob as I slid into bed, and he asked me if we had fun.

"Oh My God! I'll tell you tomorrow what happened, but it was so much fun!" I said.

Bob was always interested in hearing the details after I did anything spiritual. He was thoughtful like that. I'm sure he poked fun at me with the shop guys, but I didn't care, deep down I knew he loved me for who I was!

The next day, I heard through the grapevine that a few people were upset with my table-knocking party because no one from the other side came with messages for them! They didn't think it was that good.

This upset me, and I explained "First of all, it was a *free* event on my part, with all of my time and energy. I heard nothing but laughter that night! It was the beginning of making new friendships! They got to see things first-hand, with some unusual goings-on that never happened to me before. It was an experience for all, to feel the of the table and have some questions answered. I can't control who shows up and who doesn't!"

It was at that moment that I realized that I will never make everyone happy. Shame on those who saw something first hand, for *free*, and degraded it! That night, I experienced nothing but camaraderie along with a lot of laughter.

I thought it was great fun and entertainment on my part! That's one reason why I don't charge. I would have given those who didn't receive messages their money back, because I would have felt bad. I can't feel bad if I did it for free!

For other reasons beside this one, I haven't used the tables since that night. The date on the photos reads "10-18-2010," and Starburst and E.T. have been settled in for quite some time. People say when storing your tables, you must cover them with a white blanket to keep dust and negativity out. What do they know? Mine always sat in the basement uncovered, between readings, with no issues.

People also say that only a table with wooden legs would rise. Not true! My metal legged table works like a charm. I know because it was through E.T. that Sharon came. Energy-wise, it was the best night ever! I have to say that for me, metal legs work better than all wooden legs, but both do work, and each answers questions most respectably.

I do know that hearing people laugh at my table sessions has a big impact on me. I love hearing the laughter!

Soon, it was time for me to have lunch with my babe and tell him all about our night. He would always listen attentively with that big, shit-eating grin on his face. He loved hearing me spin my tales and I loved making him laugh.

That to me was priceless!

CHAPTER 14

Graveyard Fun

I WAS BORN ON HALLOWEEN. Yes, Halloween! My mother had me convinced when I was younger that I was the easiest of her thirteen children to deliver. She told me that she went to a Halloween Party the night I was born and (in her words) that I just slid out as soon as she reached the hospital.

I think back about how smart I was going trick-or-treating as a kid. I would always begin with my usual saying, "Trick or treat, smell my feet, give me something good to eat!"

Once the people at the door dropped a candy in my bag I would tell them that it was also my birthday. They would then drop in another candy. How clever I thought I was! Tell that to the goldmine in my mouth today!

When Halloween comes around now I think of cemeteries, not candy. Instead of looking for treats, I started a new tradition; I went looking for Spirit.

If Halloween fell on a work night, I would tell Bob before he left for work in the morning, "Hey babe don't wait up for me tonight. After work, I will just be running in for the sage. I am going to use your 35-millimeter camera. We are going to the cemeteries down the street."

I liked using his film camera and was reluctant to switch to digital.

He would always tell me to have fun and then ask who I was going with.

"I'm going to be with Dottie and Zoey. I'm dressing up for the Halloween contest at work and then we are going out to eat at Cactus Jack's."

My co-workers always treated me to plenty of cards and gifts at my welding station for my birthday. I would use my downtime to scratch off the lottery tickets I had received, to see if I had won. I did the same for them on their special days too—we were a great group of girls who worked well together!

Those who wore costumes would parade around the café for staff to vote first, second, and third place winners. I won first place for many of those contests. For me, it was such fun dressing up on my birthday and having so many co-workers join in!

One Halloween, my friend Zoey dressed as a soothsayer, kind of like a fortune-teller, medieval style! She had painted her hair silver and gold and spiked many strands straight up all around her head! Her face was painted silver and gold as well, and she wore a black cape. She carried a cauldron with runes and pretended to tell fortunes.

I don't remember what I wore that year. I had dressed as so many things over the years: a witch, a pirate, a pair of dice with another friend Elsie, a Rubik's® cube, and even a clown. I needed a costume that I could easily step out of and go back to work. Bob couldn't get over how many costumes I had created on my own and would just laugh at my silly antics. He knew the word *contest* would get my attention every time and that I would enter every one!

Throughout that night at work, I kept seeing a vision of a German shepherd around me. I asked the girls around me if any of them had a dog, particularly a German shepherd that maybe had passed in their childhood. They all said no. I started asking others whom I worked with because this vision kept coming to me throughout the night, but no one had had a German shepherd. I just put it out of my mind. I thought that I must be picking up something wrong, because it made no sense to anyone.

I loved Halloween and the two holidays that follow it: All Saint's Day and All Soul's Day. For me, those days were dedicated to honoring those who had died and gone to live with God in Heaven.

I really loved going to the cemeteries with my friends on those days to see if I could feel anyone's souls.

That particular year, after some appetizers and a drink at Cactus Jack's, the three musketeers, Dottie, Zoey and I, headed off to my house. We hit the bathroom, grabbed the sage to cleanse ourselves, and picked up Bob's camera to see what we could capture. Dottie had brought along a small digital camera so we would know right away if anything showed up.

Outside, we burned the sage and surrounded ourselves with the smoke by swishing it around us. That was for protection, to keep away negativity and prevent any evil from coming nearby. We then drove down the street in Dottie's car and parked it near the entrance of the first cemetery. There are four cemeteries on my street and we would check out as many as time would allow us to.

The first cemetery we entered had a black wrought iron gate that is always open. We wanted to get in before any cars went by because we were not supposed to be there and did not want to be seen!

Upon crossing the entrance gate, I could feel that we were not welcome. The chills went all the way up and down my spine. I told the girls who were now following me that we were not wanted here.

We didn't get very far before I could sense a woman trying to calm her crying baby and asked my friends if they could hear that as well. They both said no. I told Dottie to aim her camera to the right of me to take some pictures and I did the same.

I could sense hands trying to reach out to me from behind. I told the girls;

"I can feel so many hands trying to grab me from behind but not reaching me, and it gives me the creeps! Someone doesn't want us here and they are *not* happy!"

The girls followed behind me as I walked slowly further and further into the cemetery. I didn't want to tell them that I was really scared—the hair on my arms was standing tall, and I kept getting the chills big time! I continued walking further and further, talking and telling Dottie where to take a photo. I couldn't see any flashes, so I turned around to see why and saw that they were still at the freaking beginning of the gate! Now I really am all alone. Suddenly, I get this strong feeling of a man right behind me as I yell to the girls;

"What's the matter? Why are you still at the gate? I thought you guys were following me?"

One of them yelled back: "Once you told us they were behind you, trying to grab you, there was no way we were going to follow you!"

Now that I know I am alone, without the girls, I start running back to where they are standing. I didn't really know that my words had stopped them dead in their tracks like that, but it goes to show you that they truly believed me. Man, I really did have the heebie-jeebies at that moment, especially when I found out that I was all by myself, deep in the cemetery with an angry spirit behind me!

Suddenly, Bob's camera flashed without warning. Dottie told me to stop using the flash because anyone could see the light and kick us out. I told her that I wasn't doing anything, and I put my hands in the air to prove it. The flash kept going on and off as the lens began turning by itself in and out.

"This is creeping me out!" Zoey said.

I had an idea. I stepped out past the gate entrance to see what would happen and it all stopped! I stepped back in and it started up again, with the turning and flashing!

"Oh my God!" I would say. "This is amazing!"

I stepped in and out of the gate and we were all in awe because of what was happening with the camera. At that moment, they waited outside of the gate line, while I walked in a little further until I was in front of the chapel building. I told them that I could feel a man behind me again who didn't seem to want us here. I told Dottie to take a picture now because he was right behind me. I could feel my hands tighten up as he got closer.

As soon as she took the picture and her flash went off, she yelled, "Oh my God, Gail! Come see this!"

I ran back outside of the gate to meet them and to see why she was yelling like that. The picture she had taken included this *huge* orb. In the picture you can see that my hands were fisted tight because I was a little frightened. Trust me, there is a skeleton face inside that orb! He appears to be smiling because he had scared my two friends and now he knew that I was on my way out too!

It was amazing to see such a big orb in the picture. I was glad that Dottie had captured the spirit that had made me so tense. There were other orbs in the photo, but none quite as large as this one!

Photo by Dorothy Garon

It was time for us to move on to another cemetery. We got in Dottie's car and headed over to the next one. When the coast was clear, she drove to the middle of the cemetery and shut off the ignition so no one would see the headlights!

We got out of the car and started walking around. What a difference between these two cemeteries. This one had nicer energies and it was calmer!

"Hey girls, can you feel the difference here? This one is so much better, and no one is angry at us for being here" I told them. "We might even see some shooting stars, from what Spirit just told me."

We looked up but saw none at that moment, but you can bet that we kept looking for them as we walked, even though it was a cloudy night!

Once again, I told them where to take pictures and in what direction. Bob's camera was fine now and not going on and off by itself. Every time we saw the lights from cars going by, we would hide behind a tree so that we wouldn't be spotted and get kicked out!

We were busy talking and taking pictures but out of nowhere we could see a light coming our way. It was so dark, we couldn't tell what it was. We started running toward the car. You never know who could be out there at this time of night, especially on Halloween. When we started booking it, we heard someone yelling for us to stop what we were doing, or they would sick their dog on us. We got in the car and locked the doors. At this point, we thought that maybe it was the police. We just sat there and waited until whoever it was got to the car.

Once we saw that it was an officer, we were relieved, and rolled down our windows. He put his flashlight on us one by one and asked us where we had come from and what we were doing there. He wanted IDs from all of us.

Dottie told him; "Officer, we work nights. Tonight we went to Cactus Jack's, and because it's Halloween, we thought we could get pictures of long-lost souls in the cemetery."

"Do you all know that I can pull you in for trespassing after eight o'clock at night? No one is allowed in the cemetery after dusk!"

"Yes, we know that, but we aren't causing any harm. We are just taking pictures" I told him as I showed him the camera strapped around my neck.

He flashed his light to Zoey who was sitting quietly in the back seat. All I could do was laugh at this point.

I said, "She still has her Halloween costume on from work tonight. It is kind of hard to take all of her war paint off!"

Imagine him seeing her with that silver and gold spiked hair and the same on her face. I couldn't contain myself and laughed even harder. This night was getting funnier and funnier by the minute.

She asked him, quite embarrassed, if he knew her husband. He had to call them quite often to his place of work, because the alarms were always going off. Oddly enough, he did know him. That broke the ice!

At this point, I was still giggling at Zoey's costume, but Dottie was a little worried because it was her car that was trespassing, and she could be fined. I was finding this all very amusing, but I knew we would be okay, I could feel it! The officer then proceeded to ask us, "Why did you run?"

I told him, "It's dark out here, and all I could see was a light and no body. We didn't know if you were a serial killer or not!"

He started laughing and said, "I almost sent my German Shepherd after you all for running."

Bingo!

"That's where the dog comes into play!" I tell the girls.

By now the officer is all confused as they try to explain to him how I had told them that I kept seeing a vison of a dog all night at work. Now it all makes sense!

This officer was very pleasant once he learned that he had stopped three older ladies in a cemetery chasing spirits! Boy, he sure had a story to tell when he got back to the office. I bet they all laughed at us on this one. I know I would!

He told us it was time to leave, and no visiting more cemeteries after dusk!

"Okay, Officer," I lied, knowing that I would be back again next year. "Is it okay if we go slowly on the way out, to get more photos?"

He said to do whatever, but just be quick about it!

After snapping a few more pictures, we headed back to my house so the girls could use the bathroom. We had so much fun and we laughed about the whole night: the camera with a mind of its own, turning on and off; the big orb; the officer with the German shepherd; and Zoey's costume

"The only thing we didn't see was the shooting stars," I told them.

We hugged and said our good-byes. In a little while Dottie would be calling me on her cellphone.

"Gail, while I was taking Zoey home, we spotted the shooting stars in the sky and we both said, "Gail was right!"

I couldn't wait for the next day to tell Bob about our crazy night. He always listened to my stories with great enthusiasm, and of course I would have proof once Dottie made copies of the photo with the skeleton face in the orb.

It was hard for me to fall asleep that night because it took a long time for the excitement to wear off.

I did go back to the cemetery again and again on Halloween, but never the one with the wrought iron gate. Not yet anyways.

It seemed like my crowd would get a little bigger every Halloween. I would always hear the folks from work telling me, "Next year I'm going with you!"

The more the merrier, I thought to myself. The more the merrier!

CHAPTER 15

Moving to Hillsborough, New Hampshire

BOB AND I FINALLY MADE THE MOVE for good from Manchester to our log home in Hillsborough, New Hampshire, when I retired from Osram Sylvania. It was on my mother's birthday, December 2, 2010, that I clocked out for the last time.

It wasn't until April 2011 that we arrived with the last of our boxes to finish making this house a home. We had been bringing up packed boxes with every weekend trip so there wasn't much left for us to take at this point except for minor things and the rest of the food from the cupboards and fridge.

Bob originally wanted to sell our Manchester home when we moved, but I thought it was better to hold onto it in case something happened to him. Since I didn't drive, I needed a place to come back to and live. If something happened to me, I knew Bob would be all set in the Hillsborough home. Deep down, I knew we should hang on to this house, and so we just decided to rent it out instead.

It was a new journey for me and a reward that I had promised Bob many moons ago.

"Stay in the city with me, and I will live in the country with you when I retire!"

I always keep my promises.

I had plenty of time on my hands when Bob left for work during the day. I kept busy and walked the lake with our dog, Miss Spirit. I kayaked Emerald Lake, even before ice-out, always taking photos of its beauty. Entering photo contests was a hobby that kept me going along with practicing the drums. Pretending that I played well was fun for me.

I loved being retired and got quite settled in with my new routines. There was always a home-cooked meal ready for Bob when he came home from work at night, and I would always greet him at the door with a hug and a kiss to let him know how much I loved and missed him during the day.

Bob would kayak with me after supper and always brought along his fishing pole and a fatty. He found kayaking to be a very peaceful activity, it showed on his face. He treasured being in our new home in the country. He was a proud man, and we were finally living our dreams!

When he was happy, I was happy!

In June 2011, I started noticing a few minor things happening with Bob, but it didn't stand out enough to cause worry. I noticed that sometimes when he wore his belt, he would miss a few belt loops. I would tease him and ask who dressed him that morning, and then fix it so that the belt went through all the loops around his waist. This happened several times in the course of a month, but I still didn't see it as a red flag. I took it as Bob just being in a hurry so as not to be late to work.

It also didn't occur to me on another night when he was trying to get into the safe and couldn't remember the numbers to open it. He came into the bedroom where I was and asked me, "Wifey, I had a brain fart. What are the numbers to the safe?"

I told him, and then he went off to do whatever it was he was doing.

July 4 was coming up, and our nephews always came up to the lake to be with us for the weekend. That was their special bonding time with Bob and me. They loved the lake.

We needed to get food at the market to prepare for the long weekend and were getting ready to leave when Bob told me that he had a headache. He never got headaches! I told him to go lay down and gave him some aspirin. He didn't want to lay down—it wasn't in his nature. He hardly ever got sick. We went shopping anyway and planned for the fun-filled weekend ahead.

That night I asked him if the medicine had worked. He told me that he had felt a pop in his head but then felt better. Again, I let it go, because he said he felt better.

That weekend I noticed that Bob was talking like he had had a few too many beers, and again I chalked it up to that because he did have a few beers, but now I kept my eyes on him. Too many little things were not adding up.

The following week, when he went to work I noticed again that his belt was not going through all the loops. Now the red flag was up, and I asked him if he had been having any problems with anything. He told me that he was fine, but I was onto him and kept questioning things. There was as of yet no clear-cut sign except the nervousness in the pit of my stomach telling me that something was wrong.

Yes, something was wrong with Bob, but I didn't know quite what it was. I noticed that his smile was slightly off, and I started wondering whether he might have had a stroke. He kept going to work, telling me that he was fine. I asked if he was having anymore headaches, but he answered "no."

The following weekend we again had family up because we were all going to the Hillsborough Balloonfest. It was a Friday night, and we wanted to see our neighbor's band and the spectacular hot air balloons in their night glow!

It was at the festival, as he went to a vendor for a cup of coffee and used just one hand to stir his cream that I really noticed something wasn't right. My heart sank because now I was seeing it with my own eyes. He used one hand to pick up the stirrer while the other arm was motionless at his side. It was unnatural to see him act this way.

"Bob, why aren't you using your other hand?" I asked.

He asked me what I was talking about and again told me that he was fine! We found a seat and listened to the band as I tried to calm my own nerves. Something was wrong, and I knew it! He got upset with me because he could tell I was watching him closely. He told me to go and play with the band. I didn't want to make him upset, so I did just that.

I grabbed my tambourine and got up on stage when the next fast song came on, pretending that everything was okay! I was doing what my husband was doing and pretend everything was fine.

I could get a crowd going easily. I didn't want anyone to see the nervousness in my face, so I went to town with every beat of the song, playing and dancing while the crowd roared! I wasn't really having fun, though; instead, I was afraid for Bob.

When I got back to my chair, I saw that he had dropped his cigar and was feeling around for it under his seat, but his depth perception was way off and his grasp wasn't even close to reaching it. I picked it up and then handed it to him. He got up and stepped outside the tent to smoke his fatty.

It then became apparent to me that he was likely having a stroke. His left shoulder was showing signs of slumping lower than the right. My worries grew stronger and I knew that we had to get him to a hospital and I told him my concerns. He wanted nothing to do with that idea. He wanted to finish out the night with family. He made it perfectly clear that he was fine! I knew better by now. I was starting to resent that word, "fine."

We made it back home, and I informed the family that we would be heading out to the hospital first thing in the morning, without letting Bob hear me. I wanted to go then and there, but Bob would be angry at me if I mentioned it. I knew that once I got him in bed, I could talk some sense into him.

It was late, after midnight, and everyone was snuggled into bed. It was then that I spoke with Bob in a calm and quiet manner.

"Bob, do you trust me?" I asked.

"Yes!" he told me.

"I know that you know that something is wrong and that you need to get to a hospital. We are going in the morning. I wish we were there now!"

He made it clear that he would go in the morning, but not tonight. He was adamant about that. I rarely heard Bob raise his voice and had to trust that he would follow through with his promise. I told him that I thought he had had a mini stroke, and he agreed with me, while crying. We were both scared! I hugged him tightly until he fell asleep.

I, on the other hand didn't sleep a wink that night. I was worried that he could have a major stroke, and I needed to be awake if it happened so I could call an ambulance. It was a long, long night, and my heart skipped many a beat.

I quietly slipped out of bed to get a hospital bag ready, full of clothes for both of us. I knew it wasn't going to be good news and that he might have a long stay in the hospital, so I prepared for the worst. My fears about Bob's health forced me to think ahead without falling apart. I packed toothpaste and toothbrushes for myself and Bob and made sure that I had enough money for an emergency. I packed a towel and facecloth with changes of underwear for him and me and snacks to eat, just in case one of us got hungry waiting in the emergency room.

The fear inside of me was strong—I was scared half to death! The morning couldn't come fast enough. Bob needed help, and I knew it! I started whispering a prayer, "In the name of the Father and the Son and the Holy Spirit . . ."

I prayed like there was no tomorrow and asked God to help me through this. I laid there, listening to the sound of the alarm clock ticking the night away as my own heart beat quickly in tune to it— very quickly, as I was never so scared in my entire life until now!

In the morning I tried to move things along, and Bob was stalling once again. I had to plead with his family to have a talk with him so that we could get on the road. I felt that enough time had been wasted!

Bob finally came up from smoking his fatty downstairs, and we were off to Catholic Medical Center in Manchester. You could have heard a pin drop during the long ride as no one spoke a word.

We were dropped off at the emergency room and as we walked through those doors, I knew that our lives would never be the same.

After giving our insurance information, we took a seat, but it wasn't long before someone came for us. As we were following the nurse, Bob walked right into a door frame! I grabbed onto him and guided him the rest of the way so that it wouldn't happen again.

We were in the emergency room for at least six hours, and Bob dozed off several times. I laid my head down on his bed from my chair while I held his hand. I was so exhausted from the long night and tried to grab a few winks between tests.

I could hear voices outside of his curtained room and as I peeked out. I saw four doctors looking at Bob's MRI and conversing with one another. I told Bob that he had a group of doctors looking things over. It wasn't belong before one of them finally came in to give us some news.

I remember paying attention when this doctor began talking about a brain tumor called glioblastoma multiforme-4. The doctor explained that it was very serious and that Bob would be transferred by ambulance to a hospital in another town that was better equipped to help patients with this disease. The doctor talked a lot, and I absorbed what I could. Not once did this doctor call it cancer—not once—so I timidly asked if it was cancer, and he answered, "Yes!"

I remember thinking, "Why couldn't he just say that in the beginning without beating around the bush?" I don't think I would have known he was even talking about cancer if I hadn't have asked.

It was an aggressive type of cancer, and there was no cure. The doctor told me that he understood now why I thought Bob had had a mini stroke. They were all leaning that way until they saw the scan of the brain. We were told that we would learn more when we got to Dartmouth Hitchcock Medical Center in Lebanon, New Hampshire, where he would be seen by specialists. With that, he wished us well and left the room.

I had never heard such sobbing from my husband in all the years that I had known him. In fact, this was the first time I had ever heard him cry so loudly. I held onto him tightly for quite some time, comforting and holding him as the news sunk in.

I think I was in a state of shock! I couldn't cry, and all I could think of was my dream where Mother Mary had told me that my husband would pass before me. It seemed like it was now becoming a reality. I was so scared for him. I kept apologizing over and over as I held onto him for dear life. I knew the road ahead was going to be a bumpy one!

It would be a while before we could leave by ambulance, so I made some of the dreaded calls to give the news to our family and friends. It had to be done, and I knew that I had to be strong from here on out. It was hard for them to hear the diagnosis. Some reacted in anger, some in disbelief, and some quietly accepted the news. It was then that I decided to choose just one person from each side of the family to pass the information to, because their emotional reactions were too hard on me. I had enough to deal with taking care of my husband and didn't need the added stress of any negative comments or opinions. I needed to be strong only for Bob and myself!

I was happy that I had packed a travel bag because we would end up spending the next nine days in the hospital waiting for the specialists to make a game plan. I was happy that I had had the forethought to pack a bag and bring extra money and grateful that I had listened to my gut instincts.

The ambulance ride to Lebanon was about an hour and a half, and I sat in the front seat. I could hear Bob conversing with the man who was taking care of him in the back. Sometimes I would hear him laughing, but I knew that it was a nervous laugh. He was scared as heck and had every right to be.

All I could think was that I was glad I had retired just a few shorts months earlier. I didn't have to worry about dealing with work. My retirement was a blessing in disguise. I remembered the sign I received from the book my neighbor had given me and the words I had read that made me decide to leave work and give a five-day notice: "If you're not happy with your job, leave it!"

Boy, someone out there in the spiritual world was guiding me, and I knew I would depend on them in the days ahead! I am glad that I listened to the spirit that communicates with me.

My husband needed me more than ever, and I would be there for him, no matter what, just as we had written to each other in our wedding vows.

"No matter what!!!"

After talking with the many doctors at DHMC, we were told that Bob needed a craniotomy, and this would be the first procedure to aid us with his quality of life!

They removed 80 percent of the tumor when Bob had this surgery. As long as, he could show them that he could climb stairs, they would let him go home. It was the longest nine days ever, but soon we would be back home where we were the most comfortable.

I made all the follow-up calls and got the paperwork going. I kept a calendar of all his appointments for radiation and other treatments. Every two weeks, we were at DHMC for appointments, infusions, and lab work. Bob also did clinical trials, and I made sure that it was what *he* wanted to do. I gave him the correct dose of chemo pills at home for five days every month.

When Bob slept at night, I would be on my computer looking for a miracle. I was looking for a doctor who had a cure. Maybe there was someone out there that could save Bob's life. I looked for cures, remedies, diets, and whatever I could read to try and save my husband's life. It was sucking my energy dry. After three solid months of doing this, I just stopped. I had to accept what life he had left and decided to make the best of it. I didn't want to make myself crazy, and I had to let it be, or so I thought.

"Let go and let God," I would tell myself over and over.

I promised that I would give him the best "rest of his life" ever! I knew in my heart that I would lose him someday and that this was the time to live life to its fullest.

I decided to set up a shrine on my fireplace hearth. I put all my statues of Mother Mary and St. Joseph on the hearth and had many prayer cards with different prayers to say while my candles burned. I would do this only when I knew Bob was downstairs smoking his fatty and playing pool. I didn't want him to catch me because he would be worried for me. He stayed downstairs for hours, and it gave me the time to bargain with God. All I needed was an hour to say my prayers and ask God to take me instead of him.

You see, I was willing to give up my life for the love of my life! I was offering my life to let Bob live. It made sense to me to have God give him that miracle and to take me instead. I was older, and I had no regrets. I wanted Bob to enjoy the log cabin on the water, and so my vigil began: secretly, every day, I talked to God and Mother Mary, asking them to just take me instead. I really thought that if I prayed hard enough it could work. After all, someone out there listens to me when I speak. Right? What could it hurt, I thought to myself? I thought about those five stages of grief: *denial, anger, bargaining, depression, and acceptance.* I always wondered why *shock* wasn't in all of that! It is quite the shock when you hear words like *terminal, incurable, brain tumor!* So here I am bargaining. I wasn't in denial, and I wasn't angry, and I really don't know why. I thought, "What good it would do to be that way?", and so I came up with a positive way to give of myself and hoped that it would work!

I continued this negotiating for a couple of months until one morning when Bob came upstairs for another cup of coffee and saw me on my knees praying in front of the hearth. It was too late to hide my things, and he questioned what I was doing on the floor with statues in front of me and candles burning. I told him that I was bargaining with God and Mother Mary in prayer. I admitted that I wanted to trade places with him and had asked them to give him a miracle and to take me instead, because I was older.

Boy, the next thing I got was *shock!* Bob was yelling at me, asking why I was doing this, because he really believed that I could make it happen! He was very angry and loudly said (between swear words), "If God takes you, then what am I supposed to do without you? I can't live my life without you, Babe. You've got to stop this immediately!"

Wow! He never yelled at me like that in my entire life. And he was so mad! I never realized that he would think this way—that he actually believed it could happen if I asked. I couldn't believe that he thought I had that much power!

He wanted me to put those things away and never to pray like that again, and then he sat down next to me and started crying. All I could do was cry with him. We grieved a lot together that night. That's how I looked at it, grieving together.

That woke me up! I promised that I would stop bargaining with God. I couldn't have my husband upset like this. I hated to see him cry! That was the day I put all my statues and candles away. I didn't stop praying, but I did stop bargaining once and for all. It was that day that I went straight to *acceptance* and vowed to make the rest of Bob's life his best possible life.

My babe was in the *depression* stage. He couldn't work, couldn't drive, and sometimes he couldn't think straight. I saw it play out when the therapists would come by and show him flash cards. They showed him a picture of a comb, and he knew what it did but couldn't say the word. This therapy wasn't helping him; it was only frustrating him. I knew in my heart that this therapy was done. For sixty bucks an hour I could do that myself, but why would I, if it made him more depressed? Bob never had to worry about flash cards ever again. It seemed useless to me, to show him what he couldn't do. I wanted to show him what he could do!

He could still play poker, so that's what I considered his therapy. I rang up the family and planned several poker parties at the house to ease Bob's mind of his worries. He was slow going, but everyone made an effort to be patient with him. I saw a smile come back to his face, and that was my intention moving forward, to keep that smile on his face!

As I said before, every two weeks we had to travel to Lebanon for one day of treatment. I told Bob that after that long day was done, he would have a two-week vacation. That's how we did things: we focused on the vacation times, when there were no long car trips for transfusions or chemo, blood draws, MRIs, or scans.

Sometimes a trip to Foxwoods would be in order, or we might just have company over and play pool. We would visit with neighbors for tea or go walking around the lake. I tried to keep him busy as best as I could.

I remember when he started losing his hair, I told him that I wanted to shave my head in support of him. He told me;

"No *fucking* wife of mine is going to be bald so get it out of your head!"

That was that! I didn't argue with his logic.

I knew, from this point forward we would live our lives one day at a time.

CHAPTER 16

Moving Back to Manchester

———————

LIVING LIFE ONE DAY AT A TIME was all we could do after Bob's diagnosis, just three months after moving into our retirement home on Emerald Lake. We made each day count, deciding what activities to do depending on how Bob was feeling. We had company all the time, which kept our minds off the inevitable. Keeping up with a big log home was a lot for both of us to handle, even with the help of family and friends.

After just one year of living there, we found out how God's mysterious ways come into play. It's those little signs that make you sit up and take notice that another path is about to be crossed. It was up to us to take heed of it or not.

Our home in Manchester, New Hampshire, would be ready for renting again at the end of April. I asked Bob if he wanted to move back because things would be easier for us there. I could get him around by taxi, since I didn't drive, and the grocery store there was within walking distance of our house, unlike in the country. He said no, and that was the end of that! I promised him that I would stay with him no matter where he wanted to live, and I would put an ad in the paper to rent out our Manchester home.

A week later, Bob called me downstairs, saying that we needed to talk. I really didn't have any idea what he wanted to talk about but was quite surprised when he told me that he wanted to move back to our little cape in Manchester.

"Are you sure?" I said, "I don't have a problem staying, and living out the rest of your life here. It was a promise I made to you long before I retired!"

He said that he had thought about it quite a bit and that he wanted to move back home. He also told me that both of our families would

110

be close by, and it wouldn't be so hard for them to keep traveling back and forth. I told him that the best thing for me would be not having to wait thirty-three minutes when I called for an ambulance. Back home, we could have one in just three minutes!

In Bob's mind it was settled, we were going to move back to Manchester. We spread the word, and I thought that most on his side would be happy to hear it, but I caught slack for it. I heard that *I* was making Bob leave the home that he had built and loved so much. It was so far from the truth, but I had no time or energy to argue or worry about that now. We had to pack once again and put our house on the market.

I hired one of my best friends, Laurie, to help with packing because she was so good at it. It was only thirteen months earlier that she had helped me to pack to move here. Crazy how unexpected life is!

Before moving back home, I asked Bob if we could add a fresh coat of paint and some new rugs to make it feel like a new home, and he agreed. We hired people to pull out some of the rugs and to paint the walls in our color choices. Unbeknownst to me, Bob chose the same exact color scheme for his man cave as I had chosen for our bedroom; beige for the walls and tan carpeting. We had the exterior painted as well and swapped the red shutters for black ones. It was time for a fresh start in an old home that held many memories for us. We wanted the house to be ready by the first week of May.

Our log home was huge, so we needed to downsize our furniture. We gave away some of our bedroom pieces and let go of many other items that I knew wouldn't fit in the smaller cape. We left so much behind for the new owners. We would surely miss the pool table, where Bob got a kick out of watching us all trying to beat him. He was so good at playing pool, and in all the times we played, I only beat him once!

We left a nine-foot Christmas tree behind because it would never fit in our old home. What mattered most was being closer to family and the hospitals. Not having to stack wood was a plus, but leaving the friendships that we had made with neighbors was harder for us.

It was time to say our good-byes and to let them all know how much they meant to us at this point in our lives. They all understood why we had to leave.

We may have only lived there full-time for just over a year, but we owned the land and visited regularly over the course of many years. We would miss walking around the lake and getting in the boat like we always did after Bob came home from work.

Poor Miss Spirit had no clue what the heck was going on. She sat peacefully as the hired movers came to get the last of the boxes. Even before the movers came, truckloads of belongings had been taken out with the help of family and friends. These were taken to the storage space at Bob's business, for retrieval at a later date.

It was time to do a walk-through, just Bob and me, to make sure we didn't leave anything behind and to say good-bye to a sweet beautiful home that had come to life with our own personal touches.

We walked hand and hand into the great room and looked out through the huge glass doors at this wonderful lake that we had enjoyed so much over the years. We both had tears rolling down our faces, but we knew that this was meant to be.

We hoped that the new buyers would appreciate all the special details, but most importantly, we hoped that they would leave Bob's and my handprint and words declaring our love for one another on the retaining wall just off the back walk-out.

It was time to move on as we stepped out through the front entrance door that once held the carved wood sign, which read, "Durants". We took one last look back inside before closing the entry door. It was empty and bare, but I could picture it in my mind just how it used to be. Even though we weren't in the house long, this home held many wonderful memories! As we left, the only sound we heard was that of the door clicking shut and an engine running.

Out front, our best friends Terry and Helen were waiting to take us back home in their pick-up truck. Bob didn't cry, which surprised me. He seemed pleased to go back home, and for some reason deep down inside, I know he did this for me. He loved me that much, and he did it so that I could be a better nurse and caregiver for him. He knew I could be self-reliant in the city. He was making life easier for both of us, and I loved him for that.

It was then that I realized that the house didn't really matter to him anymore, and that our love for one another was far bigger that that log home—much bigger than anyone could ever realize. Neither of us teared up over leaving that beautiful home after that day. We had to make *new* memories in the *old* home now.

Our time was too precious to waste any tears on an inanimate object. Bob and I, along with Miss Spirit, were truly home, and it felt good to be back!

I saw the change right away as the movers placed the first couch down in the living room. Spirit jumped up and watched out her window like she had never left it. Bob went out back on the deck to smoke a fatty.

Somethings never really change, do they?

I was happy, they were happy!

CHAPTER 17

Getting Papers in Order

BOB'S HEALTH WAS GOOD ENOUGH that he decided to go away with his buddies on a fishing trip for a week to Moosehead Lake in Maine. It was set for the month of May, his birthday month.

I had made all the arrangements for them and helped Bob with packing to make sure he wouldn't forget his medicine. Before the trip, I taught Bob how to take his shots. He had to learn, since I been administering his blood-clot prevention shots and I wasn't going with them.

Using a black magic marker, I labeled a plastic bag for each day of the week, explaining how and when to take his pills. If the plastic bag had a letter "L" or an "R", he would know the shot would be on his left or right side for that particular day. His brain cancer had made him forgetful, and I hoped this technique would help him while he was away.

I wanted him to have the best time ever. I gave him $1,800.00 out of our savings and told him to treat the guys whenever possible. He asked me what I would be doing while he was gone.

"I will clean the house and take walks with Miss Spirit," I told him.

I didn't want to tell him what I was truly planning. This might be the only chance I'd have to prepare for his funeral. The time was now, because I didn't know when his last day on this earth would be. I kissed him good-bye, and we said "I love you" to each other. He told me to have fun.

"I will," I told him. You too."

This was going to be a tough week for me. How could I have fun planning a funeral for my husband? I had to be strong.

The next day, after Bob left, I went with Helen, one of my best friends, to the funeral home. Later that night I sat down and designed, on paper, what I wanted for a stone for Bob and me. It had to have meaning. It didn't take me long to think of the perfect design: two hearts, each holding a picture of us.

One of the pictures would be of our wedding day dance. How glorious we both looked. Bob was so handsome in his white suit with a red vest, and for once, I felt beautiful in my gorgeous white wedding gown with lace and beads and with red roses in my wedding veil crown. We were gazing at each other adoringly.

The other picture would be of us dancing at our nephew's wedding, our gray hairs shining in the light. This is how we looked as we aged together.

Although these two photos were taken years apart, you could still see the love we had for each other as we gazed into each other's eyes. The love was captivating and enduring after all those years, I thought.

I also had a clever idea to engrave the names of our wedding songs—Bob's song to me, "Forever & Ever, Amen," and my song to him, "The Power of Love,"— into the "V" shape of each heart.

I also wanted Bob's dad and my mom somehow represented on the stone. When I first met Bob, he had only his father, and I had just my mother. Bob's mother had died when he was young, and my father had simply run off. These were the only parents we knew growing up, and we loved them dearly. I knew we had to incorporate them into our stone somehow, as they were each such a big part of our lives.

Adding imagery for my mother was easy. She loved the color yellow, and her favorite flowers were roses, especially yellow roses. She always said that she didn't want flowers when she was dead. She wanted to be able to smell them when she was alive.

Thinking of a way to memorialize Bob's dad required a bit more thought. I remembered a picture of Bob's dad making his first communion, his hands folded tenderly. "That's it!" I thought to myself, "I'll have his praying hands holding a yellow rose." I was pleased that I had found a wonderful way to honor our parents and to show just how much we loved them.

Coming up with these ideas was simple compared to the difficult task of going to the stone company alone and trying not to break down crying. I had to be strong. I said a prayer, asking God to help me with this task. I just wanted it done. I walked a couple blocks from my house to get there in time for my appointment. As I opened the door I told myself, "You can do this Gail."

I was greeted by a very nice man at Manchester Memorial Company. We sat at a computer together to make this stone come to life using my detailed drawing. With a little bit of tweaking and the centering of my pictures inside the hearts, we brought it into existence. We went out back, and he showed me one stone with two hearts.

"Perfect" I said, "I'll take it." No need to look any further.

I don't even think I was there for an hour. I paid the salesman and shook his hand. He said he was impressed by my detailed design and explanation. He told me that in all his years of doing business, he had never seen anyone come in so prepared, knowing exactly what they wanted. My only explanation to him was that I didn't want to come back.

On my walk home, the tears ran down my cheeks. Funeral arrangements were done. The stone had been designed and was being made. Time to go buy a plot. My only hope was that Bob was having the time of his life on his vacation. Planning his arrangements was heart-wrenching, but this was the only chance I had to get it done without involving him. I liked to be on top of things, and I knew in my heart that this would be his last big trip. I couldn't waste any time.

When Bob came home, he had plenty stories to tell. He had caught some good-sized fish. He let me know how much he missed me.

"Hey, Babe, what did you do all week while I was away?"

"Oh, nothing much," I lied.

I told him I'd done a lot of cleaning but had also gone out and caught up with friends, and that I'd missed him terribly. I told him how happy I was that he'd had a chance to go away with his friends.

I'd let him know the truth of that week when I felt the time was right. It would have to be the perfect time to tell him. I didn't know when that day would be, but it would come, I just knew it.

A month later, I mentioned to Bob that I had designed a stone for us. I told him that it would be set in place by November. It was only June. I said I would tell him when it was completed. Only God knew how much time my babe had left on this earth, so before the cancer could take away his ability to walk and speak, I would give him little reminders.

When the day came, I said, "Hey, babe, the stone is in place. When you are ready, we can go to see it. I am leaving it up to you."

"Yeah, okay," he replied. I didn't bring it up again. I figured he would let me know when he felt the time was right.

It was a cold and wet December that year, but I continued to take Bob out for walks every day, even if just to the corner store, Beechmont Market. I had to keep him strong.

We loved going down to Nutt's Pond. There is a paved trail behind our house that we liked to stroll along, and we both loved watching the many animals we would see there. Sometimes we would visit neighbors or family members who lived close by. I felt that these walks kept Bob strong, and being strong meant he lived longer.

On this drizzly wet day, we headed to Shaw's, a grocery store very close to home, to get a few things for supper. Holding hands as usual, we were ready to take the corner near the store when he said, "Let's keep walking, I want to go see this stone my wifey designed!"

He took my hand and raised it to his mouth and kissed it. We walked in silence after that. It wasn't a long walk, as the cemetery was nearby. We went through the entrance, and I led the way.

"It's over here in the back next to this tree," I told Bob.

When we got there, I explained the design: the yellow rose representing my mom, his dad's praying hands from the communion photo, our wedding songs carved into the entwined hearts. He loved the pictures of us and kept calling me his "sexy babe." He asked me what kind of tree was behind the stone, but I wasn't sure, as it was hard to tell in the dead of winter.

In the next moment he was sobbing and crying so loudly that all I could do was hold on to him tightly and cry with him. I could finally release my own tears in his embrace, his arms squeezing me ever so tightly. I wanted him to know how much I was going to miss him, but also that we needed to make more memories while he was still here.

I am not sure how long we had been standing when suddenly the rains poured down on us. It was raining hard and we were not prepared for it. We were getting soaked, but we didn't care. For some strange reason I told him that even God was crying with us, that God knew how much we loved one another. Next thing I knew, he was laughing. Laughing so loudly at what I just said. Now his laughter got me laughing.

"Come on wifey, let's get to the store before we get soaked!"

"Bob" I said. "We are already soaked!"

Like two kids in love, we tried walking faster to get under cover, still holding hands. Laughing hysterically, we just didn't care at that point about getting wet. I was so happy that he had wanted to see the place where he would be put to rest. How many people get to do that? It was his decision, and it made me happy that he got to see where we would both eventually be laid to rest. That moment brought us closer than anyone will ever know.

That night, as we lay in bed and kissed each other good night, Bob quietly whispered, "Great job honey, It's beautiful."

Then he started to sing our wedding song: "I'll love you forever, forever and ever, forever and ever, amen."

I whispered, "I love you more," as we cuddled in each other's arms awaiting the arrival of a new day.

When I heard him snoring I whispered, "Thank you, God. He needed to see that!" I fell off into the soundest sleep I'd had in months.

Photo by Gail Durant

CHAPTER 18

The Last Breath

HOSPICE ARRANGED FOR A HOSPITAL BED to be brought into our home a few months before Bob ever had to use it. I remember how upset he was that it sat in our living room, and he asked me why it was there when he didn't need it.

"I am never sleeping in that bed because I want to be with you in our own king-sized bed" he told me.

I told Bob that we had to put trust in what the doctors said as they knew better than us. I honestly hoped that he would never have to use it. I told him that I would always be there for him and to try not to worry. I also told him that I had lost some weight and now my butt would fit right by his side in that bed. I always thought that hospital beds should be made at least one and a half times their size to make room for the spouse to cuddle with their partner when they are scared.

The first time Bob couldn't quite make it to the bathroom from our bedroom, I requested a urinal from hospice staff. I didn't want him to feel sad or to think that he was going to get scolded like a child would. I reminded him of all those mistakes Miss Spirit had made as a pup and how we loved her regardless. I said that I would never stop loving him for something that was out of his control. When I said "mistakes," he started laughing.

"Boy, our little girl had many of them" he said, as he patted the top of Spirit's head.

She always stayed close by and kept him great company. We were both lucky to have her. He would grab a cup of coffee and head downstairs to his man-cave with Miss Spirit following behind him. He always kept a treat in his pocket for her, and she knew it.

I would leave the cellar door open upstairs so that I could hear him just in case he had another seizure and called out my name. When I heard him playing tug-of-war with Spirit, that was a cue for me to get into the shower. I would hurry and be out in a few minutes, leaving the bathroom door open as I always worried about his attacks. You never knew when they would strike, and I had to be ready at any given time. Showers were fast, but I was happy to have some time to get one in.

That night, when Bob was sleeping, I ordered a waterproof mattress pad and night pads for our bed on the internet. I tried to be one step ahead of him even though I really didn't know what was coming in the weeks ahead. When they were delivered, I put them on the bed while he was downstairs smoking a fatty. He never knew they were there because I didn't want him to feel bad. I hid many things from him when he was sick because he had enough to worry about.

I was preparing. I ordered extra twin sheets for that hospital bed in the living room. I also bought those drinks that had all the vitamins and nutrients that he needed for when he could no longer eat.

My good friend Roberta bought us a pill crusher to help with those hard-to-swallow pills. I appreciated little gestures like that because I didn't drive and would never leave Bob alone even if I did!

Most important, I ordered Bob's cigars for the month. He smoked them like cigarettes now, but I didn't care. I had promised him that he would have whatever he wanted. It was the least I could do to make him happy, and besides the cigars kept him calm, and that was a good enough reason for me.

As far as sex went, my goal was too please him and only him. Bob had a hard time even getting an erection now. I didn't care about my needs at all and told Bob I was tired when he would ask. It really wasn't far from the truth. There were running jokes from his friends about how I would glow from sex after Bob's radiation treatments. I went with the flow so no one would know about how his health was failing rather quickly. Bob liked the fact that I made him out to be the constant lover to anyone who asked—and the fact that they believed it!

They didn't need to know the truth. I would tell them that he couldn't keep his hands off me and that chemo made him extra horny, which was true, but trying to fulfill his duties was impossible for him. I had to make him look good around his buddies, and I did. That put a smile on Bob's face, and that was all that mattered to me. Sex was the furthest thing from my mind, but cuddling, holding hands, and being quiet seemed to please both of us more. Holding each other's bodies close gave us the satisfaction that we both needed at the time. Staring into one another's eyes was the norm for us until the sleep fairy conked us out to wake to another day.

The routine would be the same every day for Bob: a coffee, a treat for Spirit, and going down the cellar to smoke a fatty. He always did his Sudoku puzzles and that would tell me how well he was doing. If he didn't scratch out the numbers because of a mistake, he was doing well. He liked the tougher puzzles but when I noticed he was having a hard time with them, I ordered easier puzzles so he could keep up with them without being reminded of his failing health. I don't even think he realized that I took the harder puzzle books away and replaced them with easier ones.

After a fall in the shower caused by a sudden paralysis to his right side, he began sleeping in that hospital bed. We had aides come in to help him shave and to change the sheets because that was too hard for me. Other than that, I had it all under control. I found a way to help with his personal care, making sure that no one would see him nude. I took care of his urinal bag and wash duties. I would lotion him up afterwards and use the shampoo caps for his hair. I always made sure he was clean smelling, using his favorite cologne talcum powder on his body and bedding.

If he had a bowel movement I would praise him because that meant he wasn't constipated, which could spell trouble. I wrote down every time he went to the bathroom to keep track for myself. I cut his mustache evenly, just as he liked it, and had my niece

Shannon come to give him a haircut so he would feel good about himself afterwards.

I was chastised by one of Bob's family for doing that.

"Why are you giving him a haircut, he's dying?" I was asked.

My response was that it made Bob feel and look good. Some people failed to appreciate the loving care I was giving him. But Bob always thanks me, and that's who mattered to me the most!

Bob would always say, "Thanks, babe, for being my nurse."

People came to visit and sat on the chair next to his bed, to talk or watch TV. Sometimes at night Spirit would jump into that seat, keeping a keen eye on her daddy.

I remember that as weeks went by and more people stopped by to visit Bob, he didn't seem to like it. It made him feel like he was dying. He asked me to tell his family not to come every day, but I told him that I couldn't do that because they would think it was my idea and not his. This is one time Bob had to tell them himself, with the words coming from his own mouth.

One afternoon, some visitors came by just after they got out of work and Bob was not happy. He said nothing, but he was a smart man and he figured out a way to end the visit so that I wouldn't get blamed. After 15 minutes of visiting, he closed his eyes and seemed to drift off to sleep. He did sleep often now, so this was not unusual. They asked if he would sleep long, and I told them that I really didn't know so they decided to leave. As I shut the kitchen door, I could hear the sound of the hospital bed rising from the living room. When I got back to the room, Bob held his finger to his lips, motioning for me to keep it quiet. He clicked the TV on with a smile.

He had found a way, all by himself, without ever having to tell anyone that he didn't want them there all the time.

I thought to myself, "Wow, his brain isn't too bad after all," and it was a secret I've kept until now.

No one could feel slighted or blame me if he asked them not to come every day himself. I thought it was brilliant!

I slept in the living room on the couch next to his bed when I wasn't sleeping in the bed with him. If he was having a bad night with pain, I would administer his morphine, just as the nurse had taught me. I would never tell him that it was morphine so that he wouldn't catch on that his time was coming near. I just told him that it would help with his pain, and he trusted me as he opened his mouth. If he didn't make any more pain sounds, we would sleep like two tired babies throughout the night.

I found that when I shut the lights off he got scared of the dark, so I learned to keep them on all night. I also made sure to keep his country music playing quietly in the background to lull him to sleep.

Our routine stayed the same every day for the next eight weeks, except that now I had to hold the cigar to his mouth because he couldn't do it for himself any longer. It didn't matter if he couldn't inhale them. The thought of a cigar next to his lips is what kept him calm. I hated that I had to keep them lit myself and that meant inhaling them for him. I did it out of love because it was worth it for me to keep him happy, though my own lungs didn't like it.

In Bob's eighth week in the hospital bed, I had to give him morphine on three different days. Though I kept a record for the nurse, I never told his or my family because I didn't want anyone to worry. I was relieved to see how the medicine comforted him.

One night, after a very long day, as we were settling down to sleep, I kissed Bob goodnight and laid down on the couch next to his bed. I was exhausted.

Suddenly I heard a wail coming from him, a sound that I had never heard before. I knew the pain was getting worse! I gave him the initial dose of morphine, but it was taking longer than normal to control his pain, so I gave him a little more as the nurse had instructed.

After an hour of this, it was clear that he needed more than I was allowed to give, so I called the agency, panicking. I saw his face change in ways that I could never imagine, something that I don't even want to describe here. Whoever answered the phone could tell from my voice that I needed someone here quickly, that I was not going to be able to administer what Bob really needed for pain meds now. The nurse showed up as fast as she could, but it still took her more than a half an hour to get Bob calm and pain-free once she arrived.

While the nurse was taking care of Bob, I made a few phone calls because I didn't want to be alone anymore. I was scared for both of us! This wasn't looking good, and I needed my family and friends around me now.

Soon I was following a regimen of administering his new pain meds every 15 minutes, some scheduled for every half hour and another one on the hour. Now I became a clock watcher with a few good friends and some sisters in my kitchen while Bob's family was in the living room spending time with him. I continued to go in and check on Bob and give him his meds using my time chart.

At this point, I didn't deny anyone access to come by because people had to say their good-byes and I stopped no one from coming in—no one, because Bob was loved by so many in his life!

After hours of people stopping by, one of Bob's family members screamed at me, telling me that it was his family's time to be alone with Bob and that it should be his immediate family only! I mean I was literally yelled at, in my own home, right in front of Bob!

At a time like this, it was time for all of us to come together for support. I yelled right back, reminding them that they had spent the entire morning with him alone and that my family loved him too, and that at this point no one was leaving. If they had a problem with that, they could leave!

It got very quiet and I surprised myself by yelling back in front of my babe, but it was time I finally stood up to a family that had been blaming me for Bob's cancer.

I also asked them who would hug me if he died. I needed my own family for support at this time, and none of them could understand that! I was happy to have people there solely for me, simply because they loved both Bob and me.

For the longest time, I was blamed for Bob's cancer and was treated so badly. I don't even want to say what happened on this day because

I am trying to be as positive as I can. I want this book to be uplifting in order to help others.

The day of Bob's death was a living hell and a nightmare that I wanted to end. It wasn't my Bob's sickness creating this nightmare but rather the people who didn't understand death. They wished it had been me dying instead of Bob, as I heard later through the grapevine.

They had no idea that I had already bargained with God to trade places with Bob, because I loved him that much. That's what love truly is, to give up your own life so that another can live!

God had other plans.

I am so grateful that I went to catechism as a child. I finally understood how those lessons, taught so long ago, and could help me now. The time was now. I had faith that Bob would soon be on his journey. I was glad that I had spoken to Bob about God and Heaven before he passed!

Thank goodness I had the reverend's wife to talk with also. She told me that caregivers get blamed a lot, but that I didn't have to understand it. I told her about all the things that were being said and done, and that I was receiving a lot of criticism for every act of love that I did for Bob. She told me that I was just like Jesus being crucified. She said Jesus suffered on the cross just as I was suffering now from their hatred. I always thought Bob's family loved me, but his illness proved otherwise. The reverend's wife told me that no one needed to be treated like this and that it was time for me to let them go.

This day would be long, and I remembered that we needed Bob to have his last rites. Some of my family members went out to the church to find a priest, to no avail. I called the nurse who took care of Bob, and she was able to find someone for us. She assured me that he would be there within a few hours.

I knew that if Bob passed before the priest arrived, his body would not be going anywhere. He would remain in our home until he received his last rites. Thank goodness the priest arrived before Bob passed on.

I was grateful at this point to have my family by my side, along with a few friends. Raised Catholic, we knew all the prayers by heart, and it helped when we said them together. Somehow, we all managed to gather in my small living room with the priest to speak of Bob's new journey to Heaven.

We prayed. He asked if someone wanted to lead in prayer and read from his bible. I told him that I would, but he wanted someone else because I was holding Bob's hand. My friend Cindy bravely read the paragraphs and did a great job.

As the priest was leaving, I tried to hand him some money, but he wouldn't take it. I followed him outside and hugged him once more and thanked him for coming last minute. I slipped my hand into his pants pocket and left three twenty-dollar bills. He just smiled and thanked me. It was so nice of him to come on such short notice, and it was the least I could do. At least Bob was still alive to hear us pray over him.

I went back inside, wondering where my energy was coming from because I hadn't slept for the last two nights. I checked in on Bob again to make sure that he was resting comfortably. I didn't want to hear that death squeal ever again. At this point I didn't want to be present when he took his last breath, and I prayed that I wouldn't be.

I went online and asked my Facebook family to pray that God would come and receive Bob. It was time for us to let him go. I knew in my heart that it was time for me to tell this to Bob. I had promised him so many weeks before that I would let him know when his time had come.

I went into the room where he was and leaned close to him. I grabbed his hand and kissed the top of it. I started talking, not caring who was listening or who was in the room with me. This was a promise between Bob and me.

"Bob," I said as the tears started falling down my cheeks, "remember when I told you that I would let you know when your time has come? Well the time is now. I will be okay, we will all be okay. It's time for you to leave us. Look for your mother's hands reaching out to you, as she will be the first to bring you to Jesus. When you see the light and those hands, know that it will be her to guide you. Don't be afraid, as we spoke of Heaven before. It's beautiful, babe, and you will see all who have gone before you. After you see your mom and all your relatives, please make sure to give my mom a hug and a kiss for me. I am sure she cannot wait to see you too!"

By now I was crying out loud as I spoke. I know he heard me because though his eyes were closed, the tears started to stream down his face. I told him that I knew he could hear me because I saw his tears as I wiped them away for him. I kept talking about how his family on both sides would miss him dearly but that we would all meet up again in due time. I told him to believe and not be afraid because he was going to a better place with no pain. I told him how much he meant to all of us and how we all loved him. Again, the tears started to fall down his cheeks, and I wiped them away once more.

I asked if anyone had anything to say, and one by one, each spoke with gentleness instead of hatred, finally getting it as they heard me include them all in my words.

When his family had finished talking to Bob, I asked some of them to go outside while I checked to make sure he hadn't soiled himself. I didn't know at the time that it would be my last time changing him. This time I asked for their help in holding him on his side. I asked them to look the other way while I cleaned him, telling Bob not to worry, that no one was looking. I thought maybe if they had a hand in helping me with his bathing, it could somehow help them to heal in their own minds.

As I was bringing the bed back up, I was asked if I had something to clear Bob's throat as he seemed to be struggling to breathe. I raised his arms as the nurse had taught me, and he seemed to be okay for the moment.

My neighbor Joan popped in to see how things were going, but she never really had the chance to say anything. As she looked into the living room, she knew exactly what was happening. She ran out, saying that he just taken his last breath, which made everyone else come into the living room where Bob was.

I was already there and was just reaching down to give Bob a kiss on the lips when his eyes opened. As we looked into each other's eyes for the very last time, he took that last breath. His baby blues opened just at the moment that my lips touched his. I looked his way and for a second time stood still.

I was the last person he got to see, and even though I didn't want it to happen that way, it did, and I am extremely grateful for that.

At that moment I watched the color in his hands change instantly to white. I held them for a moment in awe of how quickly a living body can go lifeless! I could feel the air change around me and I knew that his spirit was rising to a better place. I could feel the chills and the cold air in the warmth of the room. I heard no one and nothing around me for a split second. Time stood still once again, and then reality hit me.

I saw peace and love in that final moment, but then I cried out loudly because he just taken his last breath. Then I screamed because I thought I had killed him by putting the bed down and turning him on his side. I thought the many meds may have caused him to choke.

My oldest sister, Linda, swiftly came to my rescue, telling me, with tears in her eyes, that I hadn't killed him and that I had given him the best care ever. She told me that it was just his time! She was right, and I knew that. Quickly, I stopped blaming myself.

I wasn't believed when I told Bob's family that he had taken his last breath. They asked a family member to try to find his pulse. I knew they wouldn't find one, and my heart stopped crying instantly. He was now at peace, and it was his time.

I made a call to the VNA (Visiting Nurse Association) so they could make arrangements with the coroner's office. It would be at least two hours before they would arrive.

For some reason my train of thought went to my neighbor, Joan, who had seen that last breath and had run out. You see, she had lost her husband to colon cancer a few years back, and I was worried for her now. I told my sisters that I had to go and check on her.

Yes, the caring side of me had to go check on my neighbor. I told my family that I knew she was crying. I just knew it! Some people stayed behind to watch the house and Bob, and three people came with me (I don't even remember who.) When she opened the door, she was crying, and we all went inside and gave her a group hug. I knew this was the right thing to do, to go and make sure she was okay, even after just losing my own husband. It was important to me that she was all right.

Some of Bob's family wrote on Facebook that I was a mad woman running around telling all my neighbors that Bob was dead, but that wasn't what happened. I went to one woman's house, a neighbor and a friend to make sure she was okay.

When we got back to the house, Bob's family had left, and it was quiet. I had a huge weight lifted off my shoulders. I too finally felt peace!

It had been a long, hard road, taking care of my husband for the last year and nine months. I was tired but happy that I was able to be my husband's nurse and care for him. I wouldn't have wanted it any other way. Bob thanked me countless times, and he was the only one to do so, but again, he was all that mattered to me. Making his life the best life ever was all that mattered to me.

When the coroner came, he asked that I go to another room so that my last vision of Bob wouldn't be of him draped in a cloth as they took him out. I leaned over and kissed Bob one last time. I listened and went into my bedroom because I wanted my final memory of him to be of his baby blues staring back at me. I took Spirit with me so that she wouldn't give them a hard time, not understanding what was happening to her daddy.

After they left, we came out and the first thing Spirit did was to run and look all around the bed for her daddy. I lifted her up onto his bed so that she could remember his smells. I told her that it would just be her and me from now on. My sisters told me that the coroner had covered Bob up with a beautifully colored cloth. I was happy to hear that because we had the most colorful life together ever.

I knew soon that I would collapse from lack of sleep. As I laid down in bed, I chuckled to myself as I remembered running out to the priest and putting my hands into his pants pocket to give him some money. Putting my hands in the pants pocket of a priest! What the heck was I thinking? Sometimes I make myself laugh. I needed that, as I hadn't laughed in so long.

Tomorrow would be a new day and a new journey, without Bob. Now, I could go out and feel the sun on my face for longer than a few seconds. I had peace, real inner peace. No one telling me what I was doing wrong anymore. Just the thought of that felt like the biggest weight had been lifted from me! I didn't have to deal with angry people anymore, blaming me for my babe's death!

Bob was in a better place, and so was I. It was time to prepare for the finest celebration of his life!

Bob deserved the best and I wanted to make sure it was just that! There was no time to be wasted. I knew the spirit of his adoration for me would always be in my heart forever!

No one can ever take away the love we had for one another. It was real and exceptional. Love doesn't die just because the one you love does. True love stays with you forever.

"No matter what!" Just like we wrote in our wedding vows to one another: "For richer and for poorer, in sickness and in health. To love and honor till death do us part! No matter what!"

CHAPTER 19

Moose Sighting

SOMETIMES A SIGN CAN COME IN THE FORM OF A DISTRACTION. It may be so big that you can't miss it. For example, you're thinking of a loved one who passed, and you're sad and tears start to flow. Then out of nowhere something distracts that thought and chases away the sadness. You realize the distraction was a sign meant for you. A song on the radio catches your attention because it reminds you of them, or you catch the windblown scent of a rose, or something rather out of the ordinary occurs that has never happened to you before. You know it was meant for you! At that precise time and moment, you know in your heart that something has just interfered with your train of thought.

The day after Bob had passed, my good friend Helen wrote me a note:

> God took a very special person to sit at his side last night. It was good to know that he is no longer suffering and good to see that your best buddy has some inner peace. As I was sitting here reflecting on those special times that we shared and the laughs that we all had, a sadness overwhelmed me. Talk about a sign from God. I looked up to see a moose running up the hill in our back yard! Those of you who knew Bob know that he was always called "Moose." We have been living here for twenty plus years and have never seen a moose in our back yard! Guess that Bob just wanted to let us know that he was okay! The sadness left, and a smile came across my face. Thanks for the sign and rest in peace Bob. You will be missed.

After reading her note, the first thing I asked was, "Did you get a picture?"

She said it didn't cross her mind, as she and her husband were in shock to see it go by so quickly.

If she had time to grab her camera to take a photo, it would have looked like this.

Photo by Helen Hiltz

I knew it was just like Bob to stop to say hello and then move on to greener pastures.

This was no coincidence. Helen thoughts were on Bob, and he found a way to distract her and turn her tears to a smile!

CHAPTER 20

The Little Black Box

BOB WAS A HUGE NASCAR FAN. I chose two pictures for his obituary in the paper: in one, he wore his Marine uniform, and in the other, he had his Nascar cap on. I had a few days until the funeral, so I did a rush order of his best cigars to be put at every seating at his luncheon. I wanted everyone to have a special memento from him.

When I made the phone call, a man at the other end told me that he would send out a free gift for my huge order. The next day the cigars and labels came in. I was way too busy to open up the little black box that accompanied my order. My daughter and granddaughter were helping me put labels on the cigars. When we finished, my daughter said to me,

"You forgot to open this up," as she handed me the little black box.

I opened the box and the first word I see is NASCAR, and I can feel the tears welling up in my eyes. They don't know Bob, they've never met him. As I continued to open it, I am in shock. I ordered cigars, what does that have to do with NASCAR?

I said, "Oh My God! Bob's doing awesome with his signs." It was a lighter with the word NASCAR on it in the same colors of the hat he wore all the time. "What a sign!" I said to my daughter. That cigar company had no idea, and yet here it is in the palm of my hand. He was with us that day.

He helped me to get through the days leading up to his funeral. His signs are what hold my head up high as he never left my side, just as he promised! That's what I call visual proof!

Photos by Gail Durant

It doesn't matter if it makes no sense to anyone else about the signs you receive. What matters is the comfort they bring to your heart!

CHAPTER 21

Bob's Visitation

TWO DAYS AFTER BOB PASSED, hospice came to pick up the hospital bed that Bob had been in for the last eight weeks. The night before, I slept there so I could remember his warmth and scent before they took it away forever. It may sound bizarre to some that I spent the night in that bed, but for myself, I needed to do it. For some uncanny reason, I was hoping that I would get a visitation from him.

My daughter, whom I adopted after Bob passed, and Miss Spirit slept on the long couch. My granddaughter slept on the smaller couch. We all spent the night in the living room together. My daughter stayed out of work that whole week, and I will truly never forget her being by my side through it all. It had been a trying week, especially the last two days. I was exhausted because I hadn't slept and all I wanted to do now was get some rest.

I finally drifted off, hoping that Bob would show up in my dreams. When I woke up the next morning at 5 a.m., I remembered every detail so vividly. Bob was at his healthiest state and best shape ever when he came to visit me in my sleep.

He was in a hurry, I could see, but he took time to look my way. He waved to me with his big shit-eating grin. I saw and felt the calm and peace in his face. He was so handsome and appeared as his younger self, like he did when we had first met.

Already I felt that he had a job to do and was very happy about it. He blew me a kiss, as he always did, and I woke up. Wow, I thought to myself, I got exactly what I wanted before they came to take away the bed. It was a great feeling to see him smile!

I believe there is a heaven. I believe a part of Bob was still here after he passed. It felt so real to me, how I could not think that? I do believe that what we love on earth will be in our heaven. A weight had been lifted in just a few short days. Bob was healthy, happy, and already on an adventure. It felt great to see that!

For the last year and nine months, Bob and I had lived our lives to the fullest. I was thrust into being his caregiver, but I wouldn't have had it any other way! I didn't know what we both were in for, but I did know that it would be a long and bumpy road and that I wanted to be at his side for it all. I loved him that much!

I felt that God had given me the courage to be my husband's nurse. I wanted to be at his side and I was grateful that I could be, but I had been scared about what lay ahead. The unknown is scary, but somehow you know that you will do the right thing, one day at a time.

I made three promises to myself and Bob, to make him happy during whatever time he had left. The first was to keep him home until the very end, the second was to give him a cigar whenever he wanted one, and the third was to be there whenever he would open his eyes so that he wouldn't be frightened or think he was alone.

I made sure that I stayed with him in the living room every night. When he got scared, I would keep the light on or play country music all night, to soothe his soul.

One visitor who came to visit asked when the funeral would be, right in front of Bob. I was fit to be tied, yet I also understood what this person was going through. I knew Bob had heard it too, because from then on, the lights had to stay on all night. He would start crying and ask me if he was going to die that evening.

"Bob," I would tell him, "you've got to trust me that you're not going anywhere, anytime soon! You're eating well and still smoking your fatties, so let me be the one to tell you when its time, okay?"

"Okay, babe" he would say, "but can you sleep with me tonight?"

He didn't have to ask twice. I would climb over the bars and try to sleep sideways with him crying in my arms, as a young scared child would do with his mother. I stayed with him in that hospital bed for three nights, and believe me, those beds are not made for two people! It didn't matter. I am not sure how we ever fell asleep like that, but we did!

By the third night of sleeping this way, he woke me up to tell me he was hot.

"I'm okay now, Babe, I think you are right, I'm not dying any time soon. Do you think you can go back on the couch again? This bed isn't made for two!"

I replied, "Whatever you want babe, whatever you want, I will be here for you!"

There was only one other time that I had to sleep with him for three nights in a row, and once again, when he realized it was not his time to go, he threw me out of his bed.

I wasn't sure how much longer he had to live, but I knew I would give him all the love I had left to give. I felt very comfortable knowing that he was getting great care from me. I made all his appointments and rode with him many times in the ambulance when he suffered grand mal seizures before he became bedridden. I fed and bathed him, gave him his medications and shots, and made sure his hair and nails were trimmed. I brushed his teeth and kept his clothes and bed clean and comfortable.

I stayed with him once for nine days at the Dartmouth Hitchcock Medical Center in Lebanon, New Hampshire. I slept in the emergency room night after night as we waited for his scheduled craniotomy surgery. It was postponed over and over again due to med flight emergencies that kept coming in by helicopter. These were life or death, so Bob had to wait for many days!

It didn't matter how long it would take, I knew I would be there no matter what, because he could have died on the operating table, and I just needed to be close to him. I remember many emergencies coming in as I slept in a recliner in the emergency room. I would make people comfortable while their loved ones were getting care, get them coffee or tea, and hold their hands. I didn't know any of them, but it didn't matter. It helped me to help them.

On the third day, a man finally asked me my name and wondered what I was doing there.

He said, "Here you are helping so many, and not one of us asks you why you are here."

When I told everyone about my husband's brain tumor, they wondered where I got my strength from. I told them that I believe in God and that I had seen heaven. Plain and simple! I needed to stay busy, so I focused on others that needed me at that time. Bob was already in good hands, so helping strangers helped to keep me calm and not worry so much.

No one will ever deny that I took great care of my husband's health. I know I made him happy, as he thanked me almost every night. To me, that was all that mattered, hearing him tell me I was his "best wifey in the whole wide world"!

After my dream of Bob beaming that great big smile, looking so happy, I jumped out of bed because there was so much that I needed to do. There was no time to be wasted. I wanted the best funeral my husband could ever have. Things had to be precise.

I had been working on five individual collages that would be displayed at the funeral home. They consisted of photos of my family, his family, our family, our friends, and our trips. I had started working on those while Bob was still alive. I would go to our bedroom while he slept and start taping the pictures I'd clipped of our lives entwined together with so many loved ones around us. I tried not to forget anyone and prayed about it. I didn't want to leave anyone out by accident.

I was grateful that photography was such a fulfilling hobby of mine. Those five collages tell a wonderful story! We had shared a great journey together, and those photos don't lie. Here was Bob's same shit-eating grin, just as big as it was in my dream! In every picture, every smile tells the same story of his happiness. Just like his visits tell me that Bob is okay, and that pleases me!

CHAPTER 22

Bob's Obituary

On April 30, 2013, I slept in my own bed for the first time. I had fallen fast asleep from the pure exhaustion of preparing for Bob's funeral these past few days. Something so genuine happened just as I was beginning to wake up, when I was in-between sleep and awakening.

To me it wasn't a dream because I felt Bob's hands on my face. I truly felt his hands on my face! I remember opening my eyes and watching him gaze into mine. Then I heard him speak.

"Babe" he said, "I don't want you to cry anymore!"

We were both on our sides, looking deeply into each other's eyes, and it felt so real as I cupped my own hand over his on my cheek. I remember pushing my head into his hands to see if it would give. I could feel his hands against my head still as he held my face! He was truly there! I didn't want to wake up, if I was sleeping. I didn't want it to end at all! I wanted to hear more, but that was his only message to me. The emotions that arose from this visit were overwhelming.

This was the only experience I've ever had where it felt as though he were truly present with me because his touch was real. I saw his fully clothed body. What stood out to me the most as he lay beside me was that he wasn't in pain anymore. He appeared as his younger self, like when I first met him. He will always be handsome in my eyes!

When I was fully awake, I knew for sure that it wasn't a dream. It was that fresh. I didn't have to try and recollect what had just happened. I knew that he was physically here with me, and I had felt him! I remember thinking to myself that he was being funny, telling me not to cry! With the tough days that were to follow, there is no way I could just turn off my tears like that! Somehow, he gave me strength with that "gift of presence," and I will never forget it, for as long as I live!

I jumped out of bed filled with energy and contentment because of what had just happened. I went to retrieve my newspaper because I knew Bob's obituary in the *Union Leader* would be published that day. It read:

Robert Durant Jr. (MOOSE) died comfortably at his home surrounded by his loving wife, family and friends. He was just shy of his 50th birthday.

He was married to Gail (Adams) for almost 18 years and together for 23 years.

He served in the Marines from 1981 to 1984 and learned the trade of HVAC on airplanes during his service. He co-owned and operated Liberty Air for the past 25 years.

He was on the board of directors for Pointers Fish and Game Club for many years, always lending a hand with the many set-up targets for practice. He was also a member of Jutras Post and was quite the pool player.

He loved travelling to many places with his wife and friends and loved going to Foxwoods, playing in many Texas-hold'em poker tournaments. He always said he was ahead of the game money wise!

He loved fishing, hunting trips; deer, bear and wild boar, with his family and friends. He enjoyed nature and thought nothing of sitting in a tree to catch the peace and quiet of the woods. He had many a tale to tell in those trees! He also loved boating the many waters with his favorite cigar in his mouth, his dog at his side, and a fishing pole in his hands!

The many children in his life loved him so dearly. He was the favorite Uncle, Brother-in-law, and Grandfather. He had the kindest soul and the warmest heart. He would help anyone out in a bind if they needed him.

He was a jack-of-all trades and built his log home as a sub-contractor. He had many ideas and put his skills to work. His log home was his baby. It was magnificent with many details. He even built some of the furniture. He could do it all and it shined in his home!

Bob was a man who many adored and loved. He died with dignity and never complained. He will be missed by so many in his life whom he loved very much.

He loved to play jokes, and with the help of his wife, he once dressed as a woman so he could see what a baby shower was all about! He made one fine-looking lady and put many a smile on numerous women that day! One we will never forget!

I know that if I had more time, I could have written in much greater detail, because our life together was so full. I was in a hurry to get it submitted to the newspaper by the deadline so that it would coincide with the wake and funeral. I just hoped it captured how much Bob meant to so many, especially to me, and that I portrayed him well on such short notice.

I smile now as I re-read the obituary, thinking about the time when I dressed Bob as a woman for my sister Nancy's baby shower. On that day, I called to let her know that I had run into three of her old friends from school. I told her that they would be coming to surprise her for the shower! Right away she knew that I was up to no good and said so.

"Gail, I know you're up to something," she told me.

She knew me pretty well, but what she didn't know was that I had dressed up three men as women for the event, make-up and all, and that it was quite fun! One of the men was her baby's father, another a family friend, and of course, my babe!

Below is a picture of Bob dressed as a woman on the day that he went to my sister Nancy's baby shower. I got his clothes from the neighborhood thrift store and he looked mighty fine! There were

many laughs that day when he walked in, especially when I introduced him as Roberta!

Photo by Gail Durant

CHAPTER 23

Bob's Eulogy

—————

MAY 2, 2013, WAS THE DAY OF BOB'S WAKE AND FUNERAL. I had woken with an inner peace and strength, and I knew that everything would be okay, like Bob always told me.

I went outside in my robe to feed the birds and to feel the sun hit my face as I looked to the heavens and blew a kiss to Bob. I told him that he was going to love the way I had planned out the day in his honor. It was time to get dressed and head over to the funeral home for a fine tribute to my wonderful husband.

The wake and funeral were to be held at Phaneuf Funeral Home, which had taken care of all of the arrangements. I had superb funeral directors, and I am still friends with them to this day.

It was a Thursday, and I couldn't be any happier at the number of family and friends that came pouring through the door. It was standing room only, and it took me the entire two hours I had allotted for the wake just to hug and thank all of those who had come. I was told that over 400 people came to show their respects. I knew there would be a lot of people because Bob and I have a lot of family and friends, and I had expected as much. But for a work day, it was quite amazing how many showed up!

Flowers overflowed the viewing room as I looked around. I had placed a fishing pole in front of Bob's ashes, surrounded by photos of him with that big shit-eating grin. It goes without saying that our wedding photo was included, as that was a big day for both of us, getting married for the first time. The five collages representing all the people in our lives were on display stands all around the room and in the lobby. People were standing wall to wall.

I had planned every detail of this day, but even so there were surprises in store for me. One of our friends was a commander from the American Legion Jutras Post in Manchester, where my Bob had been a long-time member. Suddenly, four uniformed men marched in and stood at attention. One of them read a Resolution in memory of Bob's service to God and country. It read, in part ". . . in token of our common grief, a copy of this resolution transferring Robert M. Durant Jr. to Post Everlasting and to be presented to the next of kin." He turned to salute me and handed me that Resolution plaque in Bob's honor. It was a touching moment, and they all hugged me one by one. I made sure to thank them all before they left. What a nice honor for Bob, and what a great surprise for me!

Soon it was time for the eulogy, and a young priest whom I had never met before came in to lead the prayers and talk about Bob. We had met me briefly just before the service and I had no idea that I would see him again in another chapter of my life.

I had written a eulogy, but I knew that I would be too nervous to speak in front of all these people. I have always hated public speaking—so much so that I always skipped school when it came time for oral presentations. I would take the "F" grade and didn't think twice about it. So I had asked my Uncle Roland if he could read the eulogy for me because he had spoken at many funerals and was comfortable doing it. Thank goodness he obliged, as he was very good at it. He didn't mind one bit. He read:

To my husband, Moose, Love Wifey!

As I look back through the years, I say thank you to God for putting us in each other's path. After a courtship of four and half years, Bob and I got married and started this long wonderful journey as a team.

Bob was a Marine before we met, served his 4 years and learned a trade of heating and air conditioning.

Bob loved New York for deer hunting, or Maine for Bear hunting, and Tennessee for wild boar! Boy he could surely hunt! He always came back with a harvest to fill the freezers. I was finding myself starting to change and loving it, becoming a little redneck. Couldn't wait when Bob won the Moose Lottery. That meat is the bomb!

I loved hearing his stories from a tree stand. A hawk zooming in for a meal and swerving just before it hit him in the face as it wasn't that rodent he saw. How about an owl hooting on a tree branch right next to him, or the man that went to the bath room right under his tree stand and he didn't know he was there, high in the tree tops where he loved the quiet.

How can we forget "Fruitloops", the moose with one antler up and one down. I loved hearing those stories through his eyes! His beautiful baby blues!

I cannot forget the many early rising days to go fishing. Imagine me getting up early to go fishing? I found myself loving the outdoors and being in the quiet, Bob with his cigar and me with my camera, waiting for a fish-on!!! My best memory was an early fishing trip on Granite Lake and Bob says, "Quick, Babe. Get your camera out! There's a monster fish over there about 10 pounds!"

As I swiveled my seat to get the best shot, there was a man and woman on a dock naked and she was on top scurrying trying to hide herself. Bob said those were the biggest 10-pound boobies he ever saw.

"Get a picture!" he said.

I'm like, "No you get a picture!"

Needless to say, I got one for him. It was the best laugh as we told people to look at the 10-pounder we caught, and they didn't expect that picture!

Oh, he always aimed to please. Do you all remember when I dressed him like a woman, so he could go surprise Nancy at her baby shower? He had a bonnet and a suit with a skirt on, and I laughed as we couldn't find shoes, so he kept his work boots on. I applied make-up and lip gloss. Do you remember all the ladies laughing when I announced to my sister Nancy that an old friend named Roberta has come to surprise her? When Bob popped through the door, there were many a belly laugh that day!

He's a great pool player, and really loved his poker tournaments or staying home for poker nights with friends and family for many, many years! He has claimed he's still ahead money wise. He was sharp at it!

I loved that he too loved dogs. We shared many a laugh with April. She was like a child to him, and when April passed, we got Miss Spirit. I thank God for her, as she kept Bob going on the rough days as I could always hear him talking to her. She calmed him, and she loved him too!

That was her daddy! She followed him everywhere he went! Miss Spirit will surely miss him.

We loved to travel and had numerous adventures. Who could forget skinny dipping in Aruba's waters, fishing in Oswego, New York, yelling "FISH-ON", canoeing Sebago Lake in Maine and stopping for an afternoon delight on the sand bar? We did river rafting at Hoover Dam and took a gondola ride in Las Vegas, chased elk in Wyoming, and kissed at the falls in Canada. We did snorkeling in Mexico, went to beer and cigar factories in the West Indies, and walked the boardwalk in Atlantic City. How about our latest adventures of going to the beach in the winter, to Foxwoods or Mohegan Sun Casinos or just plain old kayaking on Emerald Lake? These adventures always had us smiling! My best adventure was North Conway, where he proposed to me and asked me to be his wifey! I looked at that ring over and over for many months! Who would ever think that at the age of 40, I was FINALLY getting married!

Bob was the best handy man ever. After our log home was built air-tight, he taught himself to put in floors and walls as he was the sub-contractor, watching everyone's move to make sure his castle was built right. What a beauty our home was, and it could tell many stories. We had so much company and loved having the kids, family and friends over! He was a smart man and never afraid to try anything new. He was great at everything... well maybe not everything. I always knew after the first time, that he was NOT a plumber. I won't even go there. What was done at Durant's log home, stays at Durant's log home!

Bob was an active member with Jutras Post and American Legion. He was on the board of directors for many years with Pointer Fish and Game. He was always ready to give a helping hand to anyone who needed it.

Bob was rich in friends, blended families, his and mine. We cannot forget the love he had for his two grandkids and how he loved being called Pepe!

Bob would always crack a joke and then say, "I knew I could make you laugh!"

He didn't have to try hard. Remember the fight he had with the porta potty and how he hated one-way towels?

I will miss his little dance jig after coming out of the shower. I will miss his grilling, for he was the best at it! I will truly miss his smile, his touch, his holding hands, his soft kiss and the smell of his finest cigar! The way he called me Wifey, or just the way he held me while dancing. He always saved the waltzes for me!

He was my soulmate, my confidante. Our memories will stay with me forever and he will always be close in heart. He told me he was not afraid to die, and that made me feel better for him. He knows of eternal life with Jesus, and he said he will wait for me when my day comes. I know I will see him again, but I will surely miss that man of mine. We became a great team, reading each other's thoughts, finishing each other's sentences, and loving one another, till death do us part!

How truly lucky I was to find him. A man that saw that my true beauty was inside, and I thanked him for giving me a chance to find love again.

"Forever and ever, Amen," as Bob would say!

I have to share one last thing with all of you. Bob and I talked of death and the afterlife. I asked him, "How will I know it's you? What sign am I to look for on earth? Will it be the smell of the cigar, a light flickering?"

He thought long and hard with this one. He said, "Seriously Babe, you will know I am around and anyone else for that matter, when you smell a bad fart!"

"You're going to give me bad farts to think of you? No changing your mind?" I asked.

He said, "Nope," and on that note he laughed!

One last thing I asked of him.

"Bob, do me a favor when you get to heaven. After you have a coffee with Eunice (his mom), can you have a beer with Coffee, (my mom)?"

On that he laughed again and said;

"You bet! I haven't had a beer in a long time, but I will have one in heaven!"

Thank you all here for being part of our journey. . . What a ride it has been, and I would do it all over again. We love you all!!!!

Bob, Gail and don't forget Miss Spirit!!!!

I now would like you all to hear this song as I dedicate it to Bob, my angel in the heavens, whom I will love to the end of my world.

Save the slow dances for me.

Love, Wifey

Martina McBride's song "The Dance" filled the room. I could hear the muffled sounds of crying all around me as we listened to the song play out.

Uncle Roland had done a fine job of reading that for me, and I hugged and thanked him for it.

Next came the memorial gathering at St. Agustin Cemetery, time to get the vehicles in line for the procession. I had requested military honors presenting folded flags to Bob's dad and to me. I wanted Bob's dad to have something special to remember him by.

As many of us took our positions at the cemetery, we watched two Marines open and then fold an American flag. Another Marine was playing taps in the distance. My mind wandered off somewhere as I heard the taps playing. I also heard a woodpecker tapping on a tree somewhere. I kind of chuckled because my babe had taught me to enjoy nature, and here I was not paying attention to his service. I was listening to that damn woodpecker wondering where he could be.

I was suddenly thrust back into reality as the two Marines start speaking loudly directly in front of me with the folded flags in their arms. Bob's dad stood to my left as we both be received this honor.

I don't remember all of what was said, but the beginning stayed in my mind: "The President of the United States would like to thank your husband, Robert Maurice Durant Jr. . . ."

At that moment, I gave into the tears and just hoped that I wouldn't fall apart in front of everyone. I started looking around again, off in another world with taps playing, same woodpecker tapping, Marines talking, when suddenly I noticed something that I have never seen before. Just behind Bob's headstone, in small blooms, was a magnolia tree. Who would have guessed that I would find Bob's favorite flower, the magnolia, just beginning to bloom right behind his headstone on the very day of his funeral.

We didn't know what that tree was when we had come to see his resting place for the first time together in the dead of winter. I felt like Bob was smiling down from the heavens as he knew his favorite flower was right there, blooming for me to see. What an incredible sign to receive on this day. I knew that he was at my side once again. He told me that he would never leave me.

One of the three Marines presented me with the folded American flag, then saluted me. I thanked those men in uniform for coming out to honor a man they did not know. They showed great respect to Bob that day, a fellow Marine.

CHAPTER 24

Celebration of Life Luncheon

AFTER BOB'S FUNERAL, I held a huge luncheon for all who knew us. I had the funeral director announce for everyone to join us at the Chateau Restaurant. That meant many family, friends, and co-workers. I had no idea how many would attend but I reserved seating for 170 people. I had ordered two different dinners, buffet style, for people to choose from. I wanted nothing but the best for my babe!

I put Bob's favorite cigar at every place setting with a photo of him smoking a cigar on the label. In due time they would find out the reason behind the phrase, "Better than a fart!"

Photo by Gail Durant

I also had a photo collage of Bob wearing his many hats through the years at every seating. I inserted a poem I had written among the photos, so everyone would have a nice memento of him. Before Bob had passed, he told me that he was going to send smelly farts for all to know he was around! That would be *his* sign! It was important for me that I shared this with everyone, so they too would know when he would be nearby.

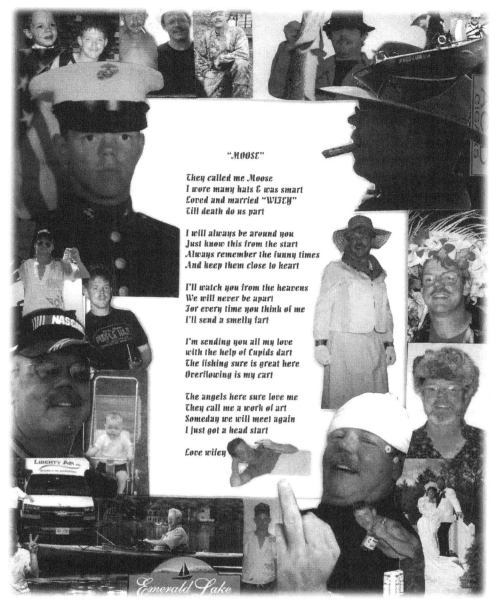

"MOOSE"

They called me Moose
I wore many hats & was smart
Loved and married "WIFEY"
Till death do us part

I will always be around you
Just know this from the start
Always remember the funny times
And keep them close to heart

I'll watch you from the heavens
We will never be apart
For every time you think of me
I'll send a smelly fart

I'm sending you all my love
with the help of Cupids dart
The fishing sure is great here
Overflowing is my cart

The angels here sure love me
They call me a work of art
Someday we will meet again
I just got a head start

Love wifey

Photo Collage by Gail Durant

As we arrived for the luncheon, some people were already complaining because there weren't any drinks being served or even available for them to purchase.

I wanted it that way. I was the only one who would be drinking at the luncheon that day. The hostess brought me some blush wine in a foam cup. As she handed it to me, she winked and said, "There will be more of that if you need it, compliments of the owner!"

It was our little secret. No one was getting drunk today—not on my watch!

This sunny day was getting brighter. Everything turned out amazing, just as I had planned for my babe. Seeing that magnolia tree had brightened my world so much and made me happy, and so did the wine!

Soon it was time for another drink, so I raised my cup to the hostess to signal for another. I ate very little and wasted no time, going around to thank everyone who had come to honor my babe!

The day turned out beautifully, and all went according to plan. I was grateful that I had given Bob the best funeral ever. I was proud of myself as I raised my cup, and I hoped by now that he had already enjoyed a beer with my mom, Coffee, and a coffee with his mom, Eunice!

"I will miss you, babe. Until we meet again, thanks for showing up!"

I brought the drink to my lips, as I knew this journey alone would be a rough one, but I am one strong woman and a survivor. I will always remember what he told me, and I drank a toast to his words: "Everything will be okay!"

A short time after the meal, after everyone had gone home, my daughter called to tell me that something crazy had just happened. She said my son-in-law didn't know how to put out a cigar, so he went to a site on his cell phone to ask the question, "How do you put out a cigar?" The response floored even him, because the reply was addressed to "Moose," which was Bob's nickname.

I think that made a believer out of him that day!

Our loved ones who have passed find many ways to make sure we don't forget them. I think this was a special message from Bob, letting him know that he was thankful that he tried that cigar in his honor. It certainly got a reaction Bob would've wanted. Moose was loud and clear! Expect the unexpected!

CHAPTER 25

Moose Farts

I OFTEN ASK BOB TO SEND ME SOMETHING if I haven't heard from him in a while.

Signs can come from people who were and still are involved in our lives to let us know they are still around us at any given moment. They can be someone very close, a work acquaintance, or a relative. It doesn't matter who it is, but they will bring what they received to your attention. In this case, it was our friend Kim, who was very close to Bob.

Be is an excellent example of a sign she received, and it blows me away. Why, you say? My husband's nick name is "MOOSE" and as I said before in my story, he told me he would leave me a smelly fart so that I would know he was around. I don't smell the fart here, but I do smile when it's brought to my attention. I tell my friend,

"Lucky you!!!" He was clearly with you on this day! *"Moose Fart"!* It was so simple and made us both smile.

Photo by Kim Helie

How could my babe resist this? I am really proud of him, as he's doing a fine job with sending his signs. All I did was ask out loud for him to send me something because I was missing him, and our friend, Kim made the delivery.

CHAPTER 26

The Dinghy

THE FUNERAL HOME RECEIVED MANY PLANTS and flower arrangements as well as prayer and mass intentions and sympathy cards on our behalf. Among them was a stuffed animal moose (which I later gave to Miss Spirit) and a statue of a man and his dog hunting and a picture frame with a fish on it. All these mementos came home with me after the funeral.

I continued to receive sympathy cards in the mail as well as flowers and plants in the days following Bob's funeral, but nothing could prepare me for the delivery of a long skinny box that was left on my porch at the end of that first week.

I couldn't imagine what was inside and would have never guessed it in a million years. It was sent to me by four of my cousins, and they had no idea how much this gift would mean to me, especially coming at this time.

In the box was a long and skinny boat that looked rather familiar. It brought me immediately back to the Indian Museum on the reservation at Foxwoods. It had been our favorite spot in the Indian Village, where everything was lifelike, and it reminded me of my babe. This boat will always remind me of our last trip to the museum together, our last adventure before Bob's health started to fail. Bob loved fishing and this part of the museum was always our favorite.

The top photo shows an exhibit at the museum portraying the Indians paddling a dugout canoe through the reeds. The Indians are coming home with the fish they caught. Bob always said, "There I am! I'm the one holding the fish!"

Photos by Gail Durant

"Who does this?" I thought to myself. "Who gives the gift of a boat when someone passes?" This truly was a remarkable sign for me, and I will treasure it always. This beautiful gift sits in my living room till this day! It was remarkable and uncanny because it brought back a great memory right away: our final adventure together at the museum, at the woods—Foxwoods that is! I will always be grateful to those who made the end of Bob's life most enjoyable. They all know who they are!

My babe was an awesome fisherman on Earth. Why would Heaven be any different?

Here is the letter I sent to my cousins telling them how much that dinghy meant to me!

> Kim & Shane, Christine & Eddie,
>
> Thank you so much for the nice boat with the candles in it. Looks great lit up at night and I have it on my coffee table. That was a sweet and thoughtful thing to do, and I appreciate it very much!
>
> Just to let you know, I truly believe in signs and receiving this boat made me think back to Bob and my last trip together. You had no idea, but we went to the Indian Museum for the 5th time at Foxwoods. This museum is truly amazing and right on their property.
>
> At the museum I thought that I was going to call an ambulance as Bob was listing, (leaning) his whole body. I was scared for sure, and we had to leave immediately and left for home as soon as we got back to the hotel and packed up. I didn't want to be in a Connecticut hospital. I remember how Bob was so upset with me as he didn't realize what was happening. He didn't want to leave, but I told him that he had to trust me, and he did!
>
> This museum is huge and lifelike as millions was spent on it. They had this type of boat (you gave me), in the water with the Indians fishing. I remember telling Bob that was him.

Your boat brought me back to this many times, as Bob and I went there with different friends.

I did go back one last time after Bob died. I find this another of Bob's signs, as you didn't know that was our last adventure together. When I opened your package, I thought to myself, "Wow this reminds me of something and then it hits me!"

It was our last adventure, our last trip together.

I am sending you pictures so you can see what I mean. If you ever go to Foxwoods, put that Mashantucket Pequot Museum on your list. It's awesome and you brought me back for just a moment to a place, Bob and I loved to go to.

You had no idea and I take it as a sign that my babe is still with me.

Thanks again, love you lots,

Cousin Gail & her angel in heaven.

CHAPTER 27

Picture Surprise

I WAS NEVER ONE TO PROCRASTINATE, so not long after Bob passed, I began going through his personal belongings in order to give some to his family and friends. I thought that they would appreciate some of his individual possessions as a remembrance of him, items like his hunting clothes, moose antlers, and bear rug, his stereo system, walkie talkies, knives, all his fishing gear, family photos, his coin collection, and other items too numerous to mention.

I also wanted to help his siblings out financially and gave each of them $3,000 from a life insurance policy that Bob had left for me. I didn't have to do it, but I wanted to, as I knew Bob would smile down on my good gesture.

Before long, his closets were empty, and it was time for me to go through some of his things from the cellar. I found his duffle bag and as I was rummaging through it, I found his digital camera with a broken lens inside. I am not sure why Bob kept this camera after I had bought him a new one for his fishing trips, but before tossing it, I opened it to make sure I wasn't throwing away anything important, like a disk.

To my amazement, I did find one inside and immediately went upstairs to load it onto my personal computer.

There were twelve photos on that disk. Each of them must have meant something to Bob, but only one stood out to me. I had never seen these photographs before, but it proved to me what I had been telling my babe right along. This photo made my heart smile because it's how I had envisioned Bob's Heaven. We had even talked about it together when he was ill.

Before he passed, I told him that God needed the finest fisherman ever and that he would be the head fishing guide. I told him that if he

wanted cigars in paradise, he will have cigars. Whatever he wanted
will be in *his* Heaven!

Here's the picture that I came across and love. It certainly made
my day!

Photo by Anonymous

Seeing this photo for the first time made me cry happy tears. I love the unexpected, and this certainly was that for me. I keep this photo close by and I like to think my babe is always this happy. What a great find!

Suddenly I remembered the picture frame I had received from our friends Darla and Bruce. They had sent a plant to the funeral home along with this frame with a fish on it. I had put it aside until I could find the perfect photo. It was unusual because the frame was horizontal, but every picture I had of Bob with his fish was vertical. I hoped to one day run across a photo I could use but had no idea that it would come from Bob himself. How seamlessly it fell into place! The two were meant to be together, his picture from the disk and the fish frame from our friends. I'd like to think that it was Bob's way of showing me that he's doing mighty fine in the fishing world of things, smoking his fatty.

I wanted to take a picture of this frame and photo to include in my book, so I placed it on my bureau, on top of my wide alarm clock. Behind it, there is a cherub planter filled with fake red roses and one yellow rose in the middle (representing my mother.) Later, as I looked at the picture I had taken, all I could do was smile again. The time on the alarm clock read 5:18. That was Bob's birth date! After taking the picture, I decided against using it because I was afraid that no one would believe me, or worse, they might think I set up the shot!

I am leaving this picture out of the book because of naysayers. At least I got another personal message from my babe that he was with me that afternoon. I embrace it and smile. I don't care what anyone else thinks. It made my day and that's all that matters to me!

It shouldn't matter what anyone else thinks about your own personal stories. It's how you feel after they happen. Keep those signs close to your heart and they will make you smile quite often and rise above the grief, if even for just a moment!

CHAPTER 28

Neon Sign

THREE WEEKS AFTER BOB PASSED, I received a message from my foster sister, Maria Estella, who resides in Las Vegas. It was May 20, 2013, to be exact, and she wrote to tell me that she was downtown when she happened to come upon this CIGARS sign and she took a picture, which she included in the message.

"Gail, this picture reminds me of Bob, and I can feel that he's here!"

I kept looking at that picture of the sign. I knew I had seen it before. I remembered that I had used a similar photo on Bob's funeral collage, which now hangs on my wall. As soon as I looked, I realized that it *was* the same exact sign! In mine, Bob was standing under that CIGARS logo with the same neon green color!

Photo by Maria DeLaVega

In 1995, Bob and I got married and honeymooned to Las Vegas. On one of our adventures, we decided to go to the downtown area. We had heard so much about the Freemont Light Experience, which is a laser light show projected onto an overhead archway that spans a few blocks. While we were waiting for the show to begin, Bob noticed the sign and said, "Hey babe, get a picture of me with a cigar in my mouth under that sign."

Photo by Gail Durant

Eighteen years later, I received the same picture from my foster sister saying that she feels Bob is here. She felt it right! He was right under that sign so many years before. I found this truly exciting that she had felt him there! I keep asking myself, "What are the odds of that?"

Of all the thousands and thousands of pictures I take, I find it funny that I remembered that day, only because Bob had asked me to take his picture. He found a way to show Maria the same sign because he knew she would tell me about it. It was precisely what Bob had wanted for me, to remember our honeymoon so long ago.

All the years Maria had lived in Las Vegas, and this sign had never caught her attention before! It hadn't meant anything to her, but after Bob passed, it meant so much more!

This photo proves that we can receive signs from our loved ones through others, no matter how far away. The message she received from Bob that day was also meant for me. It put a smile on both of our faces.

I wish I had the full photo, but as you can see I had cut it smaller for the collage, and it wasn't digital format in 1995. With all the pictures I take, I wasn't going to look for a negative just to prove a point. You've got to trust me on this one!

CHAPTER 29

"Moose" Stories

———

FAMILY MEMBERS SHARED SOME "MOOSE" STORIES WITH ME—it was their way of letting me know that my babe had crossed their mind on a few instances in their lives!

The first comes from a clipping from the "Dear Abby" syndicated column. My sister, Donna cut it out from the *Union Leader*, which is our town paper. The story was about a postal worker who had suggestions about making sure that wedding, graduation, or any other holiday cards got to the recipient. This mail carrier wrote that people should update their address books because people may have moved, or worse, could be deceased.

The clipping said to include the recipient's last name and not to use nicknames because you may think everyone knows Uncle Bob as "Moose", but if you don't have a proper last name on the letter, he may never receive it.

That was the only name used in the example of the "Dear Abby" column. It made my sister smile and she saved the clipping for me. She thought it was his way of saying hello.

Another story comes from my niece, Amanda. It had been three years since her Uncle Bob's death, and she wrote this story to us on Facebook, and in an e-mail, in her own words:

I was taking a Phlebotomy class at Manchester Community College in New Hampshire. The professor told us to choose a "hot topic" or "interesting topic" in healthcare to share with the class, and it didn't have to be phlebotomy related.

I chose glioblastoma (brain tumor,) as I knew that my Uncle Bob had it, and I have a friend, who works for a company that uses a medical device called Optune®. What Optune® does is basically disrupt the cell division so the tumors can't grow. It's not a cure, but it helps many patients and is relatively side effect free, except for some skin reactions. The device was recently FDA approved at the time of my class, so now people can get it prescribed by their doctors.

I thought this was a perfect way to share a new and innovative technology because glioblastoma affects many people. It was a way to honor my Uncle Bob, his diagnosis, his passing, and the new device that can help people. I also made a handout from the webpage to be shared with my classmates.

On the way into class on the night of the presentation, I was thinking of my Uncle Bob. In class I offered the information about brain tumors. Walking out of the building, I burst into laughter and couldn't stop smiling. The car parked right in front of the building had the license plate "Moose," and my Uncle Bob's nickname was "Moose"!

I told Amanda that was Bob's way of letting her know that he was saying hi and that he was around and saw how she had honored him. He was there to see that presentation and showed her with a Moose sign. How awesome for her that the car was in the right place at the right time just for her to see it!

I find it funny because in her Facebook message, she writes that her Uncle Bob passed in April a few years back. Her message is dated April 28, 2016, and that date was precisely three years after the exact date of his death.

Bob promised me that he would send signs, and I think he's having fun with it all! He keeps his promises!

I asked Amanda if she took a picture, but she said that it was too dark, and the car was leaving as well. It didn't matter. What she felt in her heart made her smile. That's most important of all. Now she has a story to tell.

CHAPTER 30

Loving NASCAR

My Bob loved the New Hampshire Motor Speedway in Loudon, New Hampshire, and you can bet he was there with friends when the NASCAR circuit came around. They all loved going together every year; it was their tradition. I thought it was great that the company that I worked for, Osram Sylvania, would give us free tickets twice a year to the NASCAR races for July and September. That was right up Bob's alley, as he and his friends loved going to the September races the best. I was not a big fan of loud noises, so every year he always went with his brother and the same friends, Jason and Melissa.

After Bob had passed, Melissa shared the following story with me:

Hell-o Gail. Well, here is the story that you asked me about:

I am a big believer in signs from above. This just proves that they do happen.

For many years my husband Jay and I, along with Bob and another friend of ours, would go to the NASCAR race in September. It was a tradition we all loved taking part in until Bob fell ill. He passed in April 2013, and we felt we didn't want to go to the races this particular year because our foursome was broken up and it would be too hard for all of us to go without him.

Well, Bob wanted us to go, and he sent a sign from above.

I was on Elm Street, sitting in my car, waiting for the light to change, when suddenly a police officer knocked on my window. He scared the shit out of me, and my first thought was, what the heck am I getting a ticket for now, the light is red? I rolled down my window and the police officer told me that they were picking random cars with drivers wearing their seatbelts. He told me that because I was wearing my seatbelt, I would get some tickets to the New Hampshire Motor Speedway for free. I looked around and saw two cars behind me and one to the right and left. I knew Bob had something to do with it the fact that they picked me, and I thanked him! It was for the July races, and because it was such short notice we couldn't go, so I gave them away. It was a nice sign to receive. I have no pictures of those tickets, but I have another story to share with you.

Another time I knew Bob was around me, in September. I planned to take a day off for the September race to stay at home and watch it on televison with my family. This race meant a lot to my husband Jason and me. It wouldn't be the same to go without our friend, Bob.

Then on the Friday before the race weekend, and I made a trip to a place called Camping World to buy supplies that we needed for a new camper we had bought. As I was checking out my purchases, they handed me four tickets to that race for free. Here it happens again. I walk out of the store and I look up and thank Bob for yet again another sign he has sent to me. He must want us to go to the races and carry on our tradition. This time my husband couldn't make it, but my daughter and I went and had a great time. We could feel that Bob was with us the whole time. We had great weather and enjoyed the race, the way Bob wanted us to. We got four tickets and left two seats open for my husband and Bob. Tradition had to carry on!

I love the way Bob let Melissa and Jay know that he wanted them to carry on with tradition. For this to happen twice in the same year and at two different locations was a sure sign that Bob wanted them to keep on going to a sport they loved and that he would be sitting right there along with them. I told her how amazing it was and definitely a sign for them, as they were his best buddies, whom he loved sharing this pastime with.

Photo by Melissa Tuttle

The same thing happened to me the following year on May 12, 2014, to be exact.

I was in my friend Laurie's car, and we were at a stop sign at the corner of Granite and Elm, the main street in Manchester. Police were looking randomly inside individual cars, and we thought they were looking for a person of interest. A policeman came up to the car, peered inside, and said he was conducting safety stops in Manchester. He directed us to proceed across Elm Street and told us to stop where a group of people were standing. We were told we would receive a gift for wearing our seat belts. To my amazement, the gift was a pair of NASCAR tickets!

This reminded me of my friend Melissa's story and made me think of Bob right away. A person handed us an envelope with two tickets inside for the July race. With tears in my eyes, I told Bob that I got his message loud and clear and that I knew he was around us. None of us could use the tickets, so I called Melissa that night and shared my story with her, and I asked if she and Jason could use them. They were both busy, so my nephew Joseph and his wife got to go to the race, compliments of Bob.

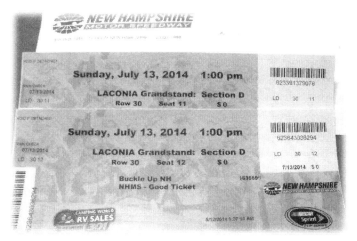

Photo by Gail Durant

That wasn't the only sign having to do with Bob loving NASCAR. One day, my friend Laurie and I had just finished up some errands when I noticed a license plate on a car in front of us that read "NASCAR" just before we turned onto my street. This incredible sign made me think of my babe once again. How I love those little reminders from him! This makes me smile and my day complete that he is still here with me.

Photo by Gail Durant

Bob loved Foxwoods, a casino on an Indian reservation in Connecticut, about a two-hour drive from where we lived. Bob loved poker and was ahead of the game in tournaments. He was a sharp poker player. I sat with him and watched many times as he played. I let the hosts know he had brain cancer and any time he could have a grand mal seizure. They would put a chair behind him so I could sit and keep a keen eye on him. I never let him out of my sight. He was a smart competitor, who kept track of his losings and winnings. Winning at poker made him smile during difficult times in his life.

"I showed them!" he would say. "I'm leaving with money in my pocket!"

We took a few trips out there before he passed to help get his mind off things. It's what he wanted to do, and I was all about making him happy. Some folks would question us going back and ask, "Again?"

"Yes, again," I would say. "It's what he loves to do with his wife at his side!"

Bob did have a claim to fame. He died being ahead in tournament poker—$1,200.00 to be exact!

Going back "to the woods" for the first time after Bob passed was hard for me, but it didn't take long before I realized that my babe was at my side once again. I took this trip with my sister Donna and her husband Bob. We took a wrong turn, and I think my Bob had something to do with that! As we turned around and came to a stop, I looked up and happened to see the street name was "Robert." I took this picture because I knew Bob was with us at that moment!

Photo by Gail Durant

After seeing that street sign, I had a feeling it was going to be a fun time at the casino for sure!

While walking around at Foxwoods, I knew my instincts were right when I spotted a NASCAR slot machine that I had never seen on my earlier trips with Bob. You could even choose your favorite race car driver, and Bob's was Clint Bowyer, #15. Bob would have been in heaven playing this, I thought to myself!

I recalled trying to get Clint Bowyer to give Bob a ride on the fast track at the speedway as a surprise, through the Make-A-Wish Foundation. I even offered $10,000 to help make it happen faster and to help out with the costs! I wish I had thought of it sooner, because the earliest it could occur would be July, and Bob didn't have that kind of time. I finally came to the realization that it would never happen.

Now here I was at Foxwoods, staring at this machine in front of me.

Photo by Gail Durant

I clicked on the name Clint Bowyer and put my money in the slot. I played a maximum bet one time.

"This is for us, Bob. I know you're here," I said as I kissed the picture of him that I always carry with me for luck. I put the picture next to the money opening. I hit the button and the cars race, and Clint's car is out in front.

"Come-on honey, you can do it!" I cheer.

The cars race round and round, and Clint drops to last place— game over! I laugh out loud! Bob used to get so angry when his man wasn't doing well in the car race, but he loved him anyway. I played one more time and then walked away. After all, it's my babe's favorite, not mine, but he was still with me. Not long afterwards, the machine was removed. I believe it was meant for me to see on this day, even though I lost a little money, I didn't care. I believe that Bob was with me my first time back.

Time to go find a slot that grabs my attention. I walked down to the next casino, as there are many at Foxwoods. I don't have to walk very far, and a little gem calls out my name. How could I resist sitting at this machine; after all, he sort of looks like my handsome guy, to boot.

Photo by Gail Durant

I pull out my card and slide my money in the slot, and in no time at all I can hear my fishing reel bringing up the Big Kahuna! My babe was at it again. He said he would stay by my side and he did. I hit a jackpot as the machine racked up my winnings! Bob and I are going fishing!

I heard the waitress calling out for drinks. I waved her down.

"What will you have, ma'am?"

"A rum and diet coke and a bottled water please. It looks like I will be fishing for the next few hours!"

I settled in with my feet up where you usually put your drink and smiled to the heavens.

"Thanks babe for showing up today." I blew Bob a kiss. I took my first sip and knew that it was going to be a nice trip after all. I could feel my babe was with me!

CHAPTER 31

Moose Says Hello

MY FRIEND LAURIE SENT ME A PICTURE that was a sign meant for her. It was a message that Bob had come by to say hello!

Laurie was very close to Bob, and he used to call her his daughter, even though she was older than him. I used to get a chuckle out of that. Laurie and I have been good friends for many years, and I knew that I could count on her, especially when Bob's health began to get worse.

I'll never forget the one and only time Bob fell in the shower and I couldn't lift him. I gave Laurie a call because she lived close by and I knew she could be here in minutes with her brother Ray to help me get him off the floor. I made sure to put undies on Bob before they arrived to give me a hand in getting him to the couch from the bathroom.

That night, I helped him into the hospital bed set up not far from the couch, and that's where he stayed for the next eight weeks until he passed. It's no wonder that Bob wanted to say hello to Laurie and to let her know that he didn't forget his daughter on the other side. I was happy for her, that she had also received one of Bob's signs. One night, after Bob's death, Laurie went to a restaurant with her boyfriend. They were surprised that they got a seat by a window in the front, because it was pretty packed, and people were waiting in line.

As she was preparing to sit down, she looked out the window and saw a truck backing in with a license plate that caught her eye. It featured a picture of a moose as well as the word "Moose," except the Os were replaced with Qs, making them look like eyes. Laurie was excited and told her boyfriend that she had to get a picture of it. She grabbed her camera from her purse and took off running outside.

"I've got to show Gail!" she told him.

Photo by Laurie Irish

Bob was letting her know that he was watching over her! She had a special place in Bob's heart, and he let her know that he was around to say hello!

When I first saw the photo, I noticed the number twelve in the lower left corner. I met Bob on the 12th. I love this license plate.

CHAPTER 32

Free Rooms

DESPITE ALL THE FOXWOODS TRIPS THAT BOB AND I TOOK, we never once got a free room. Some of our friends got free rooms regularly, but Bob and I never did. It was nice that our friends got a break, but it would have been nice if we got that same break too! We spent the same amount of money and did all the same things, such as going to shows and dining. The men played poker while the wives played slots! It made no sense. In Bob's final year, we went to Foxwoods three times, because it kept his mind off the brain cancer and it was what he wanted to do. I did anything to please my husband. Anything to see him smile!

Every year I would ask the casino host why we never got free rooms. We made use of their museum and pools with the same people. We would use our Foxwoods cards at every slot, and Bob used his at every poker table to acquire points. We were told that we probably didn't spend enough money gambling.

Our trips to Foxwoods weren't all about gambling—they were about the adventure. We used to take off during the day to Mystic, Connecticut, because there was so much to see and do there: Mystic Seaport Village, Mystic Aquarium, and the Mystic Drawbridge, where we watched the sailboats come in as we enjoyed an ice cream. We would visit the shops.

There was also an amazing Indian Museum right on the property at Foxwoods Casino, and we would visit that quite often.

Eventually, Bob and I stopped questioning why we never got free rooms like our friends did.

Bob and I always came home with money in our pockets. We never gave them our last penny. It wasn't in our nature to do so. Bob kept track of his winnings, and he always stayed ahead in the poker tournaments. He was happy that he could say that.

When Bob died, I made all the necessary calls including one to Foxwoods. I gave them his Dream Card number and told them that he had passed so he didn't need to be in their system anymore. They assured me that they would take him out of their database, and I shredded his card.

I stopped receiving brochures in his name from the casino, but I was still receiving flyers in my name for upcoming events and entertainment.

Seven months after Bob passed, he suddenly received an e-mail from Foxwoods addressed specifically to him. Since we shared an e-mail account, I saw all of his messages. I wondered what could they want after all this time. He hadn't received anything whatsoever since I had called and had his name removed from the list. Bob only used the computer to play video games or poker and rarely checked his e-mail, so he likely never would have seen that message.

When I read the message, I laughed. It was an offer for two FREE complimentary nights at one of two hotels available for the following month!

I could hardly wait to let our friends know. We finally got free rooms! I called Foxwoods to talk to someone about the mix-up, but I was told that I couldn't use the offer because they were issued in Bob's name and *he* would need to be present with proof of his identity! They were sorry and apologized. They were not sure what had happened in their database.

Go figure—I guess the trick to getting free rooms is to be deceased!

You can bet that Bob had something to do with this and that he was smiling from the heavens! He loved playing tricks on me and this was just another way to get my attention.

You've got to love that man of mine for trying to get the last laugh!

After all this time, I finally started receiving fliers in my own name for a free room, and guess what? I am not deceased, so you can bet

I will try to use it! Foxwoods holds such good memories for me, and I will go back for sure.

I know Bob had something to do with getting me a free room. We had such good times going there, and he wanted me to continue doing so, even if he was with me in spirit only!

CHAPTER 33

Finding Bob's Stash

I AM NOT SURE HOW LONG IT WAS AFTER BOB HAD PASSED that I decided to clean off his night table, but it was at least a good year. He didn't have a drawer, so it was really just a matter of removing pictures and the rubber placemat for dusting.

Before starting, I noticed a white bag under the table, from a department store. When I opened it, I found a gift that Bob had purchased and forgot to give to me. With his brain cancer, he would forget a lot of things. For me this was a nice surprise as it made me think of him the moment I found it.

It was sexy lingerie with spaghetti straps and an animal print on it. It was very pretty! Bob always bought me sexy lingerie. He was a romantic, and I loved how he always called me his sexy babe! In his eyes, I was.

I smiled when I checked the tag for size. He had bought me a large, but because my big boobs always got in the way, I needed an extra-large. He always perceived me smaller than I actually was.

I'm happy because I received a gift after he died, but I gave it away because I couldn't wear it and there was no use holding on to it. I don't remember whom I gave it to, but I'm sure I told them that it was a gift from Bob!

When I removed the rubber mat from the top of his night table so I could clean under it, I found yet another surprise.

Along with all kinds of cards that he had kept in his wallet, he had also left a hundred-dollar bill, as well as a fifty. There was a New Hampshire Resident Lifetime Combination Hunting and Fishing License, his driver's license, his permit to carry firearms, his boating license, the International Bow Hunter's Education Program card, and various credit cards.

Photo by Gail Durant

He also had a list of all the medications he used to take. I had typed it up so that we could just hand it to the receptionist at the doctor's office or hospital when they asked for it.

At first, I didn't understand why he stashed all of these things together, but eventually it made sense to me.

I remembered the day, so long ago, when Bob was sitting on his side of the bed with his back to me. I could hear him saying repeatedly, "I don't need this one and I don't need that one."

I remember asking him what he was doing, and he replied that he was cleaning out his wallet.

I didn't think much of it at the time, because he did that quite often. He hated a fat wallet. I let him be. Thinking back on it now, I can see that this time was different. He knew, because of his brain cancer, that he wouldn't have a need for those cards any longer. Why else would he remove them? Those little cards really defined who he was in life.

I was quite surprised when I found all of this because I had never found anything under that mat before when I dusted. I left it all there for some time. I knew that the next time I went to Foxwoods I would take his $150 and play for him, in his honor, to see if he would bring me some luck.

The best surprise of all was finding his Moose necklace. Our best friends, Helen and Terry, had given that to him. He used to wear so many different necklaces. He had a cross necklace made from magnetic hematite stones. He wore an eagle necklace until it broke. But before he passed away, he always wore this Moose pendant that had been made from a quarter. He would always have to take it off when he went in for an MRI and would have me hold it, so as not to lose it.

You can bet I had tears on this day. I feel that he wanted me to find this stash of his. I can almost hear him saying to himself, "Someday my wifey will find this here, and think of me." He was right!

Leaving the "Moose" necklace for me to find was his way of saying hello from the other side. My tears were happy tears!

CHAPTER 34

I Love You

Photo by Gail Durant

I THINK BACK TO THE TIME when this little card came in the mail as part of a sales solicitation. Bob was now in his hospital bed full-time at home, and I wanted to show it to him to let him know how much I loved him. I held it up to his eyes and said, "Hey, babe, read this."

I expected a response like, "I love you too."

But instead he looked at it and said, "Happy Birthday, Mom!"

I remember how my heart sank that day knowing that his cancer was getting worse. After a few minutes, I decided to try again and pretend I had a new card. I held it up to him hoping he would read something different with the same card.

"And what does this one say, Bob?" I said.

"I *fucking* told you already," he said. "It says, 'Happy Birthday Mom!'"

"You're absolutely right!" I lied. I kissed him and told him I loved him and to get some sleep. Swearing wasn't part of Bob's nature, at least not around me.

That day, I remember, was a turning point for the worse for Bob. I wondered in the back of my mind if his Mom's birthday was in April, because it was April when he brought her up out of the blue. She had died so long ago, when Bob was only 11 years old. I later asked a few members of his family when her birthday was, but no one could remember. I really don't know why, but somehow on this day I felt she was around us and he could feel it too! His time on this earth would be coming to an end very shortly. I had no idea just how soon!

Bob's words were very few after a while. Sometimes he would just stare and mumble. I tried so hard to try and understand what he was saying. I would always tell him that I loved him, but it was hard watching his lips move and hearing no response. Even so, I knew what he was saying despite his silence. I know in my heart he was telling me that he loved me back, as he always did. I just missed hearing it. I would kiss him, and he always kissed back. At least I had that to hold on to. The love was still there, no matter what!

He died later that month, at the end of April.

It was hard to live each day without hearing him tell me how much he loved me. I missed those three words more than anyone could know because we had said it to each other quite often, many times a day when he was alive.

Quite some time after Bob had passed, I visited my sister Diana at her home. She told me that she had bought something a while ago for herself but felt it never really belonged to her. She went upstairs to her bedroom and came back down carrying a sculpture. As she hands it to me she says, "Think of it as a gift from Bob," and then asked me if I knew what it meant.

I was floored. It said "I love you" in sign language!

Diana had no idea how much I missed hearing those three words! I'd like to think Bob had something to do with it all. In his dying days, his *I love yous* were as silent as the hand that sat in front of me, but that day he spoke loudly, and it didn't fall on deaf ears. Somehow, he had found yet another way to let me know he was thinking of me and still loved me.

Out of the many in my family, I always felt that this sister had a keen sixth sense and with her intuitive feelings, she had known that this statue belonged to me.

This gift sits nicely in the cabinet in my living room. I look at it every day as a reminder of how much Bob still loves me.

Like the statue of the hand, he couldn't speak, but I heard him say "I love you!" very clearly. My sister had no idea how much this meant to me that day. All because of one little solicitation in the mail that said, "I love you."

I have received two more similar cards in the mail since then and it makes me smile. Whenever I receive one, I look up to the heavens and wish Bob's mom a Happy Birthday!!!

Even though I have never met her, her picture is kept in a frame in my home because I feel she's close by with my babe. I always feel that the two of them must have been cut from the same cloth, with their goodness and kindness.

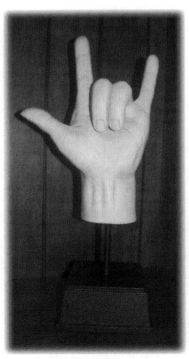

I have my own favorite detective, my search angel, Larry, who found Bob's mother's birthdate for me. I just had to know for myself. She was born June 8, 1942. My babe had it wrong. It wasn't her birthday in the month of April, but deep down I know she was right there, watching over her son, waiting to take his hand the minute he passed to the other side! My hand statue is a reminder that I am right!

Photo by Gail Durant

CHAPTER 35

Christmas Wrap

SIGNS CAN COME FROM NEAR AND FAR. My foster sister, Brenda, who lives in Las Vegas, let me know of another sign from Bob. In her own words she wrote, "Especially for you Gail, I ordered some wrapping paper from a high school fundraiser. This is *not* the Christmas wrapping paper I ordered! However, this is the Christmas wrapping paper I got! It's a sign from Bob!"

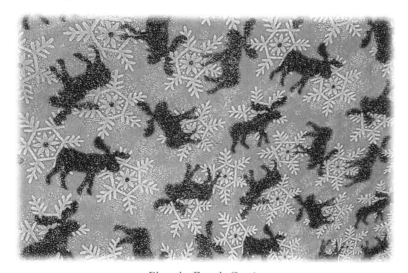

Photo by Brenda Garcia

I chuckle as I look at the picture that she sent, of Christmas wrapping paper with moose on it. How obvious to me that it was a sign for both of us. It made her day, and it made me smile too. One has to love Christmas paper with Moose on it!

What she doesn't know is that there was more meaning in that picture than just the unexpected image of the moose. First of all, the color red is my favorite color, and Bob knows that! You see, after

Bob passed, I changed his man cave in our basement into one hell of a woman cave. He never got to see it. The walls are painted in a bright red, and it is decorated for Christmas yearlong, including the Christmas tree adorned with our special ornaments. I even have snowflakes hanging down from my drop ceiling which are the same design as those in the wrapping paper.

Photo by Linda Cusson

I really believe that Bob wanted me to know that he saw what I had done to his man cave. I always wanted to keep the Christmas tree up year-round, but Bob balked at that idea. With this wrapping paper, I can assure you he found a way to let me know that he sees that I finally got my wish. Christmas year-round.

CHAPTER 36

Two Flags

———

I FIND IT FUNNY WHEN LITTLE THINGS HAPPEN that make you think twice. One day, I went to a department store to buy two small flags for his gravestone. Bob was a Marine, so I wanted to decorate his stone with red, white, and blue. But when I got home from shopping, I realized that I had forgotten the flags. It was the main reason I had gone in the first place. I don't drive, so the flags would have to wait until the next time I could get a ride to the department store.

Not long after I got home, my brother Mike, our cousin Mark, and a friend of theirs came by for a visit. Mike told me he had also just returned from the same store that I was at.

"I was just there, I said. I'm surprised we didn't see each other."

Then I told him that I went there looking for two small flags for Bob's grave and forgot them. Mike gave Mark a funny look and they both started laughing. I asked them why.

Mike proceeded to tell me that he went up an aisle in the store and saw some flags staring him in the face. He didn't know why, but he felt he had to pick up two flags.

"Two flags," he repeated.

He tells our cousin to go get them out of the car and give them to me.

He says, "I stopped by to check up on you, and I guess to deliver some flags!"

We all got a good laugh and loved the uncanniness of it all. The unexpected always amazes me!

CHAPTER 37

Dream Messages

I BELIEVE THAT OUR SEPARATION FROM THOSE WHOM WE'VE LOVED and lost will only be for a brief period before we meet again. Remember, life is short!

I feel that we will be reunited in the afterlife, once we've lived out God's final plan for us on earth.

I believe that there is a heaven. I saw it in my dreams, and I see it in the signs that I receive from those who have gone before me. I do not get signs every day, but it seems that they come when I need them the most.

We all have something on earth that reminds us of those that we've lost. We can see, smell, hear, feel, or even dream it: that one thing that triggers the thought of a loved one. For me, I *see* shadows from the corner of my eye. I *smell* the scent of Bob's cigar. I *hear* a song that holds a special meaning. I *feel* a presence that causes my hair to stand on end, or goosebumps to form, or I might even break out in a hot or cold sweat. Sometimes, loved ones will send messages in *dreams*.

The spiritual manifestations are great but are different for everyone. Only you will understand the sign that will trigger the memory of a special bond that you've had with that precious someone.

Everyone experiences these signs, when something grabs your attention!

The spiritual happenings that make me think of Bob at any given moment help me to cope, to live life without him. Receiving signs helps me to live without my loved ones for now, until I move on to greener pastures to be with them eternally.

I want to tell you a story that happened to me after Bob had passed. It was my first winter without him. There was a big snowstorm, New

Hampshire got pummeled with 15 inches of snow. I had to shovel off the two decks and make a walkway for my dog and a path for my oil man. I also had to clear the front entrance and a footpath for my mailman.

I had to go out a few times to shovel because the snow was accumulating so quickly. I did have Bob's ATV with a plow on it, and even though it was under cover, the battery was still dead because of the severe cold weather. Bob had always been the one to plow, and I never messed with it.

After the third time of going out to shovel and lifting the heavy wet snow, I started to get a dull ache in my heart and my breathing was off a little. Now that got my attention fast! I slowed down, took more breaks, and tried not push too hard, but I knew I had to finish before it iced up with the rain coming.

I tried to push the snow with the shovel handle wedged up against my belly so that I wouldn't have to lift it. At least I was getting the job done.

This dull ache and throbbing lasted three days, and it scared me, but not enough to go to the hospital. I knew that urgent care would ask my pain level on a scale of one to ten. I would have to say "one" because it wasn't real pain, but instead a dull throbbing. It was a warning sign for me and I took it that way. I had to be more careful and find other means of clearing snow.

That same week I got a call from my foster mom, Osbie. The first thing she wanted to know when I picked up the phone was if I was okay. She sounded nervous.

I lied to her and told her that I was okay and wondered why she was asking.

"Mija," she said, "I had a dream last night and Bob came to me with tears running down his face! He wanted me to call and tell you to get someone to show you how to run the ATV with the plow again!"

I was a little stunned by what she had just told me, so I asked her to repeat herself.

Then she asked me again, "Are you okay?"

"Yes," I told her, but I was thinking "how the hell could she possibly know this?" She has never been back to Manchester since she left over 45 years ago. How did she know that we had a plow on the ATV, never mind that we had an ATV at all?

My babe had sent her a message in a dream, and she delivered it.

That just proved to me once again that we are being watched over by our loved ones. This time, it was my late husband who saw something from the heavens and found a way for me to receive his message. Osbie was my receiver, and I was quite happy to hear that communication. It was the first time that Bob had come into someone else's dream to relay what he wanted to say. He knew that Osbie would follow through.

I always knew that we experience love connections from above, but this was a first for me, having it come through another person's dream. I absolutely loved it. There was never a doubt in my mind when Osbie spoke. I was just in awe of it all and happy that my babe was still watching over me!

I knew in my heart that it was time to hire someone for snow plowing and shoveling. I sold the ATV with the plow because I knew that I would never use it. I hired people to plow the driveway and shovel the walks and decks and, I am sure that Bob was pleased. Why else would he send that communication, except to get me to act?

I find it comforting that someone I love guided such a caring act from above. It shows me that our souls are still connected.

I may not be able to hold Bob's hand or kiss his lips, but his little signs give me comfort while I am still alive.

There is no doubt that the departed walk among us!

I call them my angels!

CHAPTER 38

One-Year Anniversary

1 Year Anniversary
In Loving Memory
Robert Durant Jr.
(MOOSE)

04/28/13–04/28/14

God took you early
He takes the very best
My tears still flow freely,
Even after you're laid to rest

One thing brings me comfort
To mend my broken heart
"Signs from the heavens"
And a bad smelly fart!

My dreams of you are real
As I feel you touch my face
Then you hold me tightly
With a big "MOOSE" embrace

Our memories keep me smiling
Your signs keep me alive
Your love will stay forever,
Cause I feel you at my side

Someday we will be together,
And until we meet again
Enjoy eternal life with Jesus
My Love, My Life, My Best Friend

Love your wifey, Gail.

CHAPTER 39

Dad's Visitation

My sister Diana and I both experience spiritual happenings to different degrees and enjoy sharing those moments with each other.

I have always felt that if you have a close bond with someone who meant the world to you, you could receive many, many signs from that individual after they pass. When it's someone who wasn't in your life much, you won't get as many signs, which makes sense: If the connections weren't there in real life, how could they be so in the spiritual world?

Our father, John, who most people called Jack, wasn't in our lives much, and I really don't remember how old I was when he deserted my mom and left her with thirteen children. I do remember however, that I was his favorite of all the girls, and he always called me his "Mighty Mite." I was confused when he didn't come back home at all, but as I grew up, I learned that it was for the best that he left. I do recall him drinking, gambling and making mom cry. I know we were afraid of him if he came home from work in a bad mood.

I do recollect however, that after Dad left for good we went on the welfare system, receiving food stamps and surplus food—that was when we ate the best ever! No more worrying about how we would eat if he gambled away his paycheck. When I ate boxed pizza for the first time, it felt as though we were rich! Mom fed all the neighbors and always shared with others. No matter who stopped by, you could bet that there was food being offered. I know I am like her to this day, always feeding others!

I reconnected with my father many years before he passed through written letters. I found out he was living in Huntington Beach, California. I still have his replies, with all my questions unanswered. I wanted to know how he could just leave like that, but he would never say. He also never divorced my mom, Coffee, because, as he always wrote, he still loved her. He never remarried.

That's why I was surprised when he came to me in a dream that I've never forgotten. I woke up, and the dream stayed with me. I shared it with my sister. Diana.

"Diana," I tell her, "In my dream, I was walking alone on this clear winding path in the forest. It was very dark, and I was scared as heck. I am not sure why I didn't turn around, but I kept on going further into the darkness. Suddenly, our father stepped out from behind a big tree and stared at me!"

Before I could say anymore, she exclaimed, "That was my dream! I must have told you about it before. There was snow on the ground while I was walking through a path in the woods. Dad stepped out from behind a big tree!"

"Diana, I've never heard your story before. I'm just trying to tell you mine!" I wanted her to know that I wasn't taking her story from her. "In my dream, there was no snow on the ground!"

We both realized that we each had a similar story to tell, and that it was the only visitation that either of us ever had from our father.

I asked if our dad had spoken to her. She said "yes," but she couldn't remember what he had said.

I told her that I did remember what he said to me. It wasn't much, but enough for me to remember when I woke up. He told me that I would be successful!

All alone in the forest, in the blackness of the night, those were the only words he said to me. He then stepped back behind the same tree and disappeared. I woke up with a memory so fresh that I knew that my dad had come with a message.

I find it amazing that Diana and I had comparable dreams. I'm not sure why we would have been walking in the woods alone at night, because it's not something either of us would do. I also realized that our father was not in a good place, as it was so lonely and dark.

I was happy that he had come by to deliver a message to each of us. I wish my sister could remember what he had told her. I do believe that he was trying to give us something positive to look forward too. In his world, he was showing insight and encouragement, something that he rarely showed in our world.

While I am still on the phone with my sister, she asked, "Gail, don't you feel that you are successful right now?"

I told her that I had done everything I wanted to do in life, but before I die, I just knew that this book would need to be written, so I could help children without parents, as Mother Mary had asked of me.

After receiving my dad's message, I hope and pray that this is the success he was talking about. That will make me happy, when I accomplish writing this book to help many children.

I never cared about success as long as I am happy and have no regrets, as I always finish what I set out to do. I am not in it for the money. Whatever I make on my writings will be given to charities of my choice.

I told Diana that I didn't want to be a celebrity on T.V. or rise to fame. That's not for me. That would just make me nervous, standing in front of an audience and speaking to a crowd.

It amazed me that our dreams were almost identical. If I hadn't mentioned it to her, we would have never known that we dreamt of the same visitation with our father.

I think of the word *content* when I look at being successful. We are both content with the way our lives have turned out. That's an accomplishment all on its own!

I am positive that my book is the success my dad spoke of in my dream. I also hope that he finds the light in his world, as that forest was way too dark. I can only pray that he sees the light at the end of his tunnel!

CHAPTER 40

AARP Contest

SIGNS CAN BE SMALL OR BIG. Some we don't see right away, like this next story of mine.

It was late November 2014 when I turned on the computer to read my e-mails. An announcement for an AARP contest popped up. The announcement said residents of nine cities were eligible, and my home, Manchester, New Hampshire, was on the list. The contest required an essay in 200 words or fewer telling why you love your city. You could also send in an optional photo. It was very clear that the 200-word essay was most important, but I had no time to think about it and closed the message. Maybe tomorrow.

The next day I go on my computer and the message popped up again, but I didn't recognize it at first. The word "contest" always grabs my attention, so I opened it and realized it was the same one I looked at the day before. I knew I should check it out, but again I had to be somewhere.

The third time the message caught my attention, I wasn't so busy, so I decided to look closer. I had a gut feeling about it. I pulled up the rules and regulations. This should be easy, I thought. What can I write about my city that would attract the judge's attention?

After careful thought I had an idea for a story. I don't drive. I will write about how I get around and how everything is close by. I will write how I go on the trails and take shots of wildlife behind my house and about all the animals I see in my own backyard not far from home. I will write about how I photograph deer, cormorants, mallards, great blue herons, birds, turtles, frogs, and Canada geese. I will describe our bus system and how we have cabs to get us wherever we may want to go, how I can walk to restaurants or the

Department of Motor Vehicles for a non-driver I.D. card—its right around the corner from my house. The Manchester Commons has a little bit of everything. I can even get my haircut there.

I emphasized everywhere I could get to without a driver's license. I sent in a photo of kayakers at Lake Massabesic with a great blue heron in the bushes as they paddled by. It was optional, but I knew it showed that even living in the big city we can have a little bit of country in our area. I was done in about 40 minutes. I found it hard to fit it all in with just 200 words to write. I went over the count again and again because I didn't want to be disqualified. Finally, at exactly 200 words and corrections made, I sent it off.

The holidays were coming, and soon my mind was on that. I completely forgot about the essay I sent in.

Thanksgiving came and went. Gifts I had already bought for Christmas needed to be wrapped and more shopping had to be done. Christmas cards had to be addressed with a generic letter of the year's events in my life. This is never an easy task, as I usually send out close to 200 Christmas cards. I have a lot of family and friends. Finally, I remembered that contest I had entered and wanted to see who had won and what their story was like.

It was the end of December when I checked the AARP website and learned that the "You and Your Town" contest had ended and the voting was done. I had forgotten to share my story with friends and family to get as many votes as I could. I really don't like voting contests, so I really didn't care about winning at that point. I just wanted to see the story of Manchester. I was curious how the winner wrote it up. I couldn't find any finalist list, and I hadn't received anything, so I thought, it must not be me. I let it go and didn't think much about it. Good for whomever won.

January came along, and one day when I check my e-mail, the contest title comes up in a subject line that reads, "Congratulations— You are a winner in the AARP You and Your Town Contest." I know there were many prizes to be awarded and thought maybe I had won some type of tablet, as many were being handed out. There were to be nine Grand Prize winners (one from each city), and about ninety-two tablet winners. I thought to myself, I must have won a tablet.

Then to my amazement I read that I was the Grand Prize winner for Manchester, New Hampshire: "Congratulations, Gail. You just won $10,000!"

> Congratulations – You are a winner in the AARP You and
> Your Town Contest
>
> Mon. Jan 12, 2015 at 9:53 AM
>
> Gail Durant,
>
> We're happy to let you know you're a winner in the
> AARP You and Your Town Contest! You've won $10,000.
> Congratulations!
>
> To confirm your win, please complete a Declaration of
> Compliance, Liability & Publicity Release ("Declaration".)
> It's available online by clicking here.
>
> Please fully complete the Declaration and return a signed
> original to XXXXXXX, the administrator of this promotion.
> You'll find the mailing address on top of the Declaration.
> It must be received within seven (7) calendar days of this
> email. If you do not return your Declaration within this
> timeframe, we will need to draw another winner.
>
> If you are unable to open the Declaration, download Adobe
> Acrobat Reader from the Adobe website for free.

I keep rereading this over and over. I start counting the zeros to make sure I wasn't seeing things. Tears stream down my face as I read what I need to do next. They ask for my Social Security number in the declaration, but I am a little leery. I call AARP, and after 25 minutes on the phone, they assure me that it's real and tell me to get my paperwork back to the company in charge of the contest, HelloWorld. I did one better: I called them to make sure I was not a victim of a scam.

Winning big things like this doesn't happen to me. After being reassured that it was true, I filled in the paperwork. I got a friend to take me to the post office, since I don't drive and sent in the form via certified mail. The next day another e-mail came saying that they received my information and that I might get a call next for an interview or a check in the mail sometime in March. I still couldn't believe that I had won. I will believe it when I see the check, I thought to myself.

I made a few phone calls to family members. I cry as I read them the letter. I ask them to please keep it quiet till the check comes in.

I thank my brother David for his constant reminder that something should be done with the photo of the kayakers and great blue heron. It was a winner in his eyes. I didn't think twice about it when I sent that photo in. I had to pick this one. My brother was my best critic and I trusted his advice, especially after Bob's passing.

I also called many close friends. I am not sure if they understood me as I was crying and talking at the same time. "Imagine that," I said! "I won $10,000 on a writing contest!" Right then and there it hits me big time— I finally got my sign!

Let me explain.

About six months before all this happened, I was praying every night to God and Bob to send me a sign. I wanted to write a book and help children with the money like Mother Mary asked of me. I didn't want to waste my money. I had put $10,000 in a Money Market account for my book project.

"Please," I would ask, "Should I write this book? Will people like my idea of pictures with signs? Will it be a hit so I can help many through charities?" Constant praying, "Will people understand me?" I would tell God that I know this is what I am supposed to do, but I need a sign to make sure I am moving in the right direction. "Am I to write this book?" Over and over I would ask, but no signs had come in for months. I never stopped asking. In my heart I know I need to write this book.

I just proved that I could write. *They chose me!!!!* I was the winner. My book will help many I thought. I received my answer at that moment and I thanked both God and Bob for the delivery, but it doesn't end there.

I had put away that $10,000 from a life insurance policy my husband had left for me. I put exactly that amount aside for publishing. I imagined it wouldn't cost me more than $10,000, but what did I know? I had never published before. In that moment, I realize that I am receiving the same amount I set aside for publishing. How much more of a sign could I possibly get? My answer was yes. Write the damn book!!!

It took me many months for an answer, but I finally received it. Like I said, some signs take time. I am not sure why it took so long, but in my heart I knew I was going to write one way or another. I guess I was just looking for approval from my babe. He left me one last thing that *proved* to me that he had been listening.

Three days after receiving that wonderful e-mail telling me I had won, I realize that my winning letter came on the exact same date that Bob and I met, January 12. Women don't forget these things. Bob and I celebrated January 12 and May 27 every year because I met him on January 12, and we married four years and four months later on May 27. We would go out to eat and have a few drinks in honor of these dates. My babe found a way to celebrate with me even after his passing, and I can assure you, I had a drink to that! I know in my heart that Bob *is* still proud of me.

I thanked both God and Bob that day: "Thanks for answering my prayers—I received your message loud and clear!"

Just remember that answers and messages will come forth if you are open to it. It may come fast or take a while, and sometimes not at all.

Seeing that my winning essay was about our hometown, I thought maybe our New England paper would pick up the story, but that wasn't the case. I was thinking, "How often do we hear about a contest and someone actually winning it?" I tried a few times with no luck. There must be someone who wanted a feel-good story to write.

I remembered this woman who had done many write-ups about my niece, Jodi, and her singing career. I asked if she could give me names of anyone who might take my story. Immediately she said, "I will write it!"

I said, "Great, but I won't do anything until the check comes in and it's on the up and up." I somehow still didn't believe it was real.

It wasn't long after the check arrived that I was doing a phone interview with Carol Robidoux. She runs an online news page on social media called *Manchester Ink Link*. I was intrigued with all her questions and wondered how this story would come to life. I was thrilled with her journalism experience and happy that she understood my point of view and ran with it.

This was the first step in getting my name out there—after all I had a book to write. If you want to read her whole story and my winning essay you can find it at *Manchester Ink Link* under the title, $10,000 AARP Sweepstakes Winner: "It's a sign from the Heavens!" (https://manchesterinklink.com/10000-aarp-sweepstakes-winner-its-a-sign-from-the-heavens/).

I find it interesting that I have yet to meet this woman, and yet somehow we have a connection. In fact, after a while, Carol asked me to blog for her site. She said I should spin tales with my pictures as it would give me practice for when I do start writing my book.

I wasn't sure if I could do this. What would I write about? Where would I start? I had no idea where to begin or how it would turn out. The key point is that I had to try. So I did. I started blogging for *Manchester Ink Link* and am proud to say that I like it. The best part is using my own photos in my story to make it come to life, as I have tried to do in this book.

Below is a story that I wrote for Christmas 2016. When this story came out, I loved reading the comments from people who do not know me. Some people said my story made them cry, and my pictures were amazing. Others said the story gave them chills and it gave them a memory to hang on to, when they went to La Salette as children.

When I read words like brilliant and great writing, it hits me again. Carol has given me a chance to write and I get great feedback from it. It's got to be another push from the grave. I will always appreciate Carol for giving me this opportunity and showcasing my photos. She knew nothing about me and took a chance. I owe her and one day we will meet. I am sure of that much!

The blog post, "Coming full circle at La Salette Shrine," can be found at https://manchesterinklink.com/coming-full-circle-la-salette -shrine/. It gives me great comfort to share with all of you.

Coming full circle at La Salette Shrine
Photo by Carol Robidoux

La Salette shrine overlooks Mascoma Lake
Photo by Gail Durant

Gail Durant is the queen of touching tales and quirky coincidence, although she'll tell you it's all about love and leaps of
faith. Here's another sweet story with a Christmas theme, and
lots of photos.

Being sentimental this time of year I wanted to reflect back
one day over 5 years ago. It was November 2011. It's a story
that for me comes full circle by the magic of La Salette.

My husband Bob and I were in Dartmouth Hitchcock Medical Center seeking treatment for his brain cancer. It's usually
an all-day affair. On the drive home we stopped in Enfield
NH to see this place I never heard of before. I was in awe of
it all. A hillside of 20 acres and your eyes went everywhere. I
saw the Ten Commandments on blocks of stone. There were
many statues of Stations of the Holy Cross.

You could walk up steps to the hill top and see Mascoma
Lake. You could see lights all attached to many things but
not ready to be lit up yet. That would take place later on that
night and we didn't have time for that.

We couldn't stay long, as Bob was tired. He let me run
around and take as many photos as I could. He stayed below
and enjoyed his fatty. I remember running around trying to
take all the beauty in. I never saw anything like this before. I
could feel something "Special" and sensations of it all. It was
powerful for me. I wished I could stay longer and watch the
lights come on.

"It must be spectacular," I thought to myself. They had a
statue of the two children who the Apparition of the Mother
of God had appeared to them in France in 1846. When I came
to this statue I just felt I had to kneel down and pray to it and
pray I did. "Please, I ask of you, give my husband a miracle.
He is terminal and there is no cure. If you cannot do that,
take me instead. I am older and I don't mind swapping places
with him. Eight and a half years older to be exact," I said.

I was surely bargaining with whomever would listen that day. I was crying and turned myself as I prayed so Bob wouldn't see me cry. "If you can't do that and you need him more, then let us both come back one day to see this all lit up. "I want us both to see your beauty and make another trip out here." After snapping many pictures which seemed to be a life time, we headed home to our log cabin on Emerald Lake.

That night I told Bob that I wanted to go back and see it all lit up. He promised we would go back together and fell fast asleep. It was a long and emotional day for us.

That day never came. You know the two of us going back to see it lit up. I never thought about it again as my husband's illness took priority. He died on April 28, 2013.

When making arrangements with the funeral home I told them I didn't care what priest came to say prayer as long as he was Catholic. I got to meet him just before the service to talk of Bob's life. I never did remember his name. I do however remember telling him he was so young and I even asked him "Are you sure this is what you want to do?" Yeah, me asking a priest that question. Then I proceeded to tell him he was a cute priest. He smiled. He did his service and left. I was proud of myself. I handled it all from wake, to funeral service, to Marines coming in. I know Bob was proud. He got the finest funeral ever. I made sure of it!

Fast forward 2 ½ years later. My friend's church is doing a bus trip to La Salette at Christmas time. She asked if I wanted to go.

"Hell ya," I said! I always wanted to see that lit up at Christmas time. It made me think back to Bob's promise of seeing it together. She also informed me that we would go to mass and hear a choir at Sacred Heart Parish in Lebanon, NH. We would visit the shrine first in Enfield, NH.

The day had arrived for our trip and when the bus stopped it was magical. It was so lit up with angels tooting on horns and outdoor nativity scenes with the animals, Mother Mary and Joseph and the 3 wise men. There were over 50,000 Christmas lights with many outdoor displays. It was taped off so you wouldn't fall on ice, climbing to the Stations of the Holy Cross. I was happy that I got to see all the statues, a few years earlier, up close and personal. They called this display the Festival of Lights. I snapped pictures everywhere. I finally made it here and it was so wonderful to finally see it in all its splendor.

I wished that Bob was with me as a tear rolled down my cheek. Somehow I knew he was. He was my angel watching over me. I had to believe in that much. We went inside and had a bite to eat as there is a small cafeteria with some seating. Many bus tours bring people by. It's a tradition for some folks and a spiritual journey for others. For me it was personal. I got to finally see the lights and it made me happy.

Inside another area was an International Nativity Sets Exhibit. We were told that they have at least 450 exhibits form over 50 countries. Some were gifts to the priests that do their missions there. How wonderful it was to see the different ways people around the world celebrate. They all had one common denominator, baby Jesus. Beautiful.

We soon head back on the bus as we had church to attend in another town. Our tour guide (a priest) informs us that we will go see a fellow priest that now has his own congregation and he loves it. He says the man is quite young. He will be happy to see his fellow buddy again. He said the choir will be nice to hear also.

We get to our destination and one by one we step off the bus and have to walk to the side of the church to the entrance. It was taking a while. I didn't know that young priest was outside on a cold day shaking hands with all who have arrived. He welcomed us one by one. As we turn the corner and being short I cannot fully see who it is, with so many tall ones in front of me. As I get closer and closer and I make it up the step to shake his hand I am in awe. Where have I seen this priest before? Why would I know him? We are in a different town miles away from home. It hits me like a ton of bricks. This is the young priest that did my husband's mass at the funeral home in Manchester, NH. OMG! What are the odds of that?

It comes to me full circle. My 2nd meeting with him and I felt that I was meant to be here on this day. You see my babe was with me to see the lights after all. He kept his promise. I had all I could do to not fully sob while the choir sang. I sat right in the front pew. I wanted to take it all in. In front of me was a statue of an angel and I knew mine was watching over me that night. I felt his presence for sure.

We had a snack after and I met up with this young priest and I tell him my full circle story. He says God works mysteriously and he remembered me from the short visit 2½ years earlier. Who could forget an older lady telling him he was a cute priest? It's a night I will never forget with my angel sitting at my side. I was full of Joy and Song. The ride home was sweet for me. This was a most magical night. Our lady of La Salette brought a message of reconciliation, peace and joy! But most of all my babe kept his promise to me!!! To see the Festival of Lights together. Its beauty will forever be etched in my mind.

Merry Christmas to you and all your families. May the New Year, 2017 bring you much Love, Joy, Peace & Promise & a trip to La Salette. A trip you will never regret.

In 2015 the lights almost shut down at La Salette due to the number of dwindling priests in the religious community. The facility is voted to stay open for now.

Gail Durant is the fourth-oldest from a family of thirteen children. She has lived in Manchester her whole life with the exception of one year in Hillsboro, New Hampshire. She

Bob and Gail Durant
Photo by Amanda Adams

Selfie by Gail Durant

worked for forty-one years in shoe shops, laundry and manufacturing and fully retired five years ago. She lost her husband
Bob almost three years ago to brain cancer, and is currently
writing a book about their love story, Bob's diagnosis, and the
signs she receives from him, to this day.

Proceeds from the book will go to charities to help children
in some way and also for brain cancer research. She resides
in Manchester with her dog, Miss Spirit (short for Christmas
Spirit.) She has enjoyed photography most of her life, and
loves taking random shots, and spinning the thoughts she has
into stories, with pictures.

CHAPTER 41

Second-Year Anniversary Poem

Robert Durant, Jr.
"Moose"
April 28, 2013 – April 28, 2015

I love the way you still love me
Two years since you've been gone
The signs you send for me to see
Really helps me to carry on
I am forever grateful
the promise that you kept
To be at my side forever
As if we first just met
Some words you spoke to me
Stay with me to this day
The time you patted my hand

And said
"Everything will be okay"
I find Peace with every day
To know that this is true
Till the time we meet again
Know that, "I still love you"

Love, Wifey

CHAPTER 42

Happy Birthday, Babe

Signs don't always come to me when I want them too. I don't ask very often, but when I feel the need, I always get a response, eventually. It may take a day or two, or it could come months later and sometimes not for a long while. I feel that the signs will come when they're needed most. It's important to know that the other side listens to us and will find a way to answer back in a way that we will understand! This is one of my favorite stories to tell, even though I have no photo to share.

May 18, 2015 is a date I will never forget because it would have been Bob's 52nd birthday. My girlfriends and I were headed to North Hampton, New Hampshire, to visit our good friend Ina. It had become a yearly tradition of friendship, wine, good food, and stories. We all called her home "the mansion." It is always an adventure when we get together there!

On the ride there, I told my friends that today would've been Bob's 52nd birthday. I then shout out to the heavens, "Happy Birthday, babe!"

When I did that, my friends joined in, yelling out, "Happy Birthday, Bob!"

Within minutes, our driver spotted a car passing us with a license plate that read "Moose." Now we were excited because we know Bob has heard us.

I was in the backseat and trying to get my camera out to capture a shot of the license plate. The vehicle with the "Moose" plate was driving fast and going in and out of traffic. By the time I could finally take a picture, I couldn't even read the plate because it was just too far away and very blurry.

I wish I had it here to show you as proof, but it doesn't matter. What mattered was the joy all of us shared, seeing that and knowing that Bob had heard us!

I think my friends are starting to understand what I understood long ago: Our loved ones in heaven really do listen to us. They sometimes find a way to let us know that they hear us! What a great day it was knowing my babe was with us! It's those silly little signs that can fill my heart with peace!

That made my day complete before it even started—something as silly as a license plate with the word "Moose" on it. I'm glad my friends got to see this little sign from heaven!

I think Bob made my friends believers that day! He's pretty smart like that!

CHAPTER 43

No Coincidence Here

I AM A BIG FAN OF PHOTOGRAPHY, and I love taking pictures for any contest. This day was no different. I was outside in my backyard trying to get the best angle of my angel statue with the lilac bushes growing all around it. My neighbor had just come home when I told her that I just took the winning shot for the Governor's Lilac and Wildlife Commission photo contest. I felt it was going to be a winner and wanted to let her know that. Of course, I wouldn't know until August, and that was many months away. She always caught me outside snapping photos of my garden and just said "good for you" as she went inside her home.

Photo by Gail Durant

I knew this particular photo stood out most to me from the many I took. I didn't have Bob here to help me choose a winner, as he had always done, but the angel represented him to me, and I felt it was a front runner. I called my best friend, Helen and told her so.

"Helen" I ask her, "When I win first place in this photo contest, can you take me? It's an overnight stay at the Mount Washington Hotel in Bretton Woods, New Hampshire, and I will need my buddy to drive me."

"Sure," she said, "no problem," and she chuckled, as always, at my optimism. "I will do that for you."

I told her that the photo I know will win is an angel, just like Bob.

I checked the website constantly to see if the winners were posted yet, as they usually announce in the middle of August. We were already into the third week, and I still hadn't received a call about winning. It was such a great picture, I thought to myself, but maybe I didn't win.

The winning photos were finally posted, and I saw that my angel was the first-place winner this year! I could feel the tears well up once again, as I knew Bob had something to do with this. I called Helen immediately to let her know we had to book a trip together.

She answers the phone and said, "I can't talk now as we are getting ready to eat dinner while it's hot."

"I'll make it quick!" I told her. "We will be going on a trip soon and it will be free!"

That was all I needed to say.

"You won first place in the contest?" she asked.

"Yes!" I tell her, "Call me back after you're done eating."

"Food can wait," she said, "I want to hear more!"

She was so thrilled, and it didn't faze her that it had happened just as I said it would. She was so happy for me, and soon we would be planning a trip together.

We couldn't start anything until I got the call saying that I had won, which came about three days later. I told the man on the phone that I already knew I had won because it was posted on the website before I got the call. He told me how to claim the prize and congratulated me on a first-place win! We were on a first-name basis because I had won prizes in this contest three times before, but never the first place.

He informed me that the prize was an overnight stay in the luxurious Mount Washington Hotel, in our fabulous White Mountains, with complimentary breakfast the next morning. I would be issued a voucher to present when I checked in.

Helen and her husband Terry had a camper at Fransted Family Camping in Laconia, New Hampshire, so we planned a three-day weekend together. I was finally going to see their home away from home, which I had heard so much about. I had never visited before, and I knew it would be great to finally see it in person. Terry would stay behind, relaxing at the campsite with their dog Marley, while Helen and I stayed overnight at the grand hotel. My prize was for myself and a guest only and Terry didn't mind at all, enjoying time with their dog. Terry drove straight to the campground while Helen and I began our own journey. What an adventure we had planned! We couldn't wait for the day to arrive.

We decided to go in October in order to see the fall foliage, but we were a few weeks too early to see nature's beauty in its full color. It didn't matter because it was nice to get away and do things with my best friend.

We laughed as we went to the Flume, which is a self-guided nature trail through cascading falls and rock formations in Franconia Notch, New Hampshire, something we both had done in our earlier days. We got to a certain point where you could turn around, and I looked at Helen as we both were breathing heavily from the short climb.

"Do you want to turn around and pretend we did it?" I asked her.

Her knees were bothering her, and I gave her an option. She said we should keep going and just take our time. We stopped frequently, not only to capture the beauty with photos but just to catch our breath. We were both too out of shape for these steep inclines, and we knew it. We were thrilled to have made it to the end but vowed never to go back, with much laughter.

Upon arriving at the Mount Washington Hotel, we took many glamourous photos of the grounds. It was spectacular, with fall colors just starting to come out. We walked all around the site and spent a lot of time photographing a pileated woodpecker looking for insects in a big tree in front of the hotel. It made me think of my babe right away, as he had introduced me to my first one when we had visited friends in Hillsborough, New Hampshire, a few years before. This was only the second time I had seen one, and they are certainly big and beautiful, wearing our wedding colors of red, white, and black! I think they are my favorite birds.

We had dinner early that night and were in the room by 8 p.m. The meal was fit for a queen. They didn't tell us when we ordered two salads with prime rib that the salad was a meal in itself. We laughed about that so much as we lay in our beds watching TV, with full bellies, stuffed to the gills. It wasn't long before we fell fast asleep awaiting the arrival of a new day.

The complimentary breakfast was superb. Whatever you wanted was there for the taking. I'm surprised we even ate, as our tummies were still full from the night before.

I was happy that Helen always kept umbrellas in her car because when we checked out of our glorious hotel, it was raining cats and dogs. It didn't put a damper on our plans, as Helen and I always had a great time no matter the weather.

Stopping at the Silver Cascade Falls in Crawford Notch, New Hampshire, we found it was roaring with all the rain and made for beautiful pictures. We also stopped to photograph the Ammonoosuc Upper Falls Covered Bridge and soon we were heading to the Cog Railway to travel up Mount Washington to the Observatory. Helen and I stood first in line because we wanted the front row seats. It was awesome to ride up a mountainside and take pictures of it all as we went up into the clouds. As we got closer to the Observatory, the weather worsened and we had to fight the winds and heavy rains just to get inside to be warm. It didn't matter how wet we were from the water hitting us sideways, as long as we kept our cameras dry. It was great excitement for both of us. We were two wild and care-free friends, drenched in rain, and we didn't give two hoots what we looked like. Helen had taught me that it was "all in the adventure."

What fun it was opening the windows to take photos as we drove back down over the tracks of the mountainside. We had front-row seats, and the storm was like a thrill ride. We clicked away with our cameras and held on to the open sill in front of us as the water pouring in made the floors a little slippery. Our laughter was contagious and soon the other passengers were laughing right along with us!

Once back down the mountain, we headed to Helen and Terry's camper at Fransted Family Camping in Laconia to meet up with Terry. The minute I saw it, I was brought back to the times when Bob and I had a fifth wheel on our own land, before we built our Taj Mahal on Emerald Lake. How we loved it! That's what most people remembered as our home.

I reminisced about those fun days with the fifth wheel, how our land was full of trees, and how similar our lives had been to Helen and Terry's. That land and fifth wheel was our home away from home like this camper was theirs. I could feel a tug at my heart thinking about Bob and how we had to sell the log home. There were many details in that home that we both envisioned together when we had it built. I thought about the many cherished memories we had made living on that property, and now it was just that, a memory! I was missing Bob a great deal at that moment, but I tried not to let it show.

I was soon thrust back into reality, with Terry asking if I wanted to have a look around the campground. It was pretty big, and there was a lot to see. Helen and I got into his vehicle, and he brought us to a brook that runs into the land from the Gale River. As Terry began telling us about the campsite, I noticed metal poles with what seemed like street names on them: one read "Moose River Run," another read "Liberty." I couldn't help but smile and I asked them if they saw what I did.

Photos by Gail Durant

"Hey guys," I said, "Have you ever noticed this before?"

"What?" they replied.

"Look around. Does anything catch your eye?" I asked.

I start taking pictures, and they see where I am aiming my camera. They can't believe that they've never noticed it before, until I mentioned it. I think Bob must have seen me from the heavens reminiscing, and he gave me the biggest sign ever, which made this whole trip worthwhile. At that moment that I realized once again that he hadn't really ever left my side. He will always be here in my heart, my mind, my soul, and in my pictures as proof!

Bob's nickname was "Moose" and he was co-owner of an HVAC business called Liberty Air, in Manchester, New Hampshire. How perfect to see the two signs across from one another where I stood. I was in awe of how it all fit together.

"Hey guys, this brook is part of the Gale River [my name, spelled differently], and these two signs remind me of Bob big time!" I said.

They said they would have never thought of that and were amazed too!

The signs meant so much to me at that particular moment and made me smile for the rest of the day How awesome is this? I thought to myself. My babe is with me, and I feel it! I love the unexpected!

I didn't get a picture of the Gale River sign, as it was on a busy highway, and I didn't want to get killed. After all I had a book to write!

I feel that God had his hand in my winning this contest so that Helen and I could finally have an opportunity to spend time together without our husbands. We had always travelled as couples and I had enjoyed our time together on this trip. We had been friends for many years but had never been anywhere, just the two of us.

This was the last great adventure together with my best friend, Helen. Little did we know what the future had in store for us.

CHAPTER 44

A New Home

I<small>T WASN'T LONG AFTER THAT BEAUTIFUL TRIP</small> with Helen to the White Mountains that our lives ran parallel again. She called me one day to tell me that because of the upkeep and yardwork, she and her husband could no longer put off looking for a new home.

"Are you sure this time?" I ask her.

For the last eight years, I had heard this story over and over. Helen didn't want to move from the house that she'd made a home, one that carried so many wonderful memories. She had found this place way before she ever met Terry, and it was something she was proud of.

Years later, after she had met and married Terry, the two of them celebrated every holiday with their families: Easter egg hunts, Thanksgiving dinners, Halloween tractor rides, and Christmas with their blended family. It was hard for her to give up this home that she had opened to everyone, and she fought every inch of the way whenever her husband talked about moving.

That never stopped them from continuing to look for that new home. I heard them discuss it a lot, but I would just chuckle because I knew she would stay put. Family meant a lot to her, and so did her friendships.

They would explore options to move down south, somewhere warm, always looking, but constantly staying put. That's why I questioned it now. She always resisted letting that home go.

"Terry's struggling with the upkeep and after talking to God, I know it is for the best!"

You see, she had just found out that she had uterine cancer and was scheduled for surgery to see if it had spread. There was no time to be wasted. They hired a real estate agent and started looking at houses right away. Her calls to me were always the same.

"Hey Gail, we are looking at a house today, wish us luck!"

Helen would always find something wrong with the house, the style, layout, or the cost. It was nothing new, as I had heard it all so many times before. I told her they would know when the right one came along, that they would just feel it.

They didn't have much time, as Helen wasn't sure if her cancer had spread, and she was thinking of Terry, in case anything should happen to her. He also had many bouts with health issues himself, and she was trying to make his life easier so he would no longer have to deal with mowing, shoveling, plowing, raking up leaves, and bringing trash to the dump, and so on.

One day Helen called to tell me of another house they would be looking at that weekend. When she told me the name of the street, Moose Pond Terrace, I knew in an instant that this was the place they would soon call home.

"Helen, this is it, this will be your new home!"

"Gail, we didn't even see it yet, so don't jump the gun!"

"I just feel it. Bob is helping you out after all these years of looking," I told her. "This is a sign from my babe, and you know how I am with that!"

The weekend arrived, and they went to look at this house. Helen called to say that they had put a deposit down but would have to wait to see if their offer would be accepted.

"I told you, this is your new home, and Bob is helping you in his own special way!"

"I know," she tells me, "but it isn't ours yet! I'll believe it when I get the call!"

"Helen, it will be," I tell her. "I just know it!"

Not long after, Helen posted on Facebook that they had taken a leap of faith and a magic carpet ride to finally find their new home. They would be moving within the month!

She thanked God for showing her the way.

Oh, I thanked God too, but then I sent a kiss up to the heavens, to God's angel, my babe, who had found yet another way to show he had a hand in this. His signs are wonderful! Who can argue with that!!!

Moose Pond Terrace
Photo by Gail Durant

I took this photo on the day that Helen and Terry moved into their new house, which was simply gorgeous, and the details were made for them. They now had a journey to make new memories in this new house they would officially call home!

Helen had her surgery, and God gave her a second chance at life. Her uterine cancer was in remission and had not spread.

Things were falling into place, and I was extremely happy for them both!

CHAPTER 45

Third Year Anniversary Poem

Robert Durant, Jr.
"Moose"
April 28, 2013 – April 28, 2016

Pictures on my wall

I don't need a picture in every room
To let me know you're near.
I do it so I can send kisses
Of a smile I hold so dear.
There's one of you when
You caught a big fish
Your grin was ear to ear.

Or the one with a fatty in your mouth
And holding a Budweiser beer.
A picture where you proposed to me
And we married within the year.
Our wedding picture, I love so much
In the Gazebo in '95,
A magical atmosphere.
Another picture Marines salute
This one sheds many a tear.
A folded flag, and now you're gone
But sometimes I feel you're here.
There's one photo,
Where I see your eyes
And "Santa Claus" cheeks appear.
I was the one behind the lens
And I saw it loud and clear.
Your love for me was in your smile
It's still genuine and sincere.
Yes, your pictures are still on my wall
So YOU see them
From Heaven's stratosphere.

Love, Wifey

CHAPTER 46

The Rabbit

I'M A FIRM BELIEVER THAT THERE IS A HEAVEN, and I try to prove it with pictures. I have faith that signs come from above as a healing presence. That's my take on it because I have been comforted by what I've received, and it helps me to cope with day-to-day living. There is no right or wrong way to grieve. It all comes from within you and your heart.

I make each day count. I get up, get dressed, and face another day with a positive attitude. I never know when a loved one will visit, but you can bet it will lift up my spirits even more. Just like every relationship is different, everyone experiences signs differently. The beauty of receiving signs in your own way is that the signs will make perfect sense to you and no one else.

I want to tell you more about my best friend, Helen. We had known each other for over thirty-five years, more than half my life. We were maids of honor at each other's weddings and traveled many places together with our soulmates. Of all my friends, she was the most proud of me. She used to say that she envied my lust for life. I used to feel the same way about her! We traveled far and wide with our cameras at our hips, as we were both in tune to nature and photography.

She pushed me to get a job where she worked so I could make more money. She got me to wear sexy dresses and said I had beautiful legs and I should show them off! She was my go-to person when I didn't understand financial investments and the like. Our lives entwined and were parallel. Whatever happened to her happened to me! It got to the point where if she needed a new washing machine, then I would soon need one too. It was crazy. I'd get a dog, she would get a dog. My stepson would move in and her stepdaughter would move in. It was wild, but we got used to it.

Sometimes I wish it weren't so parallel. My husband died of a brain cancer called glioblastoma. One day I received a call from Helen from the emergency room telling me she had just received the same diagnosis! We did a lot of crying and hand holding, and I was once again reliving this disease that had taken my husband's life. I knew that one day it would take her life too.

There are times when things are just out of our control, and all you can do is just show up and be there. You've got to be that ear and listen, you've got to hold your loved ones' hands and cry along with them. Helen was important to me: we had a special bond that no one could break.

When Helen fell ill, I got to tell her what her purpose in life was. I brought up stories that would make her laugh; it was all I could do, as her bestie. We started to reflect on days not so long ago.

I reminded her of the time that I got her on stage to sing the Blues Brother's song "Soul Man" as the band gave us huge sunglasses and balboas to wrap around us. We had the Jameson's crowd cheering us on. I had no problem getting up with the bands and shaking my tambourine. Helen was the opposite. She needed a rum and diet coke "and don't forget the two limes" before she would do anything like that. The next day she would tell me how much fun she had and how important I was to her in her life. At that time, she was going through a divorce, and she could find laughter hanging out with me. I remember her always asking the DJ to play one specific song that she loved every time we went out to the Jameson's Club: "I Want to Know What Love Is," which was always on the turntable when we showed up to dance the night away.

I reminded her about our recent adventures when we got lost as she drove wherever the road would take us. I was the one who got nervous in a car as we were driving around, not knowing where we were. Helen taught me that getting lost was all part of the adventure. It amazed me that wherever we went, she would always spot a rabbit.

One time she spotted one by a garbage can just as we were heading inside the fence to go to the beach in Maine.

"Gail," she would say, "look over there, it's another rabbit!"

She always noticed them before me. She had an eagle eye. I laughed as I reminded her about the time we went to a tea garden in Rhode Island, where they had beautiful flowers growing. She was so desperately trying to get my attention as she spotted another freaking rabbit.

"Gail!"

She tries to whisper to me, but I didn't hear her. I was fascinated with the flowers and pergolas with roses wrapped around them, and I was trying to take pictures. She said she had tried three times to get my attention, so she had to speak loudly, but she was afraid of scaring the rabbit away.

"Gail!" she screamed. That time I heard her, and she pointed to yet another rabbit. I think we took pictures of it for the next half hour trying to see how much closer we could get without it hopping away.

As we finally head home from the garden, I tell her that her sign to me will be a rabbit, because she sees them all the time.

"If something ever happens to you and I see the rabbit, I will know it's you. I will be the bird shitting on people if I go first."

We had a good laugh on the way home. Life was amusing to us.

As I sat at Helen's bedside, holding her hand, I reminded her about how beautiful Heaven is and how she would be greeted first by her mom. I told her I would miss her insanely, but Heaven needed her more. I asked her to give Bob a hug and a kiss for me.

I asked if I could pray for her with our friends Sue and Lori while we hovered over the hospital bed set up in her home. We were holding hands, and Helen listened attentively as we recited some prayers. I had a heart-to-heart conversation with her about how she would begin a whole new journey in Heaven. I told her that what she loved on this Earth will be there in her Heaven.

"Helen," I told her, "you will have flowers, and music with dancing, and God's beauty will be up there too, so bring your camera!"

I told her there will be lots of hearts. She loved everything about hearts because they represented love. I told her that the loved ones who have gone before her will meet up with her again. She will be surrounded by wildlife, and those freaking rabbits that follow her around will be there as well. Because God knows she was a leader, I told her He will use her abilities to lead others, as she was the chosen one for her next journey.

We did the sign of the cross and ended the prayer. I proceeded to tell Helen something that kind of bothered me, "Helen, do you remember what I told you, what your sign to me would be?"

"A rabbit," she said.

I told her that I was sorry I had said she would be a rabbit, as I probably would never see one living in the city.

"Why did I say you would come back as a rabbit? I'll never get a sign from you."

Boy was I wrong. I should have known better that it wasn't just going to be the rabbit—there would be other things that would remind me of her. Different reminders will make you think of the same person. There's more than one sign for each loved one within your heart.

Helen passed a day before my birthday, October 30, 2016. The day before the wake and funeral, she came to me in my dream, telling me to bring my camera if I wanted to see the rabbit. You can bet I stashed it inside my pocketbook just in case.

The night of the wake, I was asked to stand in the receiving line, as they considered me family. It was an honor for me. After about an hour and half, it started to slow down, so I went around to look at the collages that Helen's family had put together for her. I read the cards on the flowers, and on the boards, and looked at many photos from when Helen was just a toddler. One picture immediately made my eyes light up. I ran to get Helen's husband, Terry, and her brother, Bruce.

"You guys. Come here, I have to show you something!" I say. "Remember I told you about the rabbit?" I asked. "Helen's wearing overalls with bunnies on each pant leg in this picture!"

They could only smile as I took a picture of the picture. It made my night.

On the day of the funeral, as I was being driven over to the church, I was watching outside the car window, looking for a rabbit in the woods. I had brought my camera, as Helen had instructed. At the place where her stone rest, I couldn't focus on the service because I was looking for the stupid rabbit that Helen had told me about in my dream. It never materialized, but I did tell some of her friends at the luncheon how I would always know that she was around if I saw a rabbit. I had to let them know that it was my sign for her. I think they must have thought I was out of touch with reality as a result of losing such a dear friend.

Fifteen days later, I got my first sighting, one I never thought would materialize living in the city. It was a harvest moon night, and I decided to go to the trails behind my home to get a better picture where there were no clouds. I hadn't been on the trails much because my dog wasn't able to walk very far, and I didn't like to leave her alone for too long.

As I walked toward the path, I noticed a young girl coming out of the trail with what appeared to be a white cat cuddled in her arms. As I got closer, I saw the shape of the nose and mouth and realized it was a rabbit! My eyes welled up with tears as I approached her and asked the rabbit's name. She told me that its name was Snowball and that her name was Grace. Imagine that!

She was not afraid to have an older woman approach her crying, telling her that she had just received a sign, but I could see her eyes dart to the side. I knew there had to be a mom close by watching what was going on, as I was a stranger.

I kept patting the rabbit and asked if I could hold it. She let me take it into my arms, and it was soft and cuddly. It loved to be hugged and reminded me of Helen, who was also a hugger. I couldn't believe it—in all the years of coming to the trails, I had never seen a rabbit here.

I walked with Grace to see her Mom who was still standing in the doorway. I explained why I was crying and what a wonderful sight it was for me to see this. She asked if I wanted to see the other two rabbits they had, and she told the kids to go get them.

There was a feisty one named Brownie and the other was Button. She said the friendliest of the three was Snowball, who loved to be cuddled. I knew for certain that Snowball was Helen. I would have been afraid to hold the feisty one with its feet scrambling to get away.

Photo by Jodi Scarpa

The mother's name was Jodi, and she told me that her rabbits are usually on a leash most times in the yard. I wondered how I could have missed this, but then I realize that I hadn't been walking the trails lately because Miss Spirit could no longer walk very far. I also learned that they had just moved in five weeks earlier, which explained my not ever seeing the rabbits here. I was really floored to see a rabbit in the city. Helen had kept the promise she had made me in my dream!

Most amazingly, after Grace had leashed Snowball and stood up, I got a full view of her shirt, which had the biggest shiny aquamarine-colored heart on the front, and I cried some more. Helen also loved hearts; she wanted me to have some of her jewelry before she passed but I felt funny taking it, and I told her I would take it after she was laid to rest. Her husband Terry gave me what she had wanted me to have: mostly heart-shaped pieces, which I will treasure forever. So I knew the heart on Grace's shirt was another sign. I told Helen how I loved the way she had kept her promise.

Photo by Gail Durant

A few more things have happened to me since Helen's passing that I'd like to share with you—the silliest little things that can get you to sit up and take notice and be reminded of those who have gone before us.

A few weeks after Helen passed, I was reading my Sunday newspaper, *The Union Leader*, while watching *Wheel of Fortune* on TV. The answer to the puzzle would be a song title. As the letters kept coming up on the screen, I tried to guess, and then like magic the words came to me.

"I Want to Know What Love Is!" I screamed out the answer, even before the TV contestants did!

In a matter of seconds, I remembered that this was Helen's favorite song, the one that she always requested those many years ago. Helen had found another way to show me that that she was still around. I yelled up to the heavens and let her know that I got her message, and I thanked her for it. I feel that if I thank those on the other side, they will send more signs to me.

That was always a pet peeve of mine, people not saying "thank you." I always throw it up to my *spirit guides,* as I know they are listening, and I feel they appreciate that I thanked them.

Spirits know if you respond to their messages. Many people may not know what to look for, but I hope my stories will help readers recognize and understand the signs meant for them.

There will be times however when you and your loved ones will all be on the same page with the same sign. For example: My mother loved the song "Paper Roses." You can bet that if my family heard that song on the radio, their thoughts would instantly turn to her. All of us would respond to that song because it has significant meaning to our mom. She sang it to us all the time. Every Christmas my sisters and I and anyone else who knew the words would belt out "Paper Roses" in memory of Mom. Some of us couldn't make it through the whole song, but tears cleanse the soul.

Another sign from my bestie Helen came on a different TV program: a magician's show called *David Blaine: Beyond Magic.* I love magic and will watch anything that is mystical.

On that night, Mr. Blaine asked a woman to think of a memory. He asked if what she was thinking of related to when she was five years old. She said yes and teared up. He then had another woman come up onstage and wrote a word on her hand relating to that memory. The word was "bunny".

I was thrilled to see this, and I knew my bestie had found another way to say hello to me. Of all the words in the universe, this one was an attention grabber!

If I had seen this show while Helen was still alive, it wouldn't have meant anything to me. It wouldn't have jumped out at me or even remind me of her. However, Helen is not here, and this one tiny little word had a huge impact on me.

It was meant only for me. Helen's family doesn't think of her sign as the rabbit. They have their own memories that they've shared with her. When they recognize her signs to them, they will know she is nearby. Something, someone, some random song, will make them think of her, and when it happens, they will just know it!

I received a piece of jewelry recently from Helen's sister Jennie. It was touching that Jennie could let go of something that came from her mom, Helga, but she must have felt it belonged to me. When I opened the little box and saw the rabbit brooch with the red eyes, it made me cry. It was very nice of Jennie to let a piece of her mom go, in remembrance of Helen, just for me. It touched my heart indeed!

CHAPTER 47

The Red Wagon

SOMETIMES I CAN SEE THINGS HAPPENING IN MY MIND before they happen in real life. It doesn't occur often, but when it does, it surprises even me.

Miss Spirit and I loved walking the trails behind my house. They would lead us to Nutt's Pond. I was happy I still had her for comfort after Bob had passed. This particular day it was about 70 degrees out, so I didn't think it was too hot for Spirit to walk. My neighbor, Srdjan, came along for the stroll, as he loved being around her. We got to the area on the trail where I would always take pictures of the geese and mallards that I spotted in the water.

Suddenly, I noticed that my dog was walking funny, pacing back and forth. She vomited profusely, and diarrhea was running out of her like water. I caught her before she falls to the cement, and I laid her on her side rubbing her belly and telling her that it will be okay. I took out my phone and call 911. I just needed the number for my vet because I didn't have it on my phone, and they were located nearby, just off this trail.

"911, what is your emergency?"

I was frantic, and I told them that my dog was very sick on the trail at Nutt's Pond. I knew that vehicles could not get through and that she was too heavy for me to carry out. Tears were rolling down my cheeks as Spirit's eyes rolled back into her head, and she became lethargic.

"Ma'am, we only do human calls," they said.

"I know" I respond. "I just need to be connected to a vet's service to get help. My dog is down, and I think I am losing her. Please put me in contact with some help, please!"

They connected me to an out-of-town service who asked for my location. I repeated three times that I was in Manchester and told them exactly where, but they couldn't pinpoint where I was. Meanwhile Srdjan had reached my vet on his phone and handed the phone it to me. I asked if there is any way they could help me.

"No ma'am, we don't do that here," they say. "You would have to bring her here to us."

I thanked them and hung up while still holding my own phone in the other ear. I kept hearing, "Ma'am, we still can't pin point your location."

Suddenly, I'm not hearing anything. I am visualizing a red wagon with my dog in it, and Srdjan and me running like the dickens to save Miss Spirit. I could picture all this in my mind like it was happening in real time, Srdjan and I running down the trails for dear life. I start asking kids on the path if they have a wagon, all while I am still on the phone. I kept getting "no" for an answer and I just looked up to the heavens and wailed to God. Those poor people on the phone trying to help me out could hear me yelling, "God, PLEASE!" I say. "I just need a red wagon, I don't want to see my dog die!"

You know, that man above listens to me. There are many entrances to get on the trail and out of nowhere comes this woman pulling her three kids and a dog in a long hard plastic red wagon! I think she heard me shouting, as she was coming in because she came right over to us.

"Oh my God—miss, can I borrow your wagon?" I ask.

She tells her kids to get out and brings it to me, telling me there is an animal hospital at the end of the trail, not far from here.

"I know" I said. "It's the one I use for my dog!"

On the phone I hear the dispatcher ask if I'm all set. "Yes," I said. "I have a red wagon" and I thanked them and hung up.

The woman with the wagon said she would meet us there. Srdjan and I lift Spirit into the wagon and start running, just like I saw in my vision. Srdjan had the front and I took the back so I could keep my eye on Spirit. It felt like it took forever to get there. Srdjan is tall and fast, but I am short and before long I am out of breath because of my asthma. I tell him to slow down or he will be pulling two of us in the wagon.

Once inside, I tell the receptionist that I was the one who had called. I ran to the water dispenser and filled a cup and tried to get my dog to take a sip, but she wanted nothing to do with it, so I poured it on her head instead and rubbed it in.

Within a minute, my dog sits up and wants to jump out of the wagon like nothing ever happened! I was shaking my head in amazement, yet happy to see that she was feeling better. They took her out back and checked her out and suspected that she had heat stroke. It wasn't a hot day, but at almost fourteen years old, she had a hard time cooling herself off.

I went outside while waiting for them to finish the paperwork. The young lady was in her car with her children and their dog. I brought the red wagon over to her and thanked her again and again. Before going back inside, something told me to ask what her name is.

"It's Megan," she says and proceeds to give me her last name.

Srdjan walked home to get his car and my pocketbook so I could pay the bill. We got home safe and sound with Spirit sleeping for the rest of the night because of her ordeal. It took the wind right out of her.

The next day I went on social media to tell my story and again to thank this woman. I also asked that if anyone knew her, to please show her the write up. I got an immediate response from Megan asking how my dog was doing.

I said, "Thanks to you, she is just fine! You were my angel!"

I asked for her address, so I could send a little something for her and her children, after all their plans of a cart ride never materialized. God sent me an angel that afternoon and I wanted them all to know how much that red wagon had meant to me and my little girl.

We have since become friends on social media. One day recently, I asked if I could take some photos of her, her children, and their dog for this story. She obliged but told me they didn't have their dog anymore.

Sad to say but neither did I, but for different reasons. Six months after that ordeal my Spirit went on to greener pastures to be with her daddy. She was over fourteen years old. I was very happy that I had her love and comfort for more than three years after her daddy passed. They have yet to come in my dreams together, but in due time I know they will, no doubt about that!

I took a photo of Megan's children, Owen, Lily and Max with Srdjan at the same spot where they showed up with the red wagon that day.

From left to right: Srdjan, Max, Owen, Lily & The red wagon
Photo by Gail Durant

My book cover is a photo that I took of my husband, Bob and Miss Spirit. It's layered over a photo of a tunnel taken by my best friend, Helen. I know that Bob and Miss Spirit are together again and that's why I choose these special photos for my book cover.

As I held Spirit just before she passed, I told her that she would see her daddy again, and I saw her eyes light up for just a moment before she left this world. I hadn't used that word "daddy" in a long time. They loved each other so much, and I know they are reunited once again, just as I portrayed on the front cover of my book.

Spirit died in my arms on December 13, 2016, and I received my first sign from her on February 1, 2017. It took six weeks. My friend Kim and I were sitting in my living room when an ad for Spirit Airlines came on TV. The TV ad showed the plane with big letters on it that spelled Spirit. I never heard of this airline before. One thing for sure, it made me smile as my little girl finally let me know that she flew high to the heavens.

CHAPTER 48

Ole Hawk Eye

ANOTHER FRIEND OF MINE, COLLEEN, passed in December 2016. I received a sign that helped her family when she passed. I shared the sign that I connected with their sister, and it helped to ease their loss in her death.

I met Colleen in the projects, which are known as Elmwood Gardens. We never hung around together, but we were cordial and would always said hello whenever we saw one another. Her family were neighbors to my foster mom, Osbie. We lived side by side, so we saw each other often, yet we never really spoke.

I had heard that she was mentally challenged, so I always made sure to greet her whenever our eyes met, and her eyes showed excitement when she saw me. They came alive! She was friendly and always had a smile for me. Sometimes I could feel her staring at me after I passed, watching, always watching as I walked by.

When I think about it today, I realize that she yearned for a friendship with me because I would say hello to her when most kids wouldn't. But I was too busy back then trying to fit in myself, trying to make friends, and I didn't notice.

Life moves on and journeys take us down new roads. Our paths would cross again, but this time, it would be Colleen who reached out to me.

Years went by and Bob had recently passed. I was outside when the mailman handed me a blue envelope with a card inside. The return address had Colleen's name on it. I had no idea how she knew where I lived or how she had known my married surname. Curiosity killed the cat, and wouldn't you know it, there was a kitty cat on the front of the card!

She wrote me a little about her life and how she lived just up the street in the Beech Hill Apartments complex. She told me that she had a daughter and a cat for a pet.

She wrote of her breast cancer and how she was a volunteer at the soup kitchen. She was hoping that I would remember her because she wanted to come and visit me.

Her handwriting was printed and like a child's, but somehow this one little card really touched my heart. She included her phone number and wanted me to call her. It was the first thing I did when I walked back into my house.

When she answered the phone, I said, "Colleen, its Gail! How are you doing? I am really surprised to hear from you!"

We started talking as though we had been best friends all these years. She had broken the ice by reaching out to me. You could tell that she was excited that I had called her. I could hear it in the tone of her voice.

I was curious as to how she knew where I lived. She told me that I was outside doing yardwork when she first noticed me. She rode the bus to volunteer at the Manchester Horizons Soup Kitchen and when the bus went past my house, at the corner where I lived, she recognized me.

It wasn't long after this conversation that we planned a sleepover at my house just for us. She walked down to my house carrying a bag of flicks for us to watch together. This was the beginning of many nights of movie marathons here. I would cook for her, making sure she ate well, and sometimes she would bring the snacks. She didn't do much talking. She would just listen and watch.

She had found a new best friend in me and would become jealous if someone stopped by to visit. It would show as she would get very quiet and give me the beady-eyed stare. I could see that she wasn't happy. She wanted me all to herself! I had to teach her that I had other friends who would stop by and that she had to be kind to them. I was kind to her and she had to share me.

I reminded myself again that she was mentally challenged and acted like a child at times. Yet I could also see a mature woman who had helped the needy for many, many years, of her own free will. Because of her volunteer work, she had received an Achievement Award from the Mayor of Manchester—a huge accomplishment! I don't think she ever really understood what a big deal it was!

There would be times when I would have to say no to her staying over for two nights in a row. I was pretty busy myself, visiting the sick and trying to get some photography in. I knew that it would break her heart if she couldn't stay over as often as she liked, so I would sometimes have her come by for just one night, to please her.

Colleen didn't dwell on her cancer. She believed that it wouldn't kill her. She didn't quite understand how aggressive it was and truly believed that she would live a long life. By just believing that, she lasted longer than most people diagnosed with triple negative breast cancer.

As her cancer progressed, her visits became few and far between. I made sure that she didn't walk when she wanted to come by. I would always send a cab to bring her to and from my house so that we could still have our visits and time together. She liked coming to my home and never really invited me to hers. She lived with her daughter, and I truly believe she wanted me all to herself. I was her childhood friend in her mind. I started to understand that my kindness in just saying hello so many years ago really had a huge impact on her.

The chemo began to wear her down and make her sick. I would call to see if she was coming by, but she was always tired and started sleeping in more. Her sister Pam and I had become good friends and now we kept in touch because of Colleen's illness. She kept me informed when I couldn't reach Colleen.

When Colleen couldn't visit any longer, I would call her just to see how she was feeling and to show her that I cared. As usual, I did all the talking, and she just listened.

Colleen's sister Lisa was her caregiver. She would relay messages to Pam, who would then pass them on to me about how her doctor's visits had gone and what was said.

Colleen began having a hard time to walk and to climb stairs as the cancer spread all through her body, with some tumors shinier and bigger than quarters. Sometimes she would show them to me by lifting her blouse. She was not shy when it came to showing me her cancer up close and personal. I knew that in time I would be losing another friend, but I was glad that Colleen had no idea what was happening.

Pam called me one day to say that we could visit with Colleen at her apartment. I decided to get pizza and grinders for us to eat. That was my motherly side, trying to make sure that she ate. I was happy to finally get an invitation to meet her daughter and to see how Colleen lived.

Colleen had a love of life, and it showed in the pictures which were everywhere. I saw now that we had something very real in common. Pictures of family were all over the place!

I had no idea how much she loved me until I saw the photo I had given her of me and my dog, Spirit. She told me that when she watched TV, she had placed the picture on the coffee table so that she could see it. That was huge for me!

I will never forget that one and only visit to her home. I got to see a side of her that was just like me. I hugged her tightly when I left and let her know that I loved her, knowing that it might be the last time I would see her.

It wasn't long before her sister Pam was calling to let me know that she had passed on a cold December day. I knew immediately why she was calling. My tears were falling even before Pam got the words out, and she was crying too.

Soon after her death, a celebration of Colleen's life was planned, and somehow I knew that it would take place in my home, even though I wasn't part of her immediate family. My house ended up being the perfect option. My spirit guides had led me to offer it, and it was the right choice at the last minute because my home is where her family said Colleen was the happiest.

That morning, while preparing the food and getting ready for people to arrive, I saw a huge bird outside the kitchen window. I grabbed my camera and waited for it to peer through the picket fence next to my patio. When it looked in my direction, I saw the most watchful eyes ever. As I snapped the picture, it turned its head, looking for prey. I managed to get two shots before it took off.

In that moment, when I saw the beady eyes, I told Pam that Colleen was visiting us and that she was the hawk! Her sign would be a hawk—I felt it and I was sure of it! Those eyes were just like Colleens!

Beady!

Photo by Gail Durant

The sisters knew me well enough to believe in what I had told them. On the drive back home, after the celebration, one of the sisters saw another hawk and pulled to the side of the road to cry.

Recently, Colleen's caregiving sister, Lisa, took a photo of a visitor in her own backyard and posted it on Facebook. Pam recognized the sign immediately and brought it to my attention. I realized at that moment that it was a sign for me to put this story in my book!

Colleen had come back to give her sister, Lisa a sign to say hello! This is the picture she took. It made one hell of a believer out of Lisa that day! She has never seen a sharp-shinned hawk in her yard. Ever!

This is the same kind of hawk that had visited my yard on the day we had honored Colleen's life!

Photo by Lisa Miller

After losing my friend Colleen, I realized how much of an angel she was to me! I believe that she came back into my life after all those years to show me how to relax. After Bob had passed, I kept myself busy at all times to keep from thinking too deeply about things. She taught me to slow down, to sit and just be still.

She wasn't my mentally challenged friend—not to me anyways. She was just my friend, my angel with wings (and beady eyes) who taught me to sit still!

Before I forget, I received a special surprise from Colleen, from beyond the grave, a Christmas present. She had bought me a few things before she passed, and her sister Lisa made sure I received them. We never exchanged gifts before, so this was a really great surprise for me. The Christmas hurricane lamp is beautiful, but the other gift said it all! It was a picture frame with words that read: *Friends Forever! Truly great friends are hard to find, difficult to leave, and impossible to forget!*

That's how she saw me, and it made me cry! I put her picture in that frame as it represents how I feel about her as well! That photo is displayed now as a reminder of our friendship and how a simple hello had drawn us together.

I will miss you my friend!

Beady eyes and all!

CHAPTER 49

Fourth-Year Anniversary Poem

Robert Durant, Jr.
"Moose"
April 28, 2013 – April 28, 2017

Four years have come and gone
Since Heaven has called your name
Loving you was easy but
Life is not the same
Missing you is what I do
Until we meet again
I am hoping you are having fun
And drinking some champagne
With others who have gone after you
It is a gosh darn shame
I bet your eyes lit up
When you saw that Helen came
Our best friend in adventures
Who no longer was in pain
Did you meet with Uncle Eddie
And walked the deer terrain
By now you must be partners
In paradise's Fish and Game
How about buddy Ronnie
Jack of all trades, his claim to fame
I'm sure you two met by now
At the Budweiser fountain
I know Miss Spirit is at you side

Forever she will remain
Our faithful dog has gone above
In Heaven's new domain
One thing I learned on Earth
Something I CAN explain
That we all will come together
Cause angels love to entertain

I Love You . . . Wifey

CHAPTER 50

My Kind of Sign

ONE AFTERNOON, MY FRIEND, KAREN AND I were on our way to a poker party. We would be meeting up with a group of women for a friendly game. As she was driving up Cilley Road, I commented on the date. It was May 27, 2017 to be exact. I told her that today would have been my 22nd wedding anniversary if Bob were still alive.

Just after I said this, a car turned ahead of us at the four-way stop sign. The license plate spelled out his name: B.O.B.!

Excitedly, I pointed out the plate to my friend! To me it was Bob's way of letting me know that he had heard me talking and remembered our anniversary too!

As I was digging through my purse, searching for my camera, that car took a right turn, but we continued straight ahead and up the busy street. I didn't have the heart to ask my friend to turn around and chase the vehicle, just so I could get a picture. It really didn't matter that much to me because I had already gotten Bob's message. It was a small and silly sign, but it had made my afternoon brighter. So did winning $15 later in the poker game!

I don't think of it as a coincidence when something like this occurs. It happens to me a lot. I will see a license plate that has meaning for me, and I love that it comes at the precise moment when I say something about my babe. It never fails to amaze me, and I have to admit, it's a great comfort too!

This got me to thinking about which license plate could make my family and friends think of me? I have taken several photos over the years of plates that have caught my eye and hold special meaning to me. They remind me of myself and the way I live my life.

Someday, when I am in heaven and you see these plates around, just know that it's me saying hello!

Photo by Gail Durant

Those who know me will easily understand this one!

Photo by Gail Durant

Or this one

Photo by Gail Durant

I always say, "Gotta love it!"

Photo by Gail Durant

Bob got me to love fishing.

Photo by Gail Durant

This plate used to be one of my favorite songs and I requested it every time we went out dancing. Bob would sing it to me as we danced close. Naturally, I would have a red dress on. I wore a lot of red dresses because it's always been my favorite color.

Photo by Gail Durant

I took this photo long before my dog Spirit passed. It was taken originally because of the love I have for the unknown! This represents me, all the way! If I were to see it again now, I would know that my dog was greeting me!

Photo by Gail Durant

I am positive that we can all relate to this next license plate at one time or another in our lives. Though some might be reminded of the TV show that is not what it means to me. We are all survivors; survivors of abuse, survivors of cancer or other debilitating illnesses, survivors of the loss of our loved ones, survivors of hard labor in tough jobs and survivors of whatever life throws at us.

I know that I am a survivor and just as Bob told me, "Everything will be ok."

Photo by Gail Durant

CHAPTER 51

Coffee Mugs

I<small>N</small> A<small>UGUST</small> 2017, I started going through more boxes that I hadn't had a chance to open since moving back to Manchester. I had no time to unpack while being a caregiver to my husband, but by this time, he'd been gone now for more than four years. I began to go through more of our things from the cabin to prepare for a yard sale. Because we had moved back to a smaller house, many of our wares never got out of their boxes, so they remained neatly stored in my cellar.

I came across a white box containing two mugs, which immediately brought me back to the day that I received them. These mugs hold a special meaning for me, and I will never get rid of them! I am using one now to drink my tea as I reminisce and write! It just goes to show how full circle life's special moments come to be. It's not the material things themselves that make me happy but rather the story behind the gift!

One day, as on many other days, Bob and I were driving around looking for land to build our retirement home on. We drove the roads less travelled searching for "Land for Sale" signs. On this day, we happened to be in Hillsborough, New Hampshire.

As we drove down a dirt road, we noticed a man outside selling things in front of his home. It was a log home, and we wanted to stop and get ideas because it was our plan to build one also. We stopped to chat with this man and learned that his name was Fred. We told him how we had been looking for land for more than a year and that we had not yet found what we wanted.

He told us that he had friends who were selling their land close by and then took us to see the lots. We felt at the time that the lot size was too small for what we were planning and then walked back to his place.

I asked if I could have some water for our dog April, as it was a warm day, and she seemed thirsty. He brought us into his home to get water and to show us how proud he was of the work he had done. It was a rather cute log home. We loved how open this man was to us without ever having met us. It was also nice to see someone else's ideas firsthand. He introduced us to his wife, Ruth, who was just as hospitable!

He told us that we were in a village on Emerald Lake. It sure looked beautiful! After talking a bit, we thanked them both for their hospitality and for the water. We decided to keep going farther down the road just to see where it would take us.

Bob stopped the truck when he saw a sign lying flat on the ground that said "Land for Sale," but it wasn't in its proper place. We took a walk to look over the area and saw a little camper sitting out by the lake. It was a good-sized lot, and Bob walked the length of the lot, counting footage with his steps. I wrote down the phone number on the sign so that Bob could call later to find out if this place was really for sale.

That night Bob placed the call, and we learned that the people selling the land lived in Connecticut. They said that they could meet us in a few weeks, but in the meantime, they told us to try out the land and see if it worked for us. They said to use it as though it were our own.

We couldn't believe how nice they were, allowing us to go swimming, fishing, and to generally get a feel for how it would be if we built there.

I loved that we weren't secluded, that there were houses all around, and I loved the fact that there was a beach right next door. That really got my attention. We wouldn't have to make one on our land, and that would save us money, I thought to myself. The children in our lives would love it here!

I knew in my heart that this was going to be our new home. Bob, on the other hand, needed a little coaxing. He would have preferred more land and fewer homes nearby, but my excitement must have changed his mind. I was showing him where I could put in a 30-foot garden. Because it was a double lot, we hoped to make it into a single lot and build that log cabin that he always wanted! I needed to be around people, and I let him know that.

Within a few weeks, we were meeting the sellers, an older couple, at the site. We were the first to talk with them, but they had other buyers waiting in line if we didn't want the property. It made sense to show it to others as well, in case we didn't buy it. It was too far for them to travel back and forth to show it individually, so they set up multiple showings for the same day.

We could see the other potential buyers walking the land just like we had done. Little did they know that inside of the little camper we were already shaking hands on a deal that would make us the new property owners! No more looking. We had found a place where we could build our retirement home someday!

I found a fifth wheel in the newspaper and told Bob that I would help him to pay for it so that we could have a place to go and lay our heads during the summers. We didn't really bother with our neighbors back then, because we didn't have the time. We kept to ourselves and to our families because there were so many of us. We had company all of the time.

We did however stay in touch with Fred and his wife Ruth, and we always made a point to stop the truck when he was outside selling his wares, just to chit chat and to say hello. We let him and his wife know that we were going to be neighbors and that it was their friendliness that had made us want to retire here in the first place.

Time goes by and so do the years. Soon the fifth wheel is off the land and a log home is being built. Bob kept busy making sure the building was going as planned. He went every night after work to check the progress. We couldn't go there on weekends anymore because there was nowhere now to lay our heads. It would be awhile before we were able to stay for a weekend. A long, long while.

Eventually though, the rough work was completed, and we finally had a place to sleep, and our weekend visits started up again.

One Saturday, when we were at the town dump, a familiar female voice said hello to us. When I asked what her name was, she told me that she was Fred's daughter, Lynda, and that she knew a lot about us. She had come by our home with her dad once. I didn't remember her name, but I did remember the visit.

I told her that her dad was awesome and how gracious he was to show us his place when we had first met! She told us that her dad had passed. We were very sorry to hear that, and we both gave her a hug. I remember telling Bob that I hadn't seen him out selling his wares lately and wondered if something had happened to him. Now we knew.

I asked her if she liked to kayak, and she said yes. I asked her to join me when she had some down time. She was a partner in a consignment shop called Family Treasure Consignment in town. I thought to myself, "like father, like daughter!" She told me that she would check her schedule. Soon we were making plans with her and her boyfriend to get better acquainted!

We became close friends and kayaked Emerald Lake when time would allow, enjoying all the beauty it had to offer. We didn't see each other much, but always made a point to keep in touch whenever we made it to the lake on the weekend.

It wasn't long after this that we moved to the lake house for good. We would have her and her boyfriend over for drinks and had many laughs drinking wine and enjoying each other's company. We hit it off and enjoyed just being silly together.

We all know how this story ended: Bob became ill, and we had to move back to Manchester.

I had already started packing boxes for the move. We hadn't told Lynda and her boyfriend yet, so I called and gave them both the news. They made plans to come by at the end of the week for one last time to say their goodbyes!

Lynda worked three days on and three days off at the consignment shop, switching off with her partner. She knew her inventory well and was constantly cleaning and rearranging things to make it more presentable to her customers. She told me that she always did a walk around to check out any new inventory that had come in while she was off.

While looking around, she spotted a white box that wasn't there three days earlier. Two mugs were set up in front of the box. She told me that she was surprised to see this at that moment since it would be a perfect gift for us, knowing that they were coming by the house to say goodbye.

She said she wasn't looking to bring us a present at all but knew she had too after seeing the mugs because it seemed like a sign. She showed her boyfriend and told him how weird it was because those mugs were not in the shop three days prior!

"These mugs appeared right after we made arrangements to get together with you," she told me!

I felt that this was another full circle moment for me at the time. After all, only two mugs came in that consignment shop that day. They were definitely meant for Bob and me.

Photo by Gail Durant

Looking at the photo, I'm sure you will agree that uncanny things happen at times when you least expect them to. I know it surprised Lynda too! In her heart, she knew that these were meant just for us. Two mugs show up with her friends' names on them, friends who would soon leave Emerald Lake for good! She knew that she wouldn't see Bob again

I'd like to think that her dad, Fred had something to do with this! Thanks Fred. You even got the spelling of our names right! I hope Bob's chatting with you over a mug of coffee as you sell your wares in Heaven. Fred was the type of man who considered selling his goods to be secondary to the friendships that he made. That's where he got his enjoyment, talking with everyone who stopped by.

I will treasure these mugs and the memories they hold for the rest of my life!

Bob and I shared great times with many friends that we made at Emerald Lake. As clear as the names on these mugs, that land was meant to be our home.

CHAPTER 52

Finding My Sister Brenda

EVERY SO OFTEN SOMETHING UNCANNY HAPPENS TO ME, but the experience I am about to share with you now really blew my mind.

In the beginning of my introduction, I told you that I had 12 other siblings. That made a baker's dozen with thirteen in the family. I had a baby sister, named Brenda Lee who died in infancy of pneumonia. I was about five or six years old and can only remember the firetrucks coming to our home. It was so long ago.

I do think of my sister often and I talk to her even though she died at four months old. She is always thought of and in my prayers. I asked relatives where my sister was buried, and no one could answer that question. They thought she was buried at Pine Grove Cemetery. They didn't think she had her own stone as we were poor in those days. I was told that my sibling may be put in with someone else's plot. No one could remember who Brenda was buried with.

On this day, my cousin Lori had asked if I wanted to go to Pine Grove Cemetery and check out some information she needed from the office there. I told her I was going to ask for specific data to see if they could show me where my sister was buried. I took my camera along with me as there are plenty of flowers and wildlife to take pictures of. She got the information she needed and then I asked if they had a Brenda Lee Adams in their files. They had nothing with this name. Whomever she was buried with, no relative could recall their name. It was futile. I remember thinking that at least I had tried. We got back into the car and drove around the cemetery and I spotted wild geese up near some stones. I told my cousin to stop so I could get out and take photos with them eating the grass. I wanted to make sure the lighting was good and that there were no shadows on the shots I had taken of the geese. To my amazement, one picture made me gasp.

"OMG! Lori" I yell! Look what's on this stone!"

She couldn't believe it either. That day my sister Brenda must have known I was looking for her. Instead she found me! This may not be her stone and not the correct way of spelling her name, but I just felt this was meant for me. Here is a picture I took that day.

Photo by Gail Durant

We called her Brenda Lee. I found this ironic and again I felt a tug at my heart! If the Canada geese hadn't been there I would have never taken this photo.

"She found me"!!!

You know those small words at the bottom of the stone?

RUHET SANFT (German)

It means: Resting Gently in English.

I have my answer. Brenda is just fine. In my heart of hearts, I just know it!

I want to add to this story now because there is a happy ending since that day that I spent searching for my sister with my cousin Lori.

My sister Brenda never let me give up on trying to find her. She was always on my mind, from the time I went to bed at night and once again upon awakening. I knew that I would soon be looking for her again.

This time I asked my friend Larry to give me a hand. He's my search angel and my special PI! He's very good at tracking people down and at bringing families together. He had done it for me once already with my nieces who were reunited with their grandmother, my mother, Coffee, before she passed. Why not the departed? I thought to myself!

I gave him a call and without hesitation, he began working to try and find where my sister Brenda was buried.

On one call, he assured me that she wasn't buried in Massachusetts like some family members had thought. It was hard to recollect things that had happened so many years ago.

My 94-year-old Aunt Violet was funny. When I asked her if she could remember where Brenda had been buried, her response was:

"Do you actually think I can remember back 57 years ago?"

We only had her name and dates of birth and death to go on along with both of my parents' names, so I knew it would take him a while to find her. Sometime later, he hit pay dirt. He called to see if he could swing by with the paperwork that held the answer.

"I found out where she is buried" he told me over the phone. "I have the cemetery name. Your sister is at St. Augustin's in Manchester, New Hampshire."

"Oh My God! That's where we are all going to be buried!" I told him.

I asked if he knew which one, because there are three cemeteries in Manchester with that same name, owned by the same parish. They are spread out along the length of South Beech Street. I was hoping that it would be the one just down the street, where most of my immediate family will be laid to rest. It's also where Bob is and close enough for me to walk there. The other two are way up over the hill on South Beech Street, not an easy walk.

"I don't know" he told me. "You will have to make a few phone calls to find out which one."

I couldn't contain my excitement. Someone had finally connected all the pieces of the puzzle. Larry had done it, using only her name, date of birth and date of death. My brother, Michael had hired someone for the same purpose years ago but had come up empty handed.

I really hoped that Brenda would be in the one closest to me, that we could all be together once again.

After he dropped off the documents, which were the church listings of births, baptisms and deaths within our family, I made a call to the cemetery and was given a number to the main office at the St. Augustine rectory. The lady who answered gave me the coordinates of her gravestone. She told me that Brenda was in the older part of the cemetery.

I asked her if it was the one closest to So. Willow Street and she believed that it was. I was thrilled! That's a five-minute walk from my house! I couldn't wait to see where she was buried and how close she would be to Bob and the rest of my family.

The caretakers were very busy as it was close to Memorial Day. It was hard to reach anyone in the cemetery office. My friend and her family were going to be burying her mother's ashes on the following Monday, but I couldn't be there with her that day. I asked if she could speak to the caretaker after her mother was laid to rest, and I gave her the coordinates that were given to me to help find Brenda's grave. She agreed to help.

Soon after, I got a phone call from my friend who was being brought to a headstone by the caretaker, matching those coordinates. Using a map of the cemetery, they were walking up to a stone at that very moment! She told me that there was no Brenda Lee Adams listed on the headstone, but the name Bernard was engraved on it.

Bingo! It's all making sense now!

This woman had been friends with my mother and was apparently kind enough to help her out in her time of need. She had allowed our baby sister to be buried in her family plot.

Photo by Gail Durant

We did think of her name when we had begun looking for Brenda,
but how many stones with that name were around New Hampshire?
We didn't know where to begin to look and what if we were wrong?

To make a long story short, Brenda is buried to the left of the
mausoleum and our family plots are to the right of it! How awesome
is that? Some family members, including myself, spoke of having
Brenda moved so that she could be united with our mother after all
these years.

When I spoke with the caretaker about moving her, he told me
that her body could be decomposed after such a long time. Because
she had died at only four months of age, he explained that her bones
hadn't yet calcified fully so there may not be any remains if he dug
up her grave. There was nothing in the area where she was buried.
He had checked it with a ground probe steel rod but couldn't feel
anything.

We decided to let Brenda stay at peace, after her fifty-seven years in her resting place, where she's been all this time. How wonderful that she is in the same cemetery, so close to all of us. Finally, after all these years, we now have a place to visit our baby sister.

Thanks Larry for peace of mind. Brenda now leaves me alone. Larry told me that this was the first time ever he connected the living with the departed.

It's great to finally have a place to visit your sister's soul. Thank-You so much for that! Brenda thanks you too!

Thanks also to Mrs. Bernard, for having a kind heart, for helping to give my sister a place of rest and for giving my mother peace of mind. It was a wonderful act. Thank You for being you!!!

I hope you like tulips from my garden!

CHAPTER 53

Loving Magnolias

Photo by Gail Durant

I DON'T QUITE REMEMBER WHERE OR WHEN it was that I took a picture of this street sign, but I do know that it wasn't long after Bob had passed. It reminded me of him, and I just had to stop and get a photo. Of course, it *is* a stop sign, so we had no choice.

I think back to the time just after we had moved to our log home for good, just three months before his cancer diagnosis. Bob had to travel back and forth from Hillsborough to Manchester for his business. Being retired, I had a lot of time on my hands, so I decided to plant a garden. There was perfect spot, about 30 feet long, that divided our property from that of our neighbors, Joe and Rita. They loved the idea as well and agreed to help with getting it started, filling it with every kind of flower imaginable, each on our own side.

It was a weed- and root-ridden plot of land and was scattered with big boulders. I imagined surrounding the boulders with colorful flowers and bushes. I had this vison, and Joe and Rita agreed to help me and Bob to bring it to life! We dug and weeded out the land of tree stumps and whatever didn't belong. We had a truckload of loam delivered, and the four of us prepped the garden ready, so we could have flowers to last a lifetime!

That was the first time I found out what poison ivy looked like! I had it something terrible for three weeks, but that didn't stop me from getting the job done while the others worked their day jobs during the week. I don't know how many trips we all took to the garden suppliers for all types of blossoms, annuals and perennials, bushes, grasses and trees, but it was coming alive and looking beautiful.

Bob and I had planted flowers in the front of our home as well. The colors gave it curb appeal. It was at this time that I first learned of Bob's love for magnolias. He told me that it was his favorite flower. I was surprised because we didn't have them at our Manchester home, so it was news to me. He bought two magnolia shrubs, red and white, and planted them close to the garden. Bob had a green thumb, and when they bloomed, they were big and very beautiful!

I remember wanting to dig up those two beautiful magnolias and bring them with us to Manchester when we moved back, a year after Bob's diagnosis. They had meant so much to Bob and would always remind me of him. He had put such great care into those magnificent flowers, and I hated to leave them behind.

Our realtor frowned upon the idea because the buyers had already seen them. She said it wouldn't be right to leave two big holes in the ground if we dug them up. I knew she was right, but it didn't make me feel any better. Bob assured me that we could make more gardens when we moved back and that he would buy me a magnolia.

Bob kept his promise. We put in three more gardens, surrounded by lattice work and on one side of the fence, he planted a white magnolia, just for me. It bloomed quite well that summer. I was happy to have one at our Manchester home. It was the only year we both saw it flower because the harsh winter and our soil killed it.

When I stopped to get a picture of this Magnolia street sign, I was reminded of the day that Bob saw his headstone for the first time. I realized in that moment how lucky I am. In the dead of winter, we didn't know what the tree behind our headstone was. Only after I saw the blooms at his funeral did I realize. I learned later that St. Anthony's Cemetery had planted that magnolia tree near our plots long before we ever bought them. We were meant to be buried there!

Within a couple of years, that magnolia tree would also die, just like the ones in our garden. Just knowing that it was there, starting to bloom at Bob's funeral, was a great sign for me from Bob himself!

So yes, I had to stop and take a picture of this street sign. Even though he never saw that tree bloom, knowing that it was his favorite flower made me happy.

CHAPTER 54

Movie Messages

IN YOUR OWN LIFE, have you ever heard someone speaking from a podium and felt that their message was meant just for you? Have you ever watched a movie or a TV show and felt that the character was directing their meaning to you? Perhaps you felt the message was somehow connected to you alone and it made you take notice because it paralleled your own life at that moment! I have felt this a few times in my life, but one particular time got made me sit up and take notice.

It was August 26, 2017, and I had fallen asleep on my couch for a bit. When I awoke, I turned on the TV and rummaged through the channels because it was only 8 p.m. and that was too early to go to bed. I came across a religious station that just flashed a movie title across the screen. It was called *Je m'appelle Bernadette*. In English it's translated as *My Name is Bernadette*. I felt compelled to watch it.

I remember watching shows like this with my mother in my younger days and how we both had loved them. The movie was in French, but it had the subtitles in English, so I could follow along. It wouldn't take long for me to become very interested in this movie because I remembered a little about the story of this young lady going to a grotto in France and seeing apparitions of Mother Mary.

Given that I had had a few visits from Mother Mary in my own dreams, I was all the more intent on watching this movie. I remembered hearing the story of Bernadette a long time ago, but I had forgotten many of the details. I had seen a few versions over the years and some depicted the story a little differently. I don't ever remember seeing this particular movie before, but if I had, it didn't have a great impact on me until that day.

Most of you know that the story is about a young girl named Bernadette who goes looking for firewood at a grotto in France. Her sister and friend run ahead of her and soon she hears a rustling of the wind. As she looks toward that direction, she sees a beautiful woman with a white gown and yellow roses at both feet.

My first thought was of my mother, whose favorite flowers were yellow roses All of her children know that whenever we see them, it's a sign that our mother is saying hello.

No one else but Bernadette seems to see or hear this apparition when she asks her to keep coming back to the grotto. Many different times, followers would walk with her and kneel to pray at the grotto until this striking woman would appear again with different messages to give to the people.

Some people called Bernadette a troublemaker, some called her a liar, but many believed that she heard and saw something. They could tell that Bernadette was in awe because of her facial expressions as she stared straight ahead. One time, Bernadette asked the woman what her name was and was told, "I am The Immaculate Conception!"

Bernadette relayed the messages as she received them to the monsignor, who at first didn't know what to think.

One time the lady asked Bernadette to dig in the ground and to eat the dirt and grass and that something miraculous would happen! She did what was asked of her and was laughed at and mocked as she rubbed the dirt on her face and ate the grass. It wasn't long before a spring of water appeared out of nowhere.

After the spring appeared, many followers and believers began washing their faces and bodies with what they believed to be most holy and phenomenal. They now believed in Bernadette's visions of the lady. Some blind people splashed the water on their faces and could see again. Some who walked with canes left their canes behind.

There were many other miracles that no one could explain. Some whose lives had been filled with sickness became healthy because of the miracle of the spring water.

Bernadette was very sickly with asthma: she coughed a lot and had trouble catching her breath. Many people thought that because of her sickness, she belonged in an asylum. Most people believed that she had made up the stories of the Immaculate Conception. When she relayed the messages, she was brought in for questioning by the commissioner and was looked over by many doctors.

Bernadette held to her story over and over, no matter how many times the commissioner tried to trick her into denying what she had seen. They could find no reason to put her away.

There was no denying that this spring had miraculous healing powers and somehow Bernadette was connected to the people who went there. Many thought that she had healing powers as well and felt the need to touch her.

Bernadette's name circulated worldwide. She could have made herself famous and become very wealthy, taking her family out of poverty, if only she would travel to speak. She wanted nothing to do with fame nor with any of the money people brought to her. She asked all her followers to keep their money or use it to help others in their time of need. It was like a pay-it-forward moment in our times.

I know exactly how Bernadette felt. I wouldn't want to be in the limelight either. I could totally understand her. Sometimes I've also felt that I was chosen because of the messages I have received from Mother Mary, even though I never saw the lady's image in real life, as Bernadette did.

I feel that I would be just like her. I wouldn't want celebrity or fame. I would only want what I feel to be my truths to be told. I also say that any money made from this book will be given away to help children without parents.

That is my plan, to do as she asked of me! There is so much meaning in her message to me and so many ways of interpreting it. I could help orphanages, or children who have lost their parents to the opioid crisis or another cause altogether, as long as it is related to children. I know I will be guided when the time comes. Plain and simple!

It was toward the ending of this incredible movie when I realized that the messages given to Bernadette by Mother Superior and monsignor were meant for me on this day. I sat straight up on my couch as I read the translated words appear on the screen one sentence at a time.

As Bernadette was taking her vows to become a nun, Mother Superior gave her a new name. She asked Bernadette what her godmother's name was, and Bernadette replied, "Marie."

Just then, Mother Superior anointed her with her new name, saying, "You will now be Sister Marie Bernard."

At that moment my eyes widened! I had heard that name before! Oh My God, could it be? I paused the television and ran into my bedroom where my computer is.

It holds thousands of pictures that I have taken through the years. I needed to see just one at this precise moment! As I scrolled down looking through the pictures I at last found the one I was looking for. I stared at the photo in great amazement. I couldn't believe what I was looking at!

Here in front of me was the picture of the headstone where my late baby sister Brenda had been laid to rest, the one that I took after I finally learned where she had been buried. I remembered that my baby sister's soul had bothered my conscience so much that I needed to find her so that I could find peace.

It wasn't that long ago that her resting place had been located. She was placed with a wonderful friend of my mother's. My sister's resting place was at the headstone of Marie Bernard! That damn near blew me away. What are the odds?

Photo by Gail Durant

I went back to the living room to finish the movie. Mother Superior was handing out assignment letters, but there was none for Sister Marie Bernard. One sister had to tend some gardens away from the convent, another had to help with disabled people in nearby towns. Sister Marie Bernard had no such assignment letter. I thought it was because of her severe asthma, but the monsignor made her purpose known more clearly. As he explained this purpose, I knew that this message held a special meaning for me, so I paid close attention!

He asked Sister Marie Bernard if she knew the story of the tree that was "no good." I found it funny because just a few months before watching this movie, I had gone to Bob's graveside and saw that the magnolia tree by our headstone had died! I told the caretaker that I would send in a check to replace the tree, but it could be any tree of his choice.

"We didn't plant the magnolia tree in the first place," I told him. "It just happened to be there when I bought our plot."

I found it funny how Bob's favorite flower was the magnolia and it had bloomed on the day of his funeral. Imagine, we had never planted it, it was just there! A great sign at the time, and now the monsignor in the movie was talking about the useless tree. Today a new bush sits in its place at our headstone. The caretaker wanted Bob to be happy with another magnolia and had called to say that he planted one in his honor.

Now the monsignor in the movie was talking to Bernadette, telling her that it was good to be useless and to give to others, saying, "The tree is absolutely useless; be like this tree Bernadette, useless, but don't worry, your uselessness doesn't mean you're worthless. Be the last if you wish. Do not try to be what you are not. Be yourself, that's all! The greatest experience in life comes not from what you do but from what you give out of love, from what is given out of love!"

That line brought back such powerful memories of the negative remarks Bob's relatives made about me when Bob was dying. Somehow, and for reasons I didn't quite understand at the time, I was being blamed for causing Bob's cancer. It also got back to me that someone close to Bob had called me "useless" and a "worthless piece of shit." It was hard to understand where this was coming from because I had been doing everything in my power to make Bob comfortable and happy. It hit me hard that anyone could think of me in that way when I knew that I was neither of those things.

I'm glad I am wise in my years and never believed that I could have so much power to cause another's cancer. I knew that I gave Bob the best life and end of life possible! I never really understood why I was tossed aside by so many after losing my husband, but by doing so, they actually gave me *comfort* and *peace,* by stepping *out* of my life. I don't hear the negativity any longer. Their tossing me aside was a blessing in disguise! Today, I feel that if someone is not in my life, they do not deserve me. I give myself to so many, and I no longer waste time on those who persecute me.

How could I not think that?

No one can cause someone else's cancer—if you are ever told that, shrug it off as I did! The person who blamed me was hurting far more than I knew when my husband died. I asked God to forgive this person for me! Today I can say that I have actually prayed for him myself.

It was not my fault that Bob died! God needed him more and no one knows better than I how much I wished that God had taken me instead. That's how deep my love for my husband was! I would've traded places with him if I could have!

Because I've seen heaven, I know that I will be reunited with my husband again. Knowing and believing this helps me to live my life without him until my work here on Earth is finished.

I felt like the monsignor in the movie was talking to me and only to me. There was a message to be heard, and I could feel cold chills run through my body as I watched the dialog that appeared on the TV screen.

At the end of the movie, Bernadette said: "It's good to be useless and give to others. I said many things, but what must be remembered is what I first said. I may have forgotten, and others may have forgotten, 'The simplest story will be the best!'"

"The simplest story will be the best!" Boy, did that resonate for me. I cried when the movie ended with just that one line on the screen at the end. I truly feel that some of the messages in this movie were meant especially for me.

Mother Mary asked me to "help children without parents" and writing this book was the only way I knew how to fulfill this promise. It's a simple and truthful story in hopes of helping many to believe in the signs they receive, as many of us truly have a "need to believe"! I only hope that by writing my story I can help many others to recognize when they see a sign. Sometimes the messages may be hidden, but sometimes they ring true like an epiphany, as this movie did for me. I hope you can find your own hidden messages and just remember one thing: no one is worthless, not even a worthless tree, because to me, even a dead tree with branches has a place for a bird to sit and relax when their wings are tired!

I've received messages over the years and as I follow them, I can easily see that something has been guiding me. I have peace when someone passes because Mother Mary has shown me my Heaven. What we want in our Heaven will be there! What we love on Earth will also be there! We will meet again with those who have left before us when our day comes to leave this Earth.

Today I am here to finish the job that Mother Mary set out for me. I hope that even though I do not know what I am doing, I will make her proud of me just for trying to do as she has asked!

Mother Mary came to me at a time when I needed her most and now she is asking something of me in return.

In one dream, she appeared to me dressed as a nun, just like Bernadette. She held my hand as we flew over a convent where other nuns were looking up at us, smiling and waving. I was shocked that they could see us.

She told me that she wanted me to see something else and we flew together over an area, like a village which was covered in mud. I saw many huts filled with it, covering the furniture and belongings. The children's faces were caked with the mud and they were dirty and helpless as they looked up at us. I realized then that they could see us too, just as the nuns had. I saw their eyes widen with hope, and that's when she told me that I would be helping children like these.

There were many children, but I didn't see any adults anywhere. I asked her where the parents were, and she told me that my work on earth would be to help children without parents.

For some time after this dream, I thought that I was to write a children's book. However, my dear friend Darla gave me clarity. She said that I should write about something I know a lot about, namely signs. She told me how she knew I had a gift many years ago and that I should write about this gift to help others. At that moment I knew she was onto something.

At the time I didn't know how I would begin, but once I lost my husband, it became very clear! I spent the next two years, waking up in the middle of the night and writing down the thoughts that would eventually become my book! I filled a box with notes and ideas of all the things that came to me continuously. I wanted people to understand how I translated those signs so that they could start interpreting their own. I am hoping that my pictures will also help to show a little proof of what I believe in.

If the money from this book helps even one child, Mother Mary will know that she has chosen the right person for the job.

Do I believe that I was a chosen one?

Absolutely! Watching *Je m'appelle Bernadette* tells me so. So many messages in that movie that I couldn't ignore, but one message was loud and clear for me: *"The simplest story will be the best."*

I believe in everything I write about, because it's the truth, "Plain and simple!"

CHAPTER 55

Art Jam Bridge Fest

ONE BEAUTIFUL, SUNNY DAY IN MANCHESTER, my friend Sue and I were on one of the bridges overlooking the Merrimack River. It was September 23, 2017, and we were there for the Art Jam Bridge Fest. It was the first time ever for this event, and the bridge was closed to traffic.

We decided to go and see what it was all about, knowing that it was for a good cause. There was a fee to get onto the bridge and people were selling their arts and crafts. The daylong event was a fundraiser to help with the epidemic of overdoses related to the opioid crisis.

I found everything to be colorful, and the weather was perfect for taking pictures along the walkway of the bridge. There were teenagers in vibrant costumes roaming around, and many people were creating chalk art work on the sidewalk. There were food vendors, artists who were painting pictures to sell, and many bands playing great music, volunteering their craft.

I ran into a friend of mine named Kim and she asked if I had seen the moose canvas that a vendor was raffling off at the other end of the bridge. We told her that we had come from that way but never saw it. We had arrived early when people were still setting up. She told me that she had bought some tickets, and if she won, she was going to give it to me. She had told the lady selling the tickets that my husband's nickname was "Moose" and that she needed to win this for me.

We hugged each other goodbye, and I assured her that I would check it out! Sue and I went on our way, still exploring each table, making sure that we didn't miss a thing.

I finally saw the beautiful canvas and knew that this had to be what Kim was talking about. It had all the colors of the rainbow and was very vibrant. Most prominent was the color red, and looking at it in that moment, I felt Bob's presence. After all red is my favorite color, and Bob knew that!

I took a photo of it and told the woman selling the raffle tickets that my husband's nickname was "Moose." I said that my friend had already stopped by and talked to them about me. They remembered her and said, "Oh, you're the one she was talking about."

I told them that I was writing a book about the signs I receive from my husband, Bob, and how the money that I make selling my book will help many children out in their time of need.

I decided to take a chance and bought some tickets. I told my friend Sue that the canvas was coming home with me, but I didn't really know where I would put it. The funny part was that just a week earlier I had taken down some pictures from my bedroom wall because I wanted a change, and I hadn't put anything up in their place yet.

The woman told me to check their website the next day for the winning number. I put the tickets in my pocketbook and then we decided to get a bite to eat.

Afterwards, we went down below to the river. It's always so pretty there, and that it seemed very magical. I took photos of all the birds: cormorants, Canada geese, blue herons, and sea gulls. I was thrilled to see so many birds all getting along together, in a group, on the river. I hadn't seen anything quite so spectacular in such a long time. It was very beautiful and made my heart happy.

My friend Sue smiled patiently with me as I snapped photo after photo. She knows I'm crazy about taking pictures. We then went back to my house to play some cards and then called it a night.

The next day I did a few chores around the house, and by noon time I remembered that I hadn't checked the website to see if I was a winner yet. As I sat at my computer I saw that they had posted the winning ticket. The numbers looked familiar. My heart was racing as I ran to the kitchen and rummaged through my purse for the tickets. I ran back to my computer and saw that one ticket matched all six digits. It was then that I started crying. The tears flowed freely, as once again my babe had come through for me. I am one lucky person to feel his presence so continuously!

I called the store to let them know that I held the winning ticket and that I would be in as soon as possible to pick up the canvas. I couldn't wait to tell Sue that I had won. She was thrilled for me and gladly offered a ride to retrieve it.

I reminded the ladies that I had predicted I would be taking this home, and they said that they hoped it would be me that won and had said as much before drawing the winning ticket. They said that they had heard many personal stories from others who had loved the moose picture.

I felt my husband Bob was with me on that day, and winning the canvas proved to me once again that my feelings were right.

I knew right where to hang it. How nice to have it facing my bed as "Moose" looks down on me, watching over me perfectly as I sleep!

I love the way my husband sends his signs, loud and clear! As if he were saying, "Hi honey, I am still watching over you because I am always around!"

How can anyone argue with that?

Photo by Gail Durant

On that same day that I went to the Jam Fest, something out of the ordinary happened. As I said before, the money collected on the bridge that day was to help with the opioid crisis and drug overdoses. They had set up an enormous wall, called "Butterflies of Hope," which was decorated with almost 13,000 butterflies, handmade by students from all the area schools.

In another area, you could write the names of any loved ones who had passed away as the result of an overdose. There was a huge butterfly shaped board filled with these inscriptions honoring them. I didn't write a name at the time because I didn't know of anyone who had passed from this crisis.

Later the same day, as Sue and I walked to the Merrimack River, I saw a butterfly land on a flower and had to stop to capture the moment with my camera. It was only the second time that I had seen a butterfly that summer, and I thought how nice it was to see a real one on this particular day as this event used butterflies as a symbol of hope.

Photo by Gail Durant

That night, as I headed to bed to watch TV around 9:30 p.m., my phone rang. It was my foster sister, Cindy. She was crying and told me that my foster brother Michael was dead. She hadn't heard from him in a few days, and he wasn't responding to her texts. She lived in the apartment above him. Her husband, James and another neighbor decided to climb a ladder to look in the second- floor window where Michael lived. They wanted to make sure that he was okay. Instead, they saw him lying on the dining room floor not moving.

It wasn't long before I was with my foster family in their time of need. When I arrived, many members of the family and some friends were already there. It would be a long night waiting for the medical examiner to make his report. When he finally came out to talk with us, we learned that Michael had died of a drug overdose.

It sure was a long night and I remember finally hitting my bed at about one in the morning. Suddenly, I bolted up! I was thinking about how unusual it was that just that day I had gone to an event meant to raise awareness about the opioid epidemic. I remembered how I didn't have a name to add to the butterfly board because I didn't know anyone who had passed from a drug overdose. It was only then that it finally hit me. That one butterfly I had seen that day was a sign to me that Michael was around. Butterflies represented the crisis at this event and since Michael had already passed, he was making me aware of his presence.

The next day I wanted to let Michael's family know that his soul sign was the butterfly. Whenever they saw one, it would be his way of saying hello! It's funny that not a single person criticized me for saying this. Somehow, they all came to believe it as being true. It wasn't long before they all had their own butterfly stories to tell. It gave them hope that his spirit still carries on around them.

The next day I visited Michael's mom, my foster mom Anna, in the nursing home. Her Alzheimer's had gotten worse over time, and she didn't know who anyone was anymore. I thought this would be a good time to bring her a doll to love. My friend Sue drove me to visit her. When my foster mom saw me, she said out loud, "Uh, oh, this won't be good!"

It floored me to hear her say that. I did not tell her of her son's passing. I just tried to get her to hold the new doll. With little persuasion she kissed and hugged it and told me how beautiful the baby was. She told me how much she loved babies as she pressed her forehead to that of the baby doll and kissed it on the lips. You could see a calm come over her as she held it tightly. I knew that baby helped her to be useful and loving again as she showered the doll with lots of love.

When Sue and I left to go home, we noticed a red car that was parked right near us, and wouldn't you know it, Anna's son Michael was with us! The license plate read BTRFLY. I had no camera on me, but I showed Sue how Michael had accompanied us to visit his mom on this day! There was no doubt in my mind!

At Michael's Celebration of Life, I stood up to speak from my heart about how the butterfly would be a reminder to us of him. I wanted everyone there to understand this. I was petrified to talk in front of a crowd, but I knew that my message had to get out, even if I only spoke for a few minutes.

A month later I was still hearing my foster family tell their own stories of Michael's sign, the butterfly. It calms them, and it makes me happy that I enlightened them about this soul sign. My foster mom still loves her baby doll and doesn't let it out of her sight. It was the best thing I could think of to help her, as she has someone that she can talk too. My foster family is getting better dealing with Michael's passing as the butterfly gave them all comfort.

Thanks Michael, for showing yourself to me on the day of the art fest. I finally received your message and passed it along. Give my babe a hug for me and tell him thanks for the Moose canvas which now hangs on my wall.

I took a picture of the butterfly I saw on the day of the festival and I have yet to see another butterfly since. I know our loved ones are truly around us. I can feel it! Find your sign for a loved one's passing, and it will give you comfort also! Soul signs are always around us from that special someone! Keep your eyes open so you can feel it too!

Around the same time, on my Halloween birthday, I received a present from a good friend of mine, Nadia, who came by to visit with me. She had no idea that my foster brother Michael had passed, nor that my dog had died not too long before. She was quite shocked to hear the news of both. She happened to bring me a beautiful scarf with a butterfly. Right away I said hello to Michael. Nadia had no idea about the sign I had for Michael and his family, and when I told her the story, she called it magical.

Photo by Gail Durant

I've said it many times before and will keep reinforcing this message: if you see, receive, feel, or even hear something that makes you think of a loved one who has passed, right away know that you are right, that they have come by to say hello!

CHAPTER 56

Another "Moose" Sighting

———

To this day, friends will still call or send private messages to me when they feel Bob's presence around them. I like it when they share their experiences with me. Let's start from the beginning, with some friends we met when we lived in our dream home in Hillsborough.

Bob and I met a younger couple, Valerie and Steve, when we were selling our log home and they came to look at it. Valerie felt compelled to give me a hug immediately after walking through our front entrance. She somehow knew I needed one, and she was right! They had no idea at the time that Bob was very sick or that that was the reason we would be moving back to Manchester as soon as our house sold.

Valerie experienced spiritual things in our home that day but was nervous to share them with me. She found out soon enough that I loved hearing these things, and we realized how alike we were.

She told me that even though they were not interested in buying our home, she knew it would sell and she was right. From that one encounter, we became friends, and we still keep in touch even now with Facebook messaging.

On September 22, 2017, I received a message from her :

Gail, I want to tell you a story. Yesterday I was thinking about you and your late husband, a lot! We were on our way to the lakes region and we stopped at a diner. For some odd reason I felt like someone was tickling my nose. Strange huh? I then saw a car with a special plate on it. I got my camera out and managed to get a picture with this special plate before they drove away. You moose be kidding me! We went inside and I turned on my phone and there you were! It opened up to your wedding photo without me opening up Facebook!

Here is the picture she captured that day.

Photo by Valerie Caron

The wedding photo she was talking about had appeared in my Facebook memories just that morning. I had shared it with everyone because it made me smile. It was from our wedding day, and in it Bob was looking at me adoringly. It showed the love we had for one another as we stared into each other's eyes!

It showed up for Valerie just as she was thinking of us. After seeing the license plate, she knew that Bob was around, and she had to tell me about it. I asked her if I could use her picture and story for my book and she gladly agreed. She also wrote again to me, in her own words;

Oh Gail, the feelings that I had were so strong yesterday and this was not the first time I've had a spiritual encounter regarding you and Bob. In fact when we first met, I had one! Yes you can use the story in your book if you like, I forgot that's what your book was about. I just wanted to share it with you, so you know how much you are loved!"

These stories are very special to me. I love when someone else receives a sign from my babe and relays it back to me. It keeps his memory and spirit alive. How great is that! It's also a reminder that he is still nearby, not just for me but for others who loved him too.

I also love that a friendship was formed just from inviting strangers in to look at our house when it was up for sale. Within an hour, we were no longer strangers because Valerie gets me! She feels things just as I do, and I know we were meant to meet!

Soul signs are incredible, don't you think?

CHAPTER 57

Forever and Ever, Amen

I OFTEN THINK BACK to one of my final moments with Bob.

"Everything will be alright. Everything will be okay," he said, as he patted my hand through the bars of the hospital bed that was in our living room. I always sat by his side and slipped my hands through the bars and held his hand tightly. I couldn't look at him as I didn't want him to see the tears running down my face. He must have known his days were limited and his end was coming soon.

"You have to go on alone, Gail. You will be okay. Everything will be okay," he said.

I couldn't look at him. I was thinking how I would miss his smile and his infectious laugh, our Sunday nights in the hot tub, his gentle kiss, his hand always patting my butt calling me his "sexy babe," his jokes, his naked dancing jig just coming out of the shower. The way he said "I love you" so many times a day, his Santa Claus cheeks, his warm touch and his soft hands (for a man, they were so soft), his holding me tight and the smell of his cologne. We never went anywhere without holding hands. He would gaze into my eyes whenever he would look at me with those beautiful baby blues. So much was going through my mind that day. I turned and blew him a kiss, and he blew one back as he always did.

"I am going to miss you so much," I said. It didn't matter how many tears were running down my cheeks. "I love you so much. Make sure you send me signs because you know I will receive them." He shook his head yes as his tears started falling. "Can you promise me one more thing?" I asked. "Can you make sure you are the first to come and get me when it's my time to meet you in Heaven?"

Again, he shook his head and said, "Yes, you can count on it!"

288

I had one more question. "How am I to know it's you? What sign will you send me?"

He thought about this for a minute and said he would send me bad smelly farts!

"Really" I said, "You're gonna give me bad smelly farts?"

"Yep," he said, with the biggest shit-eating grin ever!

"Okay smelly farts it is!"

We didn't talk much more that afternoon. We sat holding hands watching *Who Wants to Be a Millionaire?* It was quiet. Nothing more needed to be said. We just had to keep remembering, "Everything will be okay!"

Four months after Bob had passed, I had to go to the hospital for tests. I had time to kill and went into the gift shop where I saw a sign that read, "If you're waiting for a sign, THIS IS IT!"

I had to get it, it made me chuckle. I asked the clerk to hold it for me while I continued to shop.

But something more meaningful was about to hit me square in the face.

"How could I have missed this?" I was thinking to myself as a second sign came into view. Written on it were the words of comfort Bob had spoken to me on that day four months ago: "Everything will be okay."

That was the first time I ever cried so deeply in a shop over a silly sign. The owner came over and asked if I was okay. Oh, my goodness, I laughed. She's asking me if I am okay!

"I have to have that sign," I tell her.

Photo by Gail Durant

"It's the last one," she said, getting it down for me. Bob was surely with me this day. I just knew it.

I decided to make the beginning of my story the ending of my story, with a little twist! My babe was surely right when he said this to me. It's almost five years since he passed, and with his *soul signs from the other side*, I know he is still with me and I *am* okay!

I receive signs from Bob all the time. It makes me smile, and yes, at times it makes me cry. It's good to let the tears flow to cleanse your soul, whether they are tears of happiness or sadness. All the signs I receive from those who have passed over make me sure that there *is* a Heaven and that our loved ones are watching over us! I hope that my proof with pictures and signs shows you just that, *there truly is a Heaven!*

I could go on and on writing about the signs I receive, but this book would never get finished, so I decided to give you one more story of a great sign I recently received from my babe. I hope you will love this last story and that it will help you to understand your own signs as they are sent to you. That will be my wish for you all "to have the need to believe and then receive!" and from there, "Believe and receive!"

Here is my latest story, and my last for this book:

It was December 2, 2017, my mother's birthday. My sister Diana had started the tradition of doing the rosary at her house on this day in honor of our mother. She invited all of the sisters and everyone brought a dish of food to share afterward. We laughed as we tried to start the rosary prayers, but we settled down as we get further into it. It was a huge honor for us to do this for our mom, Coffee.

On this night, a few sisters were sick and couldn't make it to our little tradition, so we decided to visit them afterward and bring them a plate of food. We also brought them each some long-stemmed yellow roses that our niece Jodi had sent to us for this special day! She was out of town, performing with an orchestra, but wanted to let us know that she was thinking of us. Knowing that the yellow rose always represents her grandma, she thought it would be nice for us to have something to bring home to enjoy.

My sister Diana gave us all beautiful cross ornaments to hang on our Christmas tree or to keep out yearlong, however we chose.

After visiting a couple of homes and making sure that our sisters were okay, we were ready to go home ourselves. Once in the car, we talked about going shopping someday at Hobby Lobby. My sister Kelley suggested that it was still early and that we should go now, since we really didn't have other plans. My sisters Tami, Diana and I agreed to stroll around in the store and see what new things were out. It was fun going up and down the aisles and looking at all the decorations for Christmas. I purchased a roll of wrapping paper, some squirrel ornaments, and of course, a moose ornament (like I really needed another one, but it was so colorful and cute)!

We browsed all throughout the store, making sure not to miss anything. I remember picking up a fake microphone and trying to get my kid sister Tami to sing "Paper Roses" with me. I guess I was too loud because I ended up singing by myself as she walked away. People were looking, but I didn't care. I was singing for my mom, and I knew that she could hear me.

We came around a corner where there were many painted wooden signs displayed. None of the sayings pertained to us, but some were pretty neat. Many aisles were lined with these wooden plaques, and as I came around another corner, I gasped out loud! My sister Kelley asked me what was wrong, but I just pointed to the words on the piece of wood in front of us. It made no sense to her or to my other sisters either.

I told them that Bob had dedicated this song to me on our wedding day, and that at our reception, when he was feeling pretty buzzed, he had sung it to me out loud. He was acting silly, like I had just been with my sister Tami trying to get her to sing "Paper Roses" with the fake microphone. I knew that Bob was with me right then, because it brought me immediately back to the best day of our lives, declaring our love for one another!

I thought about buying it, but one of my sisters asked me why I would buy it and where I would put it, as my home is small, and space is limited. I never did buy it, but I smiled as we walked the rest of the aisles, knowing that Bob was around. We left the store thinking about the fun time we had shopping together said our goodbyes and "I love you" as we each got dropped off, one by one. After I walked into the house, I changed and got comfy to watch some Lifetime Christmas Movies and then went to bed.

I am not sure what time my spirit guides or my subconscious woke me, but I do know that as soon as it happened, I started writing little notes about the messages that were bouncing around in my head for this story. I knew that if I didn't write them down, I would forget by the morning. That's why I always keep a pad of paper and a pen near my bed, to record those moments immediately when I am awakened from a sound sleep, so I won't forget!

My spirit guides reminded me of Bob's song again. As I woke up, I was told to sing the whole verse that precedes the words I had seen written on that piece of wood. I was also told to go back and buy that sign, because I should make it the last story in my book. What a good idea, I thought to myself. Now I knew that I had to have that sign! I would find a place for it to hang in my home. I easily fell back to sleep.

The next morning, I called my sister Kelley to see if she could take me back to the store. She told me that Hobby Lobby was closed on Sundays, but she would take me to get it after she got out of work on Monday night. I agreed and left it at that.

I kept thinking what a wonderful last story this would be, because it proved to me that Bob was still keeping his word to never leave my side. I didn't have my camera with me on the day we were at the store, so I didn't get a picture of it. I started to get a little anxious because I was worried that it would be gone if I waited too long. I knew that I needed to go to the store early in the morning.

The store opened at 9 a.m. and I asked my next-door neighbor Srdjan (who calls me "Grandma") if he would take me. I couldn't wait to tell him my newest story. He agreed to take me, and we got there at 9:30 am. I walked fast, straight to the aisle where I remembered it to be and searched the bottom shelf. I went around and up and down the many aisles with Srdjan doing the same and after three tries, we still could not find it.

I was ready to ask for help, but something told me to keep looking. I went back to the place where I thought I had seen it last and started to rummage through the pile of signs, thinking that somehow they may have laid these new signs on top of it. After going through the pile knowing that it had been on the bottom shelf, I figured that it had to have been moved by staff, or at least it was wishful thinking on my part. I just hoped that it hadn't been sold.

As I looked up, I gasped once again.

"Oh my God, here it is!" I said.

Someone had certainly moved it. It was on display just above that lower shelf, hanging on two metal rods, the only one of its kind. This time I had my camera with me and took a picture before placing it in my carriage. At that point I knew that my last story would be amazing. Now I have proof that my connection with Bob that day was real and the message that prompted me to return for the sign is validation of that.

Srdjan understood why I wanted this sign so badly. You see, before we went to the store, we had gone to the cemetery to see my husband's and my headstone. I wanted to get another picture showing why this sign held so much meaning for me. When he saw it, Srdjan put his hand to his heart and told me that it was amazing, simply amazing!

He always loves my stories about the supernatural and after hearing them countless times, he now receives and understands his own signs and lets me know when he does. His most recent occurrence involved a job opportunity that he kept receiving in an email. He reminded himself of what I had told him, that when that happens, it's meant as a sign for you and that you've got to take heed of it, and so he did. He applied, got the job, and loves it!

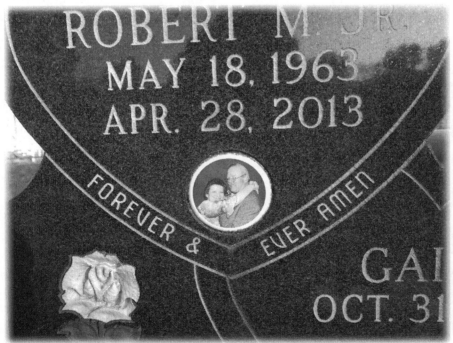

Photos by Gail Durant

Remember the beginning of this last story, I told you that Spirit wanted me to sing the first verse before the verse on this sign? Well I truly know that my babe does love me forever and ever, and I can hear him singing this song like it was yesterday when we spoke of love and said our wedding vows.

I also know that Bob is with me always, as he told me he would never leave my side. I truly believe him, because he's always sending me something, in my dreams, through a friend, words, a smell, a song, or even his touch. I get it! I feel it! I am blessed and wish that you too can be so fortunate!

Soul signs from the other side prove to me that there is a Heaven, not just because I saw it, but because something beyond our world reaches out to me. I experience things so often in my everyday life that I interpret as a connection with the other side, and I know for sure that Heaven exists. I am comforted by these communications while I live out my life without those who have passed on before me.

Believe that we will meet again, but look always for your own special gift from an adored loved one who has already risen high to the heavens!

Believe also that they are still here at your side when you need them the most! With so much that has happened to me, how could I not believe? Start asking your loved ones (out loud) to show you that they are with you, and soon you will be on your way to seeing your own signs of love from the departed. Know too that they are in a great place in the Kingdom of Heaven. It's really beautiful, so don't worry or wonder if they are okay. They are okay!

I hope you all soon receive soul signs from the other side.

God bless you!

CHAPTER 58

Fifth-Year Anniversary Poem

Robert Durant, Jr.
4/28/13–4/28/18
"Moose"

It's been five years now
Since I've been missing you

Our love is still a blessing
Which I find is nothing new

Love doesn't die because you did
I find this statement true

The memories that are in my mind
Helps to see me through

I miss your laugh and your smile
And those beautiful eyes of blue

I sure hope mom Anna
Delivered a hug from me to you

And your daughter, Laurie
Gave my message that, "I Love You"

The special bond we still have
Has tremendous value

I'll never ever let you go
We are one and stuck like glue

Yes, it's been five years now
That I am still missing you

Love . . . Wifey

CHAPTER 59

My Last Christmas Card from Bob

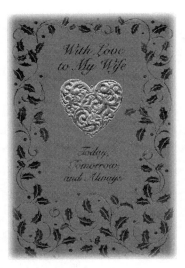

HERE IS THE LAST CHRISTMAS CARD that I received from my babe, in 2012. When he picked out cards to give to me, you could tell he took his time looking for that perfect one. I have all the cards that he ever gave to me, and he saved all those that I gave to him. The text of his message to me follows;

Hi Babe,
I Love You so much.
I want Thank You For Everything You Do For Me.
I Love You so much.
You are the Besty wife in the World
Thank you For Being There with Me.
I Love You So Much
Thank You So Much,
Love You
Bubby.

I love the heart on this card, which represents love. I love the color red, and he knew that!

What I love the most is that even when he was dying, he still declared his love for me. His handwriting shows how much he struggled to write this. His message is the best, and I will always appreciate him for thanking me when no one else did. He's the one that mattered the most, and his words of love carried me through our darkest days!

He hand-picked the best cards!

The word "Always" is why I feel he never left my side!

He signed it Bubby, he meant to write Hubby.

I love you too, Babe, "Always."

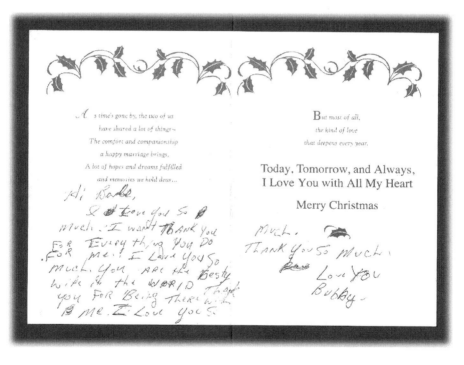

Acknowledgments

To my publisher, Deidre Randall, and her assistant Kate Crichton at Peter R. Randall Publisher LLC: Thanks so much for helping me make my book come to life. I appreciate all your efforts to make my dream come true! I couldn't have done it without your help!

Robert Durant Jr.: Thanks for loving me the way you did and for sending me soul signs from the other side! I will always love you, no matter what! I miss you so much! This love story could never happen if I never met you! You are my rock!

Jeannette Johnson: Words cannot express my gratitude for the personal advice you gave me after writing your own book, *Against All Odds*. I appreciate your help very much and our phone conversations.

Helen Hiltz: You were one of my best friends, and you encouraged me to get writing because you believed in me the most! I can picture you from Heaven with that finger, telling me to "get cracking and get that book done!" I miss and love you so much!

AARP and HelloWorld: Thanks for running that essay contest and for awarding the Grand Prize of $10,000 to me! Winning that challenge proved to me that I could write from the heart! Thank you for getting me started on my book with the winnings! You helped to make my dream come true!

My mother, Doris (Coffee) Adams: Mom, I hope you know how proud I was of you. You inspired me to write the winning story about you for a "Mother-of-the-Year" contest, my first writing success. I was pleased when you won it because it made you so happy! You gave so much love to everyone that walked through your front door. You and my foster moms Osbie Lessard and Anna Oliver made me the woman I have become today! I was the lucky one! I love you all! I miss you mom (Coffee) and Anna! Heaven is surely having a party!

Patty Hughes: Thanks for all your help for over a year, with the many hours we spent together trying to get my story to flow in my own words. I still hate tenses! You are my neighbor and co-worker but today, we are more than that. You and I have become good friends! I couldn't have done this without you! You were my personal developmental editor and the push I needed! I am happy I asked you for help. Thanks so much!

Auntie Violet Jackson: You are my biggest and oldest fan at the young age of ninety-five. You wanted every chapter as soon as it was written because you thought you would be dead before it got published. I loved that you enjoyed getting mail every week containing my book pages! Thank you for giving me hope and making me laugh with your own personal opinions!

Julie Ghent: Thank you for helping to make my book cover come alive from my own vision. You did an awesome job, and I am grateful!

To all my family and friends: All of you whom I have named in this book—thank you for giving me permission to do so and for sharing your wonderful signs and personal stories! I love you all for giving your consent. The profit from this book will help children without parents, just as Mother Mary asked of me. The children that this book will help thank you also! Some of you sit in heaven today, Helen Hiltz, Laurie Irish, and Colleen Hamer. I miss you very much. Thank you all for being a part of my life and for understanding my journey!

Angela Cruz and Sylvia Gagnon: Thank you for the feedback on the pages and for being great listeners when I was overwhelmed! Your words of encouragement helped me to carry on. I love you. Your opinions really mattered to me.

To Suzanne Phaneuf and Lorraine Curit: Thanks for just being there. I am grateful that you are both in my life! Sue, I could tell you enjoyed sharing your input with the editor and with me. Lori, thanks for always asking how the book was coming along. I love you both!

Larry Maurice: Thanks for finding my baby sister, Brenda. Without your help this chapter could not be written. I thank you from the bottom of my heart! Keep up with the great work you do!

Carol Robidoux: A woman who helped me along the way. Thanks for giving me that chance to express myself on your "Manchester

Ink Link" website and for getting my name out there. You gave me a much-needed push! We finally met and will have to have a wine date again! Thanks for believing in me!

To my siblings: Linda Fruci, Diana Katz, Michael Adams, Donna Martin, John Adams, Daniel Adams, Tami Adams, David Adams, Ann Marie Valliere, Nancy Adams, and Kelley Charest. Without you some of these stories could not be told. I love you with all my heart!

And to my sister Brenda Lee Adams: Your spirit will always be within my heart! Thanks for visiting from the other side! We will meet again! Count on it! I love you!

About the Author

Gail Durant, sixty-four years old, was born and raised in Manchester, New Hampshire. She grew up in the Elmwood Gardens projects with a family of thirteen children and her mom, Doris. She attended Memorial High School to the ninth grade and later received her G.E.D. She worked forty-one years in shoe shops, laundry and manufacturing. She found the love of her life, Bob and shared many dreams together, until brain cancer took him.

Years before Bob passed, Mother Mary visited Gail in her dreams and told her that her husband would go before her and when he did, she was asked to fulfill a job to help children without parents. She said prayers to God, Mother Mary and Bob asking for a sign if she should write a book about what she knows best (SIGNS) to help children with the proceeds she receives from selling her book. This woman's answer came in a very big way.

Gail won the grand prize of $10,000 for a 200-word essay contest and knew this sign was meant for her and started writing about her life, her love story with her husband Bob, and all sorts of signs woven in to help readers with their own signs. She illustrates with pictures of proof that there is a heaven.

Gail writes from her heart and hopes she can help many others to find their own *Soul Signs from the Other Side* after losing a loved one.